Elites after State Socialism

Elites after State Socialism

Theories and Analysis

edited by John Higley and György Lengyel

ROWMAN & LITTLEFIELD PUBLISHERS, INC.
Lanham • Boulder • New York • Oxford

ROWMAN & LITTLEFIELD PUBLISHERS, INC.

Published in the United States of America
by Rowman & Littlefield Publishers, Inc.
4720 Boston Way, Lanham, Maryland 20706
http://www.rowmanlittlefield.com

12 Hid's Copse Road
Cumnor Hill, Oxford OX2 9JJ, England

British Library Cataloguing in Publication Information Available

Library of Congress Cataloging-in-Publication Data

Elites after state socialism : theories and analysis / edited by John Higley
and György Lengyel.
     p. cm.
    "Chapter drafts were presented at two group meetings hosted by
Budapest University of Economic Sciences"—Acknowledgments.
    Includes bibliographical references and index.
    ISBN 0-8476-9896-3 (cloth : alk. paper) — ISBN 0-8476-9897-1 (paper :
alk. paper)
    1. Elite (Social sciences)—Europe, Eastern. 2. Elite (Social sciences)—
Russia. 3. Post-communism. I. Higley, John. II. Lengyel, György.

HN380.7.Z9 E42 2000
305.5′2′0947—dc21

                                      99-048270

Printed in the United States of America

♾ ™ The paper used in this publication meets the minimum requirements
of American National Standard for Information Sciences—Permanence of
Paper for Printed Library Materials, ANSI Z39.48-1992.

Contents

Acknowledgments

This book results from collaboration among an informal working group of sociologists during the past three years. Chapter drafts were presented at two group meetings hosted by the Budapest University of Economic Sciences, and we are grateful for the warm hospitality shown us on both occasions.

A third meeting, at which chapters were put into final form, was hosted by the Institute of Sociology of the Czech Academy of Sciences in Prague. There, too, the hospitality was most warm, and we are indebted to our Czech hosts. All three meetings were supported by the East–East Program of the Soros Foundation, to which we express our deep thanks. John Higley also wishes to thank the Center for East European and Eurasian Studies at the University of Texas at Austin for travel support that enabled him to participate in this collaborative effort.

Preface

Elites after State Socialism: Theories and Analysis

This book presents much new research on the configurations of political and economic elites that have emerged in the main countries of Central and Eastern Europe since the demise of state socialism a decade ago. Drawing on the most recent survey and other studies of these elites, the book concentrates on developments during the second half of the 1990s. It explores the elite circulations, differentiations, and competitions that now underpin, but in some countries also still inhibit, democratic stability and economic growth. Chapters on Bulgaria, Croatia, the Czech Republic, Eastern Germany before and after reunification, Hungary, Poland, Serbia, and Slovakia are by recognized experts in the countries. Additional chapters on elites and the use and abuse of democratic institutions in Hungary, the evolution of oil and banking elites in Russia, and the presocialist and socialist legacies that shape business elite recruitment in Bulgaria, the Czech Republic, Hungary, and Poland are by well-known American and British specialists. All of the chapters are theoretically informed, and an epilogue assesses the prospects and trajectory of elite theory "after Marxism." The book is a substantial advance in the literature on postsocialist politics and societies and in the comparative study of elites.

1

Introduction

Elite Configurations after State Socialism

John Higley and György Lengyel

This book studies the political and economic elites that held power in the main countries of Central and Eastern Europe during the 1990s, after the demise of state socialism. It examines how processes of elite unity or disunity, differentiation, and circulation were unfolding. The book's premise is that the internal workings, commitments, and actions of elites constitute basic distinctions among political and economic systems. The extent to which elites trust and cooperate with each other is crucial for constitutional and other institutional arrangements, for political and economic stability or instability, and for democratic or authoritarian political practices. In particular, elite "unity in diversity" is the sine qua non of a robust democratic polity and an effective market economy. It involves a common elite commitment to democratic institutional designs and mechanisms. It also involves a restrained elite partisanship and a reciprocal recognition by elites that they are together legitimate power-wielders. These elements of "unity in diversity" constitute an informal set of conduct-guiding orientations amounting to an elite ethos. A main question is the extent to which this ethos has emerged among Central and East European elites after state socialism.

The relation between elites and institutions is also critically important, though none of this book's contributors sees it as one-way—that elites determine institutions or vice versa. Institutions limit elite unity or disunity, differentiation, and circulation, but these elite configurations, in turn, influence the operation of institutions. In stable democracies and in what sociologists often think of as the "normal mode" of social reproduction, institutions constrain elites quite strongly. However, in times of basic reform and transformation—such as the postsocialist countries experienced during the 1990s—institutions are in flux and, consequently, elites have wider latitudes of choice and action. Gaining a better understanding of the relation between elites and institutions in countries undergoing fundamental changes is another of this book's principal aims.

ELITE CONFIGURATIONS AND POLITICAL REGIMES: A MODEL

We begin by outlining a model that distinguishes and relates patterns of elite unity or disunity, differentiation, and circulation. Combinations of these patterns constitute the critical elite conditions for different types of political regimes, including consolidated democracies. Although we, as editors, have not imposed our model on the contributors to this volume, many of the chapters employ or address parts of it, and a brief outline is therefore necessary.

Elite Unity and Differentiation

One of the model's components is a typology of national elites according to the extent of their unity or disunity and their differentiation (see Higley and Pakulski, 1995; Higley and Burton, 1997; Higley, Pakulski, and Wesolowski, 1998). In a nutshell, *elite unity or disunity* has two dimensions: normative and interactive. The normative dimension is the extent of shared beliefs and values, as well as more specific norms—most of them informal and uncodified—about political access, competition, and restrained partisanship. The interactive dimension is the extent of inclusive channels and networks through which elite persons and groups obtain relatively assured access to key decision-making centers. *Elite differentiation* is the extent to which elite groups are socially heterogeneous, organizationally diverse, and relatively autonomous from the state and each other. It is manifested by functionally distinct elite sectors (political, economic, administrative, military, religious, educational, the media, the arts, and so on), each with its own boundaries, organizations, formal and informal rules of behavior, and pecking order (Keller, 1963; Etzioni-Halevy, 1993).

Elite unity or disunity typically originates in watershed political events, such as national independence, the formation of national states, revolutions, or major political crises (Dogan and Higley, 1998). Elite differentiation occurs gradually in step with processes of industrialization and social modernization. However, differentiation may be slowed, as was the case under state socialism, if a dominant political elite requires that all functionally specialized, ostensibly autonomous elites nevertheless adhere to a single ideology, religious dogma, or ethnonationalist creed and to the party or movement that articulates it.

Figure 1.1   Configurations of National Elites (and Associated Regime Types)

		Elite Unity	
		Strong	*Weak*
	Wide	<u>Consensual Elite</u> (consolidated democracy)	<u>Fragmented Elite</u> (unconsolidated democracy) (possibly a short-lived authoritarian regime)
Elite Differentiation	*Narrow*	<u>Ideocratic Elite</u> (totalitarian or post-totalitarian regime)	<u>Divided Elite</u> (authoritarian or sultanistic regime)

Differences in the extent of unity and differentiation define the main configurations of national elites: strong or weak unity, accompanied by wide or narrow differentiation. These elite configurations are, in turn, principal determinants of political regimes: consolidated democracies where there is both strong unity and wide differentiation; authoritarian or sultanistic regimes where there is neither; totalitarian or post-totalitarian regimes where there is strong unity but narrow differentiation; and unconsolidated democracies, possibly oscillating with short-lived authoritarian regimes, where there is wide differentiation but weak unity (see figure 1.1).

The four elite configurations generate distinct sets of strategies and tactics that elite persons and groups adopt in dealing with each other. Individuals and groups making up a *consensual elite* are unconstrained by a single ideological blueprint or other telos of change, and they engage freely in competitions and rivalries with well-understood rules. There is high certainty about the rules and about the practices that flow from them, but low certainty about political outcomes, with today's winners likely to become tomorrow's losers, though no person or group suffers mortally for losing (Przeworski, 1991).

By sharp contrast, the strategies and tactics pursued by individuals and groups making up a *divided elite* approximate continual warfare, the stakes in which are not just government power, but also political freedom and sometimes life itself. Conflicts and struggles are colored by deep hostilities, they take place in the virtual absence of communication between elite camps, and power usurpations are widely expected. Politics approximate

free-for-all struggles and they have an erratic, oppressive character. Whatever low political certainties there may be depend upon effective domination and exclusion. Because of the distrusts and hatreds that pervade a
divided elite, breaking out of the configuration is extremely difficult; it
probably requires a sudden, deliberate, and fundamental elite settlement
that can only occur in a profound crisis that threatens the interests of all
main elite groups more or less equally (Higley and Burton, 1998).

The strategies and tactics characteristic of a *fragmented elite* arise from the
rapid proliferation of diverse political, economic, cultural, and other groups
that accompany many democratic transitions, especially transitions involving
sudden regime collapses or implosions (for example, Czechoslovakia at the
end of 1989, the Soviet Union in 1991). Tentative and partial elite pacts and
armistices aimed at staving off open political warfare may be fashioned, but
no elite ethos of unity in diversity develops. Instead, conflicts remain heated
and a "party of power" is likely to emerge and throw its weight around. But
whereas strategies and tactics in a divided elite involve sharp polarizations
and exclusions, with opponents typically regarding each other as mortal enemies in unchecked struggles, those in a fragmented elite involve more complex maneuvers across multiple and cross-cutting cleavages that skew the outcomes of, but do not prevent, democratic competitions (for example,
Bulgaria and Slovakia under the heavy-handed Bulgarian Socialist Party
[BSP] and Meciar governments, respectively, during much of the 1990s).

Finally, strategies and tactics in an *ideocratic elite* approximate, at least on
their surface, a value-oriented quest involving the sorts of calculations that
Max Weber termed "substantive." During their early phases, all of the state
socialist regimes (except perhaps Poland) exhibited these features. Even if
a single doctrine or other telos no longer strongly guides elite actions—as
in a "mature post-totalitarian regime" like Hungary during the 1980s (Linz
and Stepan, 1996: 42–51)—the doctrine continues to provide the idiom for
elite domination. While on the surface accepting the idiom, however, substantially differentiated and discordant elite groups jockey for political
influence through personalized patronage networks.

Elite Circulation

The linkage between elite circulation and the configurations that elites have
displayed after state socialism is one of this book's main topics. As described by
Mosca (1939) and Pareto (1935), elite circulation takes several patterns, the
most clear-cut of which are circulation through inheritance (what is today
often termed "elite reproduction") and circulation through revolution. The
key aspects of elite circulation are its *scope*—the horizontal range of the positions affected and the vertical depth from which those entering elite positions
come—and its *mode,* that is, the speed and manner in which it occurs. With

respect to scope, one must ask if the range of circulation is narrow or wide—if only the most prominent and politically exposed position-holders are replaced, or if holders of elite positions are changed across the board. One must at the same time ask if the scope of circulation is shallow or deep—if most new elites are drawn from second-echelon ("deputy") positions within existing political and social hierarchies, or if they come from far down political and social hierarchies or even from outside them (for example, disaporas, prisons, underground movements). The horizontal range and vertical depth of circulations tend to co-vary. For example, wide circulations typically bring to power and influence many persons previously distant from elite positions. The other key question about elite circulation concerns its mode—its speed and manner. Circulations may be sudden and coerced, as in violent revolutionary overthrows, or gradual and peaceful, with elites being replaced incrementally through voluntary resignations, retirements, and individual transfers.

By dichotomizing the scope and mode of elite circulation, we may distinguish four patterns (see figure 1.2).

Figure 1.2 Patterns of Elite Circulation

		Scope	
		Wide & Deep	*Narrow & Shallow*
	Gradual & *Peaceful*	Classic Circulation	Reproduction Circulation
Mode			
	Sudden & *Coerced*	Replacement Circulation	Quasi-Replacement Circulation

Classic circulation is roughly what Mosca and Pareto regarded as essential for elite renewal and thus for stable and effective rulership. It is positionally wide and socially deep in scope, but gradual and peaceful in mode. Classic circulation is conducive to the creation and persistence of consensual elites. It is great enough in scope to replace inflexible and intransigent political leaders and cliques with more conciliatory persons disposed, by virtue of their previous exclusions or subordinations, toward a more inclusionary politics. Also, its gradual and peaceful mode requires substantial negotiation and cooperation between dominant and ascending individuals and groups. Classic circulation is, in short, a process of gradual elite change conducive to a "live and let live" posture among all important elite groups. It contributes to an ethos of unity in diversity, which, once created, ensures the relatively smooth turnover of elites by avoiding social closure and keeping positions open to persons from different rungs on political and social ladders.

Replacement circulation, like classic circulation, is positionally wide and socially deep in scope, but its mode is much more sudden and coerced. It typically involves the overthrow and liquidation of ruling elites by violent revolution, though it may also occur, as in much of Central and Eastern Europe after World War II, through foreign military conquest and the imposition of a new set of elites. In its revolutionary variant, replacement circulation depends on mutually destructive struggles between existing elites that enable a small, doctrinaire, and previously peripheral counter-elite to seize power and sweep aside all who were previously dominant. Replacement circulation is conducive to the creation of an ideocratic elite (and totalitarian regime) because in order to consolidate power a triumphant counter-elite is strongly inclined to require all who henceforth aspire to elite positions to adhere to its particular doctrine and organization.

Reproduction circulation is positionally narrow and socially shallow in scope, but gradual and peaceful in mode. Typically, a dominant elite group abandons or greatly modifies its doctrinal stance and engages in a "musical chairs" exchange of positions in order to survive. Through these maneuvers, most elite persons cling to power and elite status, but, as in musical chairs, some fail to find a place and are excluded. No large change in the social profiles of elites occurs, though the hasty, often illicit efforts to obtain safe places contribute greatly to elite fragmentation.

Finally, quasi-replacement circulation is similarly narrow and shallow in scope, but its mode is more sudden and coerced. It typically occurs within an already divided elite configuration and it usually involves a palace coup by which one political clique displaces the ascendant clique from the uppermost political positions. The newly ascendant clique may display a different leadership style, but it effects no basic change in the character of politics, which remain poisonous and violent.

The Model Summarized

The model's several components are assembled in figure 1.3. There are, obviously, major problems in determining "how much" unity or disunity, differentiation, and circulation are "enough" to constitute each main elite configuration. The dilemma of the half-empty or half-full glass of water is highly apposite. Until comparative research on elites yields systematic data sets with which to construct reliable measures of "how much" is "enough," informed judgments of individual cases, using available research findings, are the best one can do in applying the model. We are sorely aware that such judgments can easily become tendentious. Despite these problems and dangers, we will offer some judgments about elite configurations in the main countries of Central and Eastern Europe during the 1990s. Before doing so, however, let us discuss one further set of complexities that are relevant to the postsocialist countries, namely, the relations between elite change and institutional change.

Figure 1.3　A Model Relating Elite Unity, Differentiation, and Circulation to Types of Regimes

Classic Circulation	Reproduction Circulation
scope: wide & deep	scope: narrow & shallow
mode: gradual & peaceful	mode: gradual & peaceful

ELITE UNITY

	Strong	*Weak*
	CONSENSUAL ELITE	FRAGMENTED ELITE
	-ethos of "unity in diversity"	-weak or no shared ethos
	-norms of restrained partisanship,	-reciprocal distrust and suspicion
Wide	compromise	
	-networks dense and interconnected	-networks dense and segmented
	Regime: consolidated	Regime: unconsolidated
ELITE	democracy	democracy
DIFFEREN-		
TIATION	IDEOCRATIC ELITE	DIVIDED ELITE
	-single belief system	-deeply opposed beliefs
	-networks run through	-networks confined to
Narrow	highly centralized party or movement	opposing camps, one of which dominates
	Regimes: totalitarian or post-totalitarian	Regimes: authoritarian or sultanistic

⤴	⤵
Replacement Circulation	Quasi-Replacement Circulation
scope: wide & deep	scope: narrow & shallow
mode: sudden & enforced	mode: sudden & enforced

ELITE CHANGE AND INSTITUTIONAL CHANGE

The social and political transformations from state socialism had many unintended and varied consequences. This is not to say that they had no common goals, however. Such goals were evident in the striking similarity of postsocialist institutional designs across most Central and East European countries. Nearly everywhere, political and economic institutions bearing a strong family resemblance were created, and this resemblance was almost as great as the resemblance that the old state socialist institutional designs displayed. The similarity of postsocialist designs stemmed from elites who defined the goals of transformation in largely the same way.

It is necessary to distinguish between institutional designs and institutional mechanisms. Institutional designs are the structural elements of social reproduction, first and foremost constitutions and market economies. Institutional mechanisms are the more specific instruments for implementing designs, for example, electoral rules and privatization programs. Elites play a seminal role in shaping institutional designs, but institutional mechanisms do much to pattern the channels and ways in which elites compete and are recruited. Despite the strong family resemblance of postsocialist institutional designs in Central and Eastern Europe, our studies show that institutional mechanisms have differed significantly between the countries in routinizing elite competition and recruitment.

This was also the case under state socialism. Key elements of institutional design were common to the state socialist regimes: social reproduction through collective ownership; state redistribution of the economic surplus; the dominance of a hegemonic party acting in society's name; the uniform profession of a single ideology by elites and all who aspired to elite positions. Yet, these common elements of state socialist institutional designs allowed for important differences in institutional mechanisms—as between the early and late phases of state socialism, and as between the several state socialist regimes. In its early phase, state socialism involved ideologically driven mass mobilizations, strong coercive measures, party and state penetration of all social spheres, and a largely one-way communication between ruling elites and subservient mass populations. In state socialism's late phase, mass mobilizations were replaced by more prosaic regulatory efforts, political coercion and penetration subsided, and ruling elites had more varied relations with a range of social categories and increasingly differentiated elite groups. Likewise, there were substantial differences between the state socialist regimes in the ways in which their political, economic, and other institutional mechanisms operated: much less uniform and harsh in Poland and Yugoslavia, for example, than in the Soviet Union, Bulgaria, and Romania.

The basic difference between the institutional changes that occurred before and after state socialism's demise was that the former were intended to reproduce state socialism while the latter were meant to transcend it. However, unintended side effects accompanied both sets of changes. Those that occurred in the late phase of state socialism altered the content of socialist ideology, transformed the public discourse, created more intricate and cooptative relations between ruling elites and the intelligentsia, and enabled new elite groups to form in opposition to the state socialist order. In chapter 6, for example, Christian Welzel examines the unintended effects of changing institutional mechanisms in the German Democratic Republic during the 1980s. He shows that they had important consequences for elite formation and institutional functioning in eastern Germany during the 1990s.

Despite such variations under state socialism, it was elites—some of them new, many of them holdovers from state socialism—that bore the primary responsibility for shaping the postsocialist orders. Much depended on their wise and unwise decisions, on their communication with mass publics to shape a new public discourse, and, most important, on their relations with each other. Where elites entered into accommodations and peaceful competitions (Hungary and Poland and, with reservations, the Czech Republic), much also depended on whether their fledgling "unity in diversity" stemmed mainly from a defensive perception of domestic and foreign threats or from a more fundamental consensus about postsocialist institutional designs and mechanisms. In chapter 4, Rudolf Tökés shows that even in one of the real success stories of the 1990s, Hungary, elites engaged in an elaborate feathering of their own nests. As often as not, Tökés argues, this involved the abuse of newly created democratic institutions.

ELITE CHANGE DURING THE TRANSITION YEARS, 1988–94

To assess the utility of our elite model and provide background for the chapters that follow, let us canvass the main elite and regime developments in the principal Central and East European countries during the 1990s. It is clearly recognized that the democratic transitions from state socialism in Poland and Hungary were of a negotiated or pacted kind. This was a more limited feature of the transition in Czechoslovakia, too. In this respect, the transitions were conducive to the emergence of consensual elites in Poland and Hungary and, more circuitously, in the Czech Republic after its independence at the beginning of 1993.

A key reason was the way in which elite circulation in each of these countries approximated the classic pattern: relatively wide and deep in scope, relatively gradual and peaceful ("velvet") in mode. The 1989 roundtables in Warsaw and Budapest, as well as the briefer roundtable negotiations in Prague, were preceded by the political articulation of opposition elites: most dramatically in Poland with the emergence of Solidarity nine years earlier; more gradually with the steady emergence of reformist and technocratic factions in Hungary under the Kadar regime during the 1970s and 1980s; quite unevenly in Czechoslovakia with the Prague Spring in 1968, its harsh repression, and the small but symbolically important group of Charter 77 dissidents during the 1980s. Especially in Poland and Hungary, these developments under state socialism gradually altered elite composition (Hanley, Yershova, and Anderson, 1995; Wasilewski and Wnuk-Lipinski, 1995; Szelényi, 1995).

The roundtables in Warsaw, Budapest, and Prague during 1989 produced a broad elite consensus about the desirability—or at least the inevitability—of democratic reforms. Opposition elites were accommodated in the politically inclusive negotiations, but during the year or two that followed, many of the less experienced and more idealistic opposition leaders, together with the leaders who had been most directly in charge of the old state socialist regimes, were eased out through democratic elections, the demobilization and splintering of reform movements, and the formation of political parties to contest elections. In Czechoslovakia, a power bid by the former Communist and newly populist leader, Vladimír Meciar, and his Movement for a Democratic Slovakia (HZDS), contributed to a "velvet divorce" between the Czech and Slovak lands at the end of 1992. As recounted by Pavel Machonin and Milan Tucek in chapter 2, this bolstered the unity of Czech elites by removing the divisive Czech–Slovak ethnic rivalry and the policy clashes that arose from the unequal Czech and Slovak economic situations. But, as described by John A. Gould and Soňa Szomolányi in chapter 3, the Slovak elite emerged from the divorce fragmented along political, ideological, and ethnic lines. Meciar and his HZDS were entrenched but locked in a bitter fight with political opponents who pushed for democratic reforms, more rapid privatization, and minority rights.

Research on the extent of elite circulation supports this depiction of elite change during the transition years in Poland, Hungary, and the two parts of Czechoslovakia. Studying what happened to the nomenklatura elites of Poland and Hungary between 1988 and 1993, Jacek Wasilewski (1998) analyzed large samples of those elites to reach the following conclusions: (1) members of all nomenklatura elite sectors moved in more or less equal proportions to command positions in private business; (2) three nomenklatura elite groups—those in the Communist Party apparatus and those in the economic and cultural nomenklaturas—were virtually eliminated from top political positions; (3) roughly a quarter of the state socialist government bureaucrats retained their posts in the postsocialist governments; (4) overall, half of the members of the 1988 nomenklatura elites of Hungary and Poland continued to hold elite positions in 1993, albeit usually not the same positions; (5) if elderly nomenklatura elite members who retired between 1988 and 1993 were excluded, the ratio of 1988 nomenklatura elite members who still held some elite position in 1993 to those who lost elite status during those years was 21:10 in Hungary, and 19:10 in Poland.

Clearly, the scope of elite circulation in Hungary and Poland was quite large. In chapter 12, Ákos Róna-Tas and Joszef Böröcz augment Wasilewski's analysis by showing that by 1993 new business elites in Hungary and Poland, as well as the Czech Republic and Bulgaria, constituted distinct formations. One measure of their distinctiveness was the large numbers of new business leaders who were descendants of grandparents (but not, significantly, of parents) who had been successful in business during the presocialist era.

Research on patterns of elite circulation in Czechoslovakia and then in the separate Czech and Slovak republics during the transition years also appears to accord with our model. In chapter 2, Machonin and Tucek show that a wide and rapid circulation of the Czech political elite occurred in the Velvet Revolution of November and December 1989 and the June 1990 parliamentary election. However, this circulation was not as much of a break with what had gone before as it first seemed because it involved the return to power of a number of 1968 reformers, accompanied by 1980s dissidents such as Václav Havel. Political elite circulation continued in the next parliamentary elections, in June 1992, when liberal right-of-center forces in the Czech territories and an ethnonationalist elite group that had been tied to the old state socialist regime in the Slovak territories, led by Meciar, defeated the 1968 reformers and 1980s dissidents. In chapter 3, Gould and Szomolányi recount how Meciar and his associates entrenched themselves in top Slovak positions before and after the divorce from the Czechs, whereas, as Machonin and Tucek show in chapter 2, circulation in the Czech territories continued to be quite wide in its range and depth, even though people who had been middle-level technocrats and managers in the state socialist regime rose to elite positions after 1992. Comparing the overall circulations of Czech and Slovak elites during the transition years, the Czech pattern was more nearly of the classic kind, while the Slovak pattern approximated reproduction.

In our model, the reproduction pattern is associated with fragmented elites, in which, though there is adherence to democratic elections, there is at most a limited elite tolerance of opponents that stops well short of the unity-in-diversity ethos. We will say more about the fragmentation of Slovak elites since independence at the end of 1992. Here, however, we want to note that the scope of elite circulation in Bulgaria was similarly narrow and shallow, though there, too, its mode was gradual and peaceful via haphazard, frequently deadlocked, and quite inconclusive roundtable negotiations during the first five months of 1990. After ousting Communist Party Secretary Todor Zhivkov in early November 1989, large parts of the state socialist establishment, including reformers, nationalists, and political opportunists, formed an ideologically loose coalition of convenience in the Bulgarian Socialist Party (BSP), which was the linear descendant of the old Communist Party. These groups continued to dominate, but not monopolize, elite positions in the postsocialist regime. Like Meciar's HZDS in Slovakia, the BSP elite constituted a "party of power" anchored in governmental bodies and government-controlled industrial conglomerates, as Dobrinka Kostova points out in chapter 11. Political opposition was marginalized and harassed, though not suppressed (Nikolov, 1998). A brief and ineffective opposition coalition government during 1991–92 gave way to a caretaker government of technocrats that was supported by, and was favorable to, the BSP establishment until the BSP recaptured government power in the December 1994 elections. During the transition years, in short, there was neither a fundamental elite accommodation nor a major elite circulation in Bulgaria. Former apparatchiks together with state socialist technocrats dominated the postsocialist regime. Wider and deeper circulation, possibly accompanied by some steps toward an elite accommodation, did not begin until the harrowing financial crisis that Bulgaria experienced in the mid-1990s, to which we will return below.

Regime transitions in Serbia and Croatia involved de facto palace coups that slowed the dismantling of ideocratic elites. In 1987, when Serbia still formed the core of Yugoslavia, Slobodan Milosevic, the new president of the Serb League of Communists, used Serb appeals for help against the Albanian ethnic majority in Kosovo as a pretext for staging an internal party coup. He replaced reformist leaders with his own henchmen and cloaked himself in Serb nationalist garb in order to stave off ultranationalists, who were emerging rapidly as a powerful challenging force (Woodward, 1995: 89). Milosevic's preemptive move enabled him and his entourage to survive the breakup of Yugoslavia during 1991 and to remain dominant in the rump Yugoslav state, which retained strong authoritarian features despite democratic trappings. A significant number of people took advantage of the subsequent warfare with Croatia and with Muslim and Croat forces in Bosnia, as well as the international sanctions imposed on Serbia, to get rich illegally and enter business and other elite positions. But as Mladen Lazic shows in chapter 7, as late as 1997 fully 60 percent of the Serb business elite consisted of people who had held high positions in the state socialist regime, while the political elite remained centered on Milosevic and his cronies. Concomitant with a very limited regime transition, elite circulation in Serbia did not go much beyond the quasi-replacement pattern, and it was unaccompanied by pacts, negotiations, or other attempts at elite accommodation.

In May 1990, when Croatia was still a Yugoslav republic, former Yugoslav army general Franjo Tudjman, who had also donned the ethnonationalist mantle, led his Croatian Democratic Union (HDZ) to victory in the first multiparty elections, winning 41.5 percent of the popular vote but capturing two-thirds of the seats in parliament. Controlling parliament, Tudjman was immediately elected by it to the Croatian presidency, and from that position he and his lieutenants launched an intensive nationalist campaign that quickly drove most holdover Communists from elite positions and made Tudjman and the HDZ crushingly dominant. Dusko Sekulic and Zeljka Sporer show in chapter 8 that the scope of this circulation was much more sweeping than that of the Serb quasi-replacement pattern, and its mode was sufficiently sudden (though not overtly violent) to approximate a replacement circulation. Indeed, in their nationalist zeal, the new ruling Croatian elites have since displayed, as Sekulic and Sporer discuss, some behaviors characteristic of the ideocratic configuration that usually arises from a replacement circulation. However, the Croatian regime probably falls short of the totalitarian type because meaningfully democratic elections continue to be held, and they are contested by parties and movements that are openly and strongly opposed to Tudjman and the ruling HDZ (in addition to chapter 8, see Pusic, 1998).

To summarize, ruling elites in Serbia and Croatia relied heavily on nationalist rather than socialist tenets to justify their ascendancy during the transitions to postsocialist regimes. These political–ideological about-faces, aided by coup-like displacements of top state socialist cliques, obviated the need for accommodations with opposition elites, and neither transition was of the negotiated or pacted kind. The scope of elite circulation was narrow and shallow in Serbia but much wider and deeper in Croatia; its mode was fairly sudden and coerced in both countries. Despite ostensibly democratic institutions, the postsocialist Serbian regime was in fact authoritarian, with the entrenched political elite maintaining its nationalist stance and virtually declaring war on its opponents. The latter were excluded from power and suppressed, and many opposition figures sought shelter abroad. The Croatian transition, by contrast, involved a more sweeping replacement of the old state socialist elites. It was effected initially through a democratic election but completed by the consolidation of an uncomfortably authoritarian regime dominated by Franco Tudjman and his ultranationalist HDZ.

The countries we have examined to this point hardly exhaust the Central and East European cases. We think, however, that they provided relatively clear examples, during the transition years, of the elite configurations and circulation patterns we have posited: relatively strong features of consensual elites and classic circulations in Poland, Hungary, and the Czech Republic; clearly fragmented elites and reproduction circulations in Slovakia and Bulgaria; a divided elite involving quasi-replacement circulation in Serbia; and, in Croatia, a divided elite whose dominant camp, led by Tudjman, came to power as a consequence of the intense ethnonationalist pressures that tore the Yugoslav state socialist regime apart and that fostered a circulation closer to the replacement pattern.

What about Russia? Attempts to achieve an accommodation among Soviet and then Russian elites during the transition years clearly failed, and the reasons for this failure have been discussed quite extensively (for example, Brudny, 1995; Higley and Pakulski, 1995). Interviews that David Lane (1997) conducted during 1993 and 1994 with more than a hundred members of both the Gorbachev and the Yeltsin political elite cohorts uncovered much disunity among them. Because of their dispersion into many groups and factions at both national and regional levels, the Soviet and Russian elites are best viewed as fragmented before, during, and after the U.S.S.R.

regime collapse at the end of 1991. Consistent with this view, data on Russian elite circulation during and since the transition years indicate a strong reproduction pattern, and we will discuss these data below.

ELITE CHANGE SINCE THE TRANSITION YEARS

Political developments in Poland, Hungary, and the Czech Republic during the second half of the 1990s strongly indicated the strengthening of consensual elites. In Poland, the 1989 roundtable agreement, renegotiated in 1990, laid the ground for a broad and lasting elite consensus. Elites embraced not only democratic institutions and procedures, but also such strategic goals as rapid privatization and joining both NATO and the European Union (EU). The consensus persisted in spite of substantial elite turnover, institutional changes such as a new constitution and three successive sets of electoral rules, and important policy differences between, for example, liberal reformers and the Peasant Party. As was widely noted during Poland's 1997 parliamentary election campaign, leaders of the major parties and blocks found it difficult to distinguish themselves from their rivals in more than cosmetic ways. Debates centered on the pace of marketizing reforms and the specific features of democratic institutions, but not on the desirability of either. The main disputes were over the scope of presidential power, the extent of welfare rights, and the relations between church and state, especially as regards policy toward abortion.

On the surface, relations between Polish elite groups looked tense. Rapid turnovers in government office holding, jockeying among Solidarity factions, and institutional ambiguities under the "little constitution" that was in force between 1990 and 1997 made for a weak collective elite identity (Pankow, 1998). But neither these fragmenting tendencies nor the former Communists' electoral successes in 1993 and 1995, under the umbrella of the Democratic Left Alliance (SLD), threatened the underlying consensus achieved in 1989–90. In chapter 5, Bogdan Mach and Wlodzimierz Wesolowski chart the extent of this elite "transformational correctness" as they measured it in 1996. They uncover strikingly similar attitudes among all major party elites about what democratic politics involve and how they should be played. The 1997 constitutional referendum and parliamentary elections clearly reflected the underlying elite consensus. Both the referendum and the elections proceeded successfully and peacefully, albeit with rather low levels of public interest and participation. The referendum approved a new constitution, which was widely regarded as a victory for the SLD government, while the parliamentary elections ended with the center–right Solidarity Electoral Alliance (AWS) winning the largest share of Sejm seats (201 of 460). Protracted but civilized negotiations eventually produced a coalition government consisting of the AWS and the liberal Freedom Union (UW). This change of government—Poland's fourth since 1989—was as peaceful as previous ones, and the subsequent cohabitation of the SLD president, Aleksander Kwasniewski, with the center–right government headed by Jerzy Buzek proved quite harmonious during its first eighteen months. In short, developments during the second half of the 1990s were consistent with Mach and Wesolowski's 1996 data indicating that a consensual elite and a consolidated democratic regime were emerging in Poland (see also Wasilewski, 1998; Smolar, 1998).

Hungarian and Czech developments after 1994 followed a similar trajectory. The victory of the formerly communist Socialists in Hungary's May 1994 elections did nothing to undermine the substantial elite consensus embodied by the 1989 roundtable in Budapest. In the 1994 elections, small and disaffected left- and right-wing elite groups gained no significant support, and the government alternation that followed was less acrimonious than the Polish alternations to that point. The Socialist victory came less as a surprise than as an expectable return to power by the original state socialist reformers. Moreover, marked continuities with the old state socialist order were apparent in the economic elite, as György Lengyel and Attila Bartha show in chapter 9. This is not to say that elite politics in Hungary have involved only smooth sailing. In chapter 4, Rudolf Tőkés scrutinizes the still jumbled and contested terrain of Hungary's new democratic institutions, as well as the ample patronage practices and ties that can be observed in the parliament's workings. Overall, however, research on Hungarian political and economic elites reveals a pattern of gradual and peaceful elite circulation that has diminished continuities between the state socialist and postsocialist periods, featured increased levels of education and administrative experience, and been accompanied by relatively high levels of personal satisfaction among elites (see chapters 5 and 9). The picture is one of ever more professionalized political and business leaders engaged in the restrained (but always ragged) competitions characteristic of a consensual elite operating a consolidated democratic regime.

As already noted, the velvet divorce between the Czech and Slovak lands at the end of 1992 contributed to the unity of Czech elites by removing main sources of ethnic and economic conflicts. Czech independence opened up numerous elite positions for younger technocratic and professional aspirants, a development that Machonin and Tucek discuss in chapter 2. In spite of personal animosities between "the two Václavs" (President Havel and Prime Minister Klaus), a democratic consensus encompassed virtually all elite groups. At the strategic level, Klaus's governing coalition of Civic Democrats (ODS) and several other parties, as well as the opposition Social Democrats, all stressed their support of EU and NATO membership, and privatization. They differed over privatization's pace and mode, as well as over governing styles and welfare policies. However, these differences seemed less pronounced than in Poland, where many leaders of the strong trade union movement, including the remnants of Solidarity, hotly resisted the "shock therapy" instituted by Leszek Balcerowicz in 1992. The Czech trade union elite by and large supported economic reforms and cooperated with the Klaus government.

Another difference from Poland, and one that contributed to the principal Czech elite groups' unity, was the presence of an unreformed Communist Party (the KSCM) that was too small to mobilize much public discontent but that could handily be blamed for state socialism's failures. Thus, while in the 1993 Polish and 1994 Hungarian elections, strong former Communist parties—the main component of the SLD and the MSzP, respectively—harnessed widespread economic frustrations to stage political comebacks, in the Czech Republic it was the Social Democrats, largely unconnected to the old regime, who profited most from popular discontents. These discontents, which are documented with survey data by Machonin and Tucek in chapter 2, enabled the Social Democrats to emerge as victors in the parliamentary elections of September 1998. However, because they failed to win a majority of parliamentary seats, the Social Democrats had to choose between forming a coalition government or setting up a minority government on their own. To nearly everyone's surprise, a secret pact between the Social Democrat and Civic Democrat party leaders in late 1998 safeguarded the Social Democrats against tactical no-confidence votes and enabled them to form a minority government on their own. Machonin and Tucek cautiously view this pact as the most recent evidence of consensus and unity in the Czech political elite.

Developments among Slovak and Bulgarian elites were less auspicious for democratic politics and robust economies during most of the 1990s. Slovakia's divorce from the Czech lands at the end of 1992 was at once a result of Slovak opposition to major postsocialist economic reforms and a basis for avoiding reforms subsequently. This avoidance contributed to fragmentation, even political polarization, between pro-reform and pro-Western liberal elites on the one side and defensive nationalist elites on the other. As detailed by Gould and Szomolányi in chapter 3, under the coalition governments led by Vladimír Meciar, HZDS membership was a criterion for appointment to key administrative posts, so that a strongly clientelist and oligarchic power structure emerged. A bitter, long-lasting confrontation between Meciar, the prime minister, and Michal Kovac, the president, indicated substantial elite disunity, as did the readiness of the Meciar forces to play fast and loose with democratic procedures in order to retain power. The debacle of a May 1997 referendum about altering rules for choosing the president further increased elite tensions. During 1998, however, the proverbial worm began to turn due to an all-out mobilization of anti-Meciar elite groups, helped by international condemnation of the Meciar regime and by the end of a period of deficit-financed economic growth. Gould and Szomolányi discuss how increased cooperation among opposition elite groups resulted in a broad electoral coalition that managed to defeat the HZDS and its allies in the October 1998 elections. Gould and Szomolányi speculate that this elite coalition and the broad-based government to which it led marked the start of a convergence among Slovakia's fragmented elites.

Bulgarian elites were similarly fragmented during most of the 1990s. Partly due to divisions among the many parties making up the opposition Union of Democratic Forces (ODS), the Socialists (BSP) remained dominant through 1996. However, toward the end of that year, and amid virtual economic collapse, the situation began to change with the election of ODS leader Petar Stoyanov to the presidency, the resignation of BSP prime minister Zhan Videnov, and widening splits among elite groups supporting the BSP over obviously failed economic policies. Large demonstrations in Sofia and other cities in early 1997 led to the removal of BSP supporters from local councils and to the scheduling of early parliamentary elections. These elections, in April 1997, were won overwhelmingly by the ODS forces, which constructed a reform-oriented government. No doubt recalling how its first attempt at governing disintegrated during 1992, this second ODS government fostered a closing of elite ranks around a democratic-reformist program. However, elite conflicts and distrusts remained great, elite differentiation remained limited, and a democratic-reformist consensus was weak at best—as Kostova finds in chapter 11. Although the principal Bulgarian elites tried to paper over their lack of unity with appeals for national solidarity, they remained fragmented at the end of the 1990s.

During the first half of the decade, it was difficult to establish which elite configuration—divided or fragmented—was emerging in Russia. Analyses of elite circulation revealed a strong reproduction pattern. For example, Wasilewski (1998) calculated that when retirees were excluded the ratio of 1988 nomenklatura elite members who retained elite positions in 1993 to those who lost such positions was 88:10 (compared with the 20:10 ratios he found in Hungary and Poland, noted above). Synthesizing a number of studies and themselves analyzing the fates of 3,610 executive, party, parliamentary, regional, and economic-business elite position holders from the Brezhnev government in 1980 through to the Yeltsin government at the end of 1993, Stephen White and Olga Kryshtanovskaya (1998) similarly concluded that only 10 percent of the Yeltsin elite were new to power circles; the other 90 percent had spent an average of 11.4 years in nomenklatura (though not necessarily elite) positions before the U.S.S.R.'s collapse in 1991.

As already mentioned, David Lane (1997) found through interview research in 1994 that Russian elites were split down the middle as to whether the Soviet regime had been basically healthy or irretrievably flawed and as to what might have been done to save it (institutional reforms or a basic overhaul). Lane also found that in 1994 Russian elites were similarly divided over the Yeltsin regime's goals and policies. Bearing in mind the attempted coup in August 1991, the unpacted democratic transition that followed, the violent showdown between Yeltsin and parliament on the streets of Moscow in 1993, and the many indications in the disastrous Chechnya intervention of 1994–95 that the military and security forces were going their own ways, a classification of the Russian elite during the first half of the 1990s as fundamentally divided and as awaiting the installation of an authoritarian regime was certainly plausible.

Russian elite developments during the mid- and late 1990s were not much easier to interpret. To be sure, no overtly authoritarian regime took power; instead, the Yeltsin government's ability to control political and economic developments in the country simply diminished. It became more difficult, if not impossible, to discern the well-articulated and deeply opposed elite camps that indicate a divided configuration. The differentiation of elite groups was too great. Numerous business and parastatal groups competed, often ruthlessly (as, for example, in the "bankers' war" during 1997) with each other; a congeries of squabbling party elites existed; relatively autonomous but internally divided military and state security groups were apparent; several trade union federations were in the field; powerful provincial governors and regional associations dotted the political landscape; a relatively efficient but uncertainly autonomous central bank wielded significant economic power; an influential collective farm lobby exerted pressures on the Duma; a bloated presidential entourage, a variety of watchdog media organizations, and a resurgent Orthodox Church, not to mention organized and powerful criminal groups, were all in evidence. All of these formations fought to control the assets of a "soft state" that was largely unable to enforce its laws and decrees (Remington, 1997). Relatively free, fair, and participatory elections were held for the Duma in December 1995 and for the presidency in June 1996. Dire forecasts that the presidential election would be canceled or thoroughly rigged proved incorrect. But these indicators of increasing elite moderation and adaptation to peaceful electoral contests were offset by bitter policy disputes and much elite mistrust, fueled by Yeltsin's erratic health and behavior, as well as by economic disarray and manifold social tensions.

Summarizing findings from his new study of the Russian oil elite and the political groups with which it interacts, David Lane, in chapter 10, examines the chaotic condition of Russian elites in the late 1990s. He shows that there is nothing approximating a consensual elite. But he also shows that a kaleidoscope of conflicting interests, rather than some deep and unbridgeable chasm, characterized elite politics at the end of the 1990s. To Lane's assessment we add that, though serious conflicts between Russian elites clearly persist, each electoral contest has been more peaceful and orderly than the one preceding it, and each standoff between the executive and parliament (post-1993) has been defused or circumvented. In short, a fragmented, rather than a divided, elite appears to exist in Russia, and the political regime is best regarded as an unconsolidated democracy. That said, the vulnerability of a fragmented elite to sudden, violent explosions that produce a more authoritarian regime cannot be ignored in the Russian case.

CONCLUSIONS

During the years of transition from state socialism in Central and Eastern Europe—from roughly 1988 to 1994—elite change involved important accommodations and the emergence of what looked increasingly like an ethos of unity in diversity, assisted by deep, gradual, and peaceful circulations, in Hungary, Poland, and the Czech part of the former Czechoslovakia. However, in the other countries studied in this book—Slovakia, Bulgaria, Russia, Serbia, and Croatia—few such changes occurred. Politics in these latter countries were dominated by holdover "parties of power" that rode roughshod over their opponents. In Slovakia, Bulgaria, and Russia, the elites were probably more fragmented than divided, as indicated by substantial elite sectoral differentiation and the proliferation of opposition groups in the political elite. But for most of the decade in these countries, populists and technocrats who survived the collapse of state socialism were in the driver's seat. The situation was worse in Serbia and Croatia, where a palace coup in the former and an electorally engineered elite replacement in the latter, as well as the exchange of Communist banners for ultranationalist ones by elites in both countries, ruled out any elite accommodation and produced only nominally democratic regimes.

Since the transition years—during the second half of the 1990s—electoral victories by opposition elites in Bulgaria and Slovakia and the successful conduct of two national elections in Russia indicated a firming of formal democratic processes, though no evidence of greater elite unity was apparent in any of the three countries. Meanwhile, elite divisions in Serbia and Croatia remained deep. In mid-1999 it was conceivable that the Serb regime's efforts to cling to power through a brutal assertion of Serb nationalism in Kosovo would lead to the regime's destruction at the hands of NATO.

BIBLIOGRAPHY

Brudny, Yitzhak M. 1995. "Ruslan Khasbulatov, Aleksandr Rutskoi, and Intraelite Conflict in Postcommunist Russia, 1991–1994." In *Patterns in Post-Soviet Leadership,* ed. Timothy J. Colton and Robert C. Tucker. Boulder, Colo.: Westview.

Burton, Michael, and John Higley. 1998. "Political Crises and Elite Settlements." In *Elites, Crises, and the Origins of Regimes,* ed. M. Dogan and J. Higley. Lanham, Md.: Rowman & Littlefield Publishers.

Chehabi, H. E., and Juan J. Linz, eds. 1998. *Sultanistic Regimes.* Baltimore: Johns Hopkins University Press.

Dogan, Mattei, and John Higley. 1998. "Elites, Crises, and Regimes in Comparative Analysis." In *Elites, Crises, and the Origins of Regimes,* ed. M. Dogan and J. Higley. Lanham, Md.: Rowman & Littlefield Publishers.

Etzioni-Halevy, Eva. 1993. *The Elite Connection: Problems and Potential in Western Democracy.* Boston: Basil Blackwell.

Hanley, Eric, Natasha Yershova, and Richard Anderson. 1995. "Russia: Old Wine in a New Bottle? The Circulation and Reproduction of Russian Elites, 1983–1993." Special issue, *Theory and Society* 24 (October): 639–68.

Higley, John, and Michael Burton. 1997. "Types of Elites in Postcommunist Eastern Europe." *International Politics* 34 (June): 153–68.

————. 1998. "Elite Settlements and the Taming of Politics." *Government and Opposition* 33 (Winter): 98–115.

Higley, John, and Jan Pakulski. 1995. "Elite Transformation in Central and Eastern Europe." *Australian Journal of Political Science* 30 (October): 415–35.

Higley, John, Jan Pakulski, and Wlodzimeriez Wesolowski. 1998. "Elite Change and Democratic Regimes in Eastern Europe." In *Postcommunist Elites and Democracy in Eastern Europe,* ed. J. Higley, J. Pakulski, and W. Wesolowski. London: Macmillan.

Keller, Susanne. 1963. *Beyond the Ruling Class: Strategic Elites in Modern Society.* New York: Random House.

Lane, David. 1997. "Russian Political Elites, 1991–1995: Recruitment and Renewal." *International Politics* 34 (June): 169–92.

Linz, Juan J., and Alfred Stepan. 1996. *Problems of Democratic Transition and Consolidation.* Baltimore: Johns Hopkins University Press.

Mosca, Gaetano. 1939. *The Ruling Class.* New York: McGraw-Hill.

Nikolov, Stephen E. 1998. "Bulgaria: A Quasi-Elite." In *Postcommunist Elites and Democracy in Eastern Europe,* ed. J. Higley, J. Pakulski, and W. Wesolowski. London: Macmillan.

Pankow, Irena. 1998. "A Self-Portrait of the Polish Political Elite." In *Postcommunist Elites and Democracy in Eastern Europe,* ed. J. Higley, J. Pakulski, and W. Wesolowski. London: Macmillan.

Pareto, Vilfredo. 1935. *The Mind and Society.* New York: Harcourt, Brace.

Przeworski, Adam. 1991. *Democracy and the Market.* New York: Cambridge University Press.

Pusic, Vesna. 1998. "Croatia at the Crossroads." *Journal of Democracy* 9 (January): 111–24.

Remington, Thomas F. 1997. "Democratization and the New Political Order in Russia." In *Democratic Changes and Authoritarian Reactions in Russia, Ukraine, Belarus, and Modova,* ed. K. Dawisha and B. Parrott. New York: Cambridge University Press.

Smolar, Aleksander. 1998. "Poland's Emerging Party System." *Journal of Democracy* 9 (April): 122–33.

Szelényi, Ivan, ed. 1995. "Circulation and Reproduction of Elites during the Postcommunist Transformation of Eastern Europe." Special issue, *Theory and Society* 24 (October).

Voslensky, Michael. 1984. *Nomenklatura: Anatomy of the Soviet Ruling Class.* London: Bodley Head.

Wasilewski, Jacek. 1998. "Hungary, Poland, and Russia: The Fate of Nomenklatura Elites." In *Elites, Crises, and the Origins of Regimes,* ed. M. Dogan and J. Higley. Lanham, Md.: Rowman & Littlefield Publishers.

Wasilewski, Jacek, and Edmund Wnuk-Lipinski. 1995. "Poland: The Winding Road from Communist to Post-Solidarity Elite." *Theory and Society* 24 (October): 669–96.

White, Stephen, and Olga Kryshtanovskaya. 1998. "Russia: Elite Continuity and Change." In *Elites, Crises, and the Origins of Regimes,* ed. M. Dogan and J. Higley. Lanham, Md.: Rowman & Littlefield Publishers.

Woodward, Susan L. 1995. *Balkan Tragedy: Chaos and Dissolution after the Cold War.* Washington, D.C.: Brookings.

Part I

Political Elite Change

2

Czech Republic

New Elites and Social Change

Pavel Machonin and Milan Tucek

The collapse of state socialism in Central and Eastern Europe at the end of the 1980s and the region's ensuing political, economic, and social changes have done much to reawaken the interest of political scientists and sociologists in the study of elites. From the start it has been clear that elites have played key roles. Central and Eastern Europe should be seen as a new domain in which to apply and evaluate classical and modern theories about elites in light of the empirical research that can now be conducted there. Let us say immediately that we reject the more or less absolute division of societies into elite and non-elite categories so prominent in the works of Machiavelli, Mosca, Pareto, Sorel, and even C. Wright Mills. However, we regard Pareto's famous distinction between the "circulation" and "slow transformation" of elites as useful for studying social change (Pareto, 1935: paras. 1427–32). Some analysts of the Central and East European transitions have reformulated Pareto's distinction in terms of elite "circulation" versus "reproduction" (Szelényi and Treiman, 1991: 279–80; Mateju, 1997: 63–65). For us—as students of stratification, social mobility, and social change—it makes sense to speak of a broad "social elite" that encompasses not only political but also economic and cultural (or intellectual) segments (cf. Machonin and Tucek, 1996: 154–67). Together with occupationally based social strata and classes, the social elite is an important aspect of societal differentiation. Its members are not only those who occupy high positions in powerful organizational and institutional hierarchies; they are also individuals with high social statuses that involve influence, education, complex work, income, lifestyle, and prestige. The social elite plays important and multiple roles in the functioning and change of political, economic, and cultural institutions. It is an inescapable feature of any modern society, though we do not regard it as independent of the larger stratification or class structure. It is essential to study how changes in all these societal components, not just the social elite, occur together.

Accordingly, we are skeptical about the thesis that in transitions from state socialist systems "We are dealing with a specific type of causality between economic, political, and social processes, a causality that has been shaped much more by 'blueprints' prepared by political elites than by 'conditional laws of history'" (Mateju, 1995: 221). We do not deny that elites have played active roles in these transitions, particularly in their early phases. But we think that empirical studies that take account of longer-term changes in stratification and class systems demonstrate the interdependence of elite and non-elite change and cast doubt on any strongly "elitist" explanation. An analysis of Czechoslovakia before, during, and after the collapse of state socialism in 1989 and of the Czech Republic after it emerged as an independent state at the beginning of 1993 reveals the interdependence of elite and wider social change.

THE GENESIS OF NEW ELITES UNDER STATE SOCIALISM

Between 1938 and 1989, the Czech people lived, other than for brief interludes, under totalitarian rule, first under six years of Nazi occupation, and then, after 1947, under a state socialist regime. The dominant features of the state socialist regime were an economy with very limited market relationships and a social order that was avowedly egalitarian and even antimeritocratic in the distribution of incomes and the diversity of lifestyles. These were, of course, abstract features of the regime; there were important concrete deviations, as well as changing circumstances that periodically strengthened or weakened the regime's basic features.[1] The reason for stressing these features is to underscore how long the extreme conditions of totalitarian and antimeritocratic rule influenced the daily life of Czech society and how profound their influence necessarily was. Various economists, political scientists, and sociologists have discussed the consequences of this long totalitarian rule, concentrating especially on how it kept the society relatively backward compared to West European societies and how it must now undergo a lengthy catch-up process (see, for example, Habermas, 1990).

Among some theorists and analysts these obvious facts have given rise to skepticism about the formation of groups that can serve as the political and social engines of postsocialist development (cf. Touraine, 1991; Minck and Szurek, 1992). In one respect, at least, this skepticism is warranted. Unlike classic democratic revolutions, the transition from state socialism was not powered by large and well-formed social classes that existed in the "womb" of the state socialist regime. In Czechoslovakia before 1989, virtually no significant or officially sanctioned private economic activities took place, while gradations of income and wealth were very flat (Vecernik, 1969; 1995). A high congruence had gradually developed between education levels and the complexity of occupational positions, on the one hand, and between earnings and power positions, on the other. Moreover, these two status-forming factors stood in unusual disharmony. This meant that there was no relatively large group of people with high educational and occupational qualifications and corresponding economic resources and power positions; there was, in short, no developed middle class (Machonin and Tucek, 1994). A somewhat similar situation existed, of course, in most other state socialist countries (Slomczynski, 1994).

The absence of a social formation "predestined" by its economic status to lead the transition did not mean, however, that there were no groups capable of leading a transition. When we applied a multidimensional measure of social status to occupational survey data for 1984, various groups whose educational and cultural credentials, and in most cases whose jobs, substantially exceeded their earnings and other economic circumstances, as well as their political influence, could be identified (Machonin and Tucek, 1994: 82). The proportion of Communist Party members in these groups was significantly lower than in the economically active population as a whole. The groups' members displayed low rates of participation in the political activities required by the regime, and they were prevented from attaining higher professional and managerial positions (with correspondingly higher incomes) by various other factors. One of these was the age barrier that operated in favor of older people affiliated with the Communist Party after the Prague Spring movement was repressed by the Soviet-led occupation in August 1968. Another was the gender barrier that operated in favor of males. A third was the flat income distribution curve that affected most occupational positions requiring higher education and involving complex work tasks. These career barriers affected many noncommunists, as well as some younger Party members and activists. In sum, there was considerable status inconsistency under the state socialist regime, and it is plausible to think that this disposed many people to adopt disallegiant, even radically dissident, attitudes and behaviors toward it (Lenski, 1966).

A modified version of the so-called "second society" theory can be put to good use when considering the situation of Czechoslovaks prior to 1989. This theory was developed by Hungarian economists and sociologists to capture the consequences of economic reforms carried out by the regime in Budapest from the 1970s onwards (Hankiss, 1988), and it is also applicable to Poland where "systemic" social and political conflicts (Adamski, 1990) led to the famous roundtable negotiations between Communist and Solidarity elites in 1988–89. In Czechoslovakia, a "second society" developed mainly at the micro and unofficial level of households, families, cooperatives, small plants, and informal groups of friends and dissidents (Machonin, 1993). Official statistics and sociological surveys did not capture the real earnings and wealth of many of these groups and milieus. It is plausible to think that a part of the ruling political, economic, and cultural elites, as well as the largely noncommunist upper-middle occupational and educational strata with inconsistent statuses, were accumulating quite substantial amounts of economic capital, together with important amounts of information (cultural capital) about and contacts (social capital) with the more advanced countries of Western Europe (Bourdieu, 1986; Mateju and Rehakova, 1994). Because of the aforementioned political, age, and gender barriers, however, these various forms of capital could not be used in any open way to stimulate modernization and economic progress. The same could also be said, incidentally, about many skilled manual workers, whose earnings were, owing to the official egalitarian system, relatively high, and who were able to participate in the "gray economy" by providing goods and services superior to those provided in the official economy. However, the chances that manual workers would rise to elite, rather than middle-class, statuses after the regime's downfall were not great.

To summarize: despite the absence of clear-cut groups with identifiable and significant amounts of private income and property, a range of people holding middle-level positions inconsistent with their economic and political statuses, on the one side, and often with their education and other cultural and social capital, on the other, formed a fairly distinct echelon in Czechoslovakia under state socialism. Dissatisfied not only with the Soviet-supported regime and its undemocratic nature, but also with their specific personal and family situations, these people were disposed toward political and social change, perhaps of a radical kind, especially given their experiences after the Prague Spring in 1968. People harmed by the wave of persecutions during the 1970s, together with their offspring, belonged to the same or similar social groupings, and these groupings also contained people who were active in the dissident movement. In terms of official positions and incomes, they did not differ much from other social groups; but informally, they were social pools from which new elites could emerge.

THE FORMATION OF NEW ELITES

During the period between the Velvet Revolution in November 1989 and the emergence of a sovereign Czech Republic in January 1993, after the "velvet divorce" from Slovakia, an almost complete circulation of the political elite, and especially of the core "power elite," took place. We have described the details of this circulation elsewhere (Machonin, 1994: 81–83; Machonin and Tucek, 1994: 85–88). Here we render it in more synthetic and general terms that also take account of economic and cultural elite circulation during the same period.

The elite circulation resulted from a combination of external and internal political and socioeconomic pressures. The external pressure was the general movement of postsocialist societies towards liberal and pluralistic democracies that was stimulated by the powerful political support of the Western democracies and by their promises of economic aid. Countervailing external pressures that might have shored up the weakened state socialist regime were undercut by the apparent collapse of the Soviet empire in Central and Eastern Europe. This collapse motivated Czechs and their neighbor populations to undertake political and social changes substantial enough to distinguish themselves from other parts of the collapsing Soviet empire. The internal pressures for change consisted of widespread discontent with the Communist regime and the readiness of the specific groups already mentioned to replace the obsolete political and social system with a quite different one.

In the Czech lands, the Communist Party leadership, which had "liberated" itself from the reform Communists of the Prague Spring by means of purges during the 1970s, was totally isolated from the population. In this situation, the Party leadership not only lost the Soviet Union's support but was even pressured by the Soviets to relinquish power. Unlike its Hungarian and Polish counterparts, however, the Czech Party leadership refused to acknowledge its historic defeat and refused to try to reconstruct the Party along reformist lines that might eventually regain popular support. This distinctive isolation and stubbornness of the Czech Communist leaders actually contributed to a smooth circulation of political elites because it enabled them to be swept aside without elaborate negotiations. In short order, the beginning of economic reform and the first steps toward greater societal differentiation formed the bases for a comprehensive political elite circulation.

This circulation unfolded in several dramatic steps. First, in November 1989 the leading adherents of the state socialist system exited from the power elite, mostly in a voluntary way, and people more acceptable to the population replaced them within the Party. In June 1990, in the first freely contested elections held since 1946, even those Communist political leaders who were prepared to support significant regime change were defeated, and a new federal government was formed by Civic Forum in coalition with Slovak noncommunist democratic movements. Civic Forum was itself a coalition of noncommunist and liberal dissenting groups, former reform Communists who had lost out when the Prague Spring was terminated, and groups of neoliberals who had not been strongly connected to dissenting groups but who urged a program of radical economic reform. Within this broad coalition, a major battle over the pace and scope of economic reform broke out almost immediately, and the neoliberal faction eventually prevailed over those advocating a more Keynesian program.

Until the neoliberals triumphed, however, the political initiative lay with the groups of dissenters and former reform Communists who were bent on constructing a democratic political system. These groups drew their support from a congeries of individuals and families injured by the state socialist system, from intellectuals and others committed to democratic principles, and from Czechs whose national pride made them resent the Soviet-supported regime and the lack of sovereignty that it represented. The Velvet Revolution activists enjoyed, in short, broad public support. But the eventual victory of the neoliberals within the emerging political elite changed the situation substantially. Their victory corresponded to rapid changes that were taking place in the wider society.

Accelerated social differentiation and the opening up of political positions provided incentives for many of the people who held inconsistent social statuses in the "second society" of the old state socialist regime. To be sure, only a small minority of these had been victims of the regime or active dissenters against it, and some of them, in fact, had resigned from the Party as late as November 1989. However, their economic, educational, and occupational locations and status inconsistencies disposed them toward activities that not only transgressed what had been permissible under the old regime, but also now, in the postsocialist era, violated many norms of the humanist and liberal–democratic dissenters who spearheaded the Velvet Revolution. These individuals quickly seized many of the opportunities that greater social differentiation and political liberalization provided. Some gained election to parliament as Civic Forum candidates in the 1990 election; many embarked on new municipal, economic, administrative, and cultural careers in their localities, companies, offices, and cultural institutions. Others acted to form, more or less spontaneously, small-scale private enterprises or to start such enterprises under a government-initiated program. Still others sought and gained restitution of property and investments that had been confiscated from them or their relatives under Communist rule.[2]

For most of these people, the new opportunities inclined them toward the neoliberal stream within Civic Forum, and this led, in turn, to the birth of several right-of-center, market-oriented parties. In particular, conservative neoliberals, led by Václav Klaus, attracted wide support among professionals, bureaucrats, and even many skilled manual workers. Partly in reaction to this turn of events, some left-of-center groups, especially the Social Democrats (who traced their affiliations back to the interwar and early postwar period) dissociated themselves from Civic Forum. In this situation, right-of-center forces won the 1992 parliamentary elections. Some small centrist parties, as well as the democratic left, represented mainly by the Social Democrats, formed the opposition to Klaus's dominant Civic Democratic Party (ODS). The Communists, with a still significant delegation in parliament, as well as a smaller group of right-wing "republican" radicals, also remained outside the governing coalition. The political power elite was thus limited to right-of-center, primarily neoliberal politicians, supported by the Christian Democrats. In principle, this broke with the ideological and political tradition of the Prague Spring and even with that of the anticommunist dissenters of the 1980s. The latter came to be represented more or less exclusively by the president, Václav Havel, whose powers were, however, quite limited constitutionally. The pattern approximated that of a "disunified elite" (Field and Higley, 1980: 35).

These changes in the makeup of the political elite were intensified by the dissolution of the Czechoslovak Federation at the start of 1993. The simultaneous victories of the ODS in the Czech lands and Vladimír Meciar's Movement for a Democratic Slovakia in the Slovak lands in the June 1992 elections created a curious situation. At the national level, the two leading and more or less dominant parties after those elections each represented clear minorities of the combined Czechoslovak electorate. Therefore, neither had a strong incentive to hold a national referendum about the country's future, and this was an important reason why the divorce between the Czechs and the Slovaks was engineered behind the scenes and occurred without popular approval. The divorce involved disbanding the elected federal parliament, and this had two significant effects on Czech elites. By removing Slovak political forces it shifted the remaining Czech political spectrum further to the right, and by eliminating scores of senior federal parliamentarians it produced a noticeably younger core political elite in Prague.

The ODS's ascendancy was followed by corresponding personnel changes in the rapidly expanding Czech state administration and in numerous regional offices of the various ministries. Augmented by changes resulting from municipal elections, new career fields for many younger supporters of the ODS and its allies opened up. Compared to political elite circulation, however, bureaucratic elite circulation was more gradual and limited because many administrative personnel who had acquired their first jobs under state socialism actually moved to elite and subelite bureaucratic positions under the postsocialist governments. At the municipal level, bureaucratic elite circulation was frequently the product of local circumstances, so that its extent varied considerably among big cities, medium-sized and small towns, and villages.

Paralleling the circulation of political and bureaucratic elites were less radical changes in the economic elite. The most obvious change was the emergence of owners and entrepreneurs. This was of great social and psychological importance. In a society where there had been an almost total absence of self-employed persons, a category of self-employed persons amounting to about 13 percent of those holding full-time jobs (perhaps 20 percent of all full-time and part-time jobholders) emerged within five years.[3] The great bulk of these self-employed persons did not have employees, and most of the few who did had only a handful. They were small businessmen, tradesmen, craftsmen, service providers—in short, the urban "petite bourgeoisie." Our data show that half of these people came from the skilled working class. There was as yet no significant group of farmers who owned large amounts of land. In the cities and towns, though many houses and properties were subjected to restitution, they were either quickly sold by their owners or used for rental incomes. These considerations suggest that the emergence of a fairly broad private economic sector has, in fact, had little to do with the formation of an economic elite.

A smaller part of the economic elite has instead been formed out of the relatively few proprietors, with or without significant numbers of employees, who have been active in the information, commerce, and business services sectors (including the "gray market" parts of these sectors) and who are able to accumulate enough capital to emerge as "self-made" men. Very often, these people hold only secondary-level education credentials. Augmenting these Horatio Algers is a variety of important managers of privatized state enterprises who profited greatly from the privatizing process. There are still others who took second jobs in the private sector before they left leading administrative posts in the old regime, and who then switched wholly to these private sector jobs and climbed rapidly to leading economic statuses.

The remainder of the self-employed component of the economic elite— namely, owners of middle-sized companies with significant numbers of employees and/or important amounts of capital—emerged through the restitution of sizable properties, through the privatization of retail, service, and manufacturing enterprises, through the foundation of companies with foreign assistance, or through the exploitation of connections in the gray and black markets. Hence, the obvious suspicion with which many Czechs regard the new entrepreneurs. In any event, the resources controlled by these entrepreneurs are seldom, if ever, sufficient to enable them to compete with the truly large companies set up by foreigners or deriving from the privatization of major state-owned enterprises. Perhaps the new entrepreneurs will eventually accumulate enough capital and/or employees to compete with these "big boys," but this is likely to take a long time and it is doubtful if it will ever be the main channel to economic elite status.

The decisive part of the new economic elite consists, instead, of the leaders of large industrial and service companies, almost all of them established by foreign capital or by major privatization activities. From its start, the ODS government gave priority to the rapid privatization of large enterprises.

Throughout the 1990s, there has been a battle to determine which of the following groups will control these privatized enterprises: private investment funds that have been an unexpectedly strong by-product of voucher privatization; banks and other financial institutions; the enterprise managers themselves; current or former top bureaucrats and politicians; foreign capitalists and/or managers; or various ad hoc coalitions of people from all these groups. The banks and other financial institutions appear to be the likely victors, but the battle is still not ended, and this means that the sociological profile of the economic elite is even now somewhat unclear.

There are, nevertheless, some interesting distinctions to be observed among the backgrounds of the most important competitors for economic elite status. The staffs of financial institutions and business service firms are relatively young and have few connections to the old state socialist system, though the top positions in these firms tend to be held by people who had experience in the old system. The managers of privatized state enterprises, by contrast, began their careers under state socialism, and they tend to be more expert in technological matters. The same is true of most high-level bureaucrats in economic ministries and state regulatory agencies. It is obvious, in other words, that economic elite circulation has not been as comprehensive as political elite circulation. The economic elite's composition has changed more slowly and has resulted partly from the normal life cycle (accelerated somewhat by political considerations), partly from ongoing structural change (mainly the increased size of the tertiary sector), and partly from changes in the occupational order itself (for example, the relative and absolute increases in the number of people working in information services with business, as opposed to technical, training).

Limited data for the cultural elite suggest that circulation has not been as great as in the political elite, but has probably been more extensive than in the economic elite. In the natural sciences and many other cultural spheres, professional credentials and demonstrated expertise remain decisive for attaining high-level positions. In the humanities, fine arts, journalism, and the social sciences, ideological affinities and political profiles play important roles. The neoliberal ODS government was not inclined to provide large-scale financial support to the sciences, to the universities, or to other bases of the cultural elite; it instead tried to transfer support for cultural activities from the public to the private sector. Accordingly, the numbers of people employed in cultural spheres declined or stagnated, and their salary levels also declined or stagnated relative to salaries in other occupations.

These trends are reasons why the most vocal dissatisfaction and protests during the 1990s came not from the working class but, rather, from members of the health-care professions, teachers, and those in science, research, and cultural institutions (for example, public libraries).[4] Compared with the economic elite, gradual life-cycle shifts in the cultural elite's composition have been accelerated by political considerations. However, it must also be said that the new postsocialist political and social order allows more space for opposition ideological streams, unconventional cultural activities, and the development of a commercialized mass culture connected to the mass media and entertainment industries. This permits many cultural activities to be carried out on an unofficial, often amateur basis, so that there are contradictory tendencies in the cultural sphere, and their complexities have so far prevented a comprehensive and persuasive study of the new cultural elite's makeup.

Putting all these changes together, we can in general say that, by the mid-1990s, the Czech state and society were led by moderately conservative elites supported primarily by younger and middle-aged generations of relatively well-educated and enterprising people, who were oriented toward Western patterns of behavior and outlook. Dominating the elite stratum as a whole were owners of large- and middle-sized enterprises, professional politicians, higher state officials, and higher managers and professionals in the financial, legal, and general administrative spheres. There were, nevertheless, significant differences between the profiles of the political, economic, and cultural elites. The political elite was sharply divided between the right-of-center holders of government power and their centrist and left-of-center opponents. The economic elite's pecking order remained fluid, with enterprise owners, bankers, and managers competing for controlling positions. The cultural elite was divided into older and younger segments, different educational specializations and professional activities, and different income levels stemming from location in the private or public sphere.

MOBILITY TO ELITE STATUSES BETWEEN 1988 AND 1993

The formula of "winners and losers" in postsocialist transformations exaggerates the linearity and irreversibility of changes in elite fortunes. It is better to remember that the same elite group can lose its relative position in one phase only to gain it back, perhaps with dividends, in a later phase. If we look at the processes of intrageneration mobility among people attaining or aspiring to elite statuses since 1989 we can see both setbacks and advances among different Czech elite groups.

A previous analysis of Czech data collected in the multicountry survey study of "Social Stratification and the Circulation of Elites in Eastern Europe after 1989," which was carried out in the spring of 1993, yielded two social categories that were highly relevant for elite recruitment: the stable and the mobile. From a sample of 2,769 persons who were economically active in both 1988 and 1993, a total of 12 percent were higher professionals or entrepreneurs. In the stable category were people who held higher professional positions. They constituted 8 percent of the sample of persons from 1988 who were economically active. In 1993, 91.6 percent of the same persons were still located in such positions, while 8.4 percent had become entrepreneurs. In this stable category, 57.7 percent had tertiary and 36.7 percent had secondary educational credentials. Their earnings were, on average, relatively high, as was the cultural level of their leisure activities. Three-quarters were male and just over three-fifths were over forty years of age. Four-fifths lived in towns and cities—40 percent in large cities. They disposed of large amounts of political and social capital. Thirty percent had been members of the Communist Party in 1988, though all but a sixth of them left the Party after November 1989. In 1993, they gave significantly greater support to the two leading right-of-center liberal parties than did the whole population, though many people with stable upper positions also supported the Social Democrats. Their self-placement on a prestige scale in 1993 was generally high.

In the mobile category were those who ascended from lower to higher occupational positions between 1988 and 1993. They made up 4 percent of the economically active population in the latter year. In 1993, half of these upwardly mobile people, some of who reached elite positions, were higher professionals and half were entrepreneurs with employees. If second jobs are counted, 62 percent of the upwardly mobile were entrepreneurs. The proportion of upwardly mobile persons with tertiary education (18 percent) was considerably higher than the population average, though persons with secondary education (43 percent) and less than secondary education (39 percent) predominated. Nearly half of the upwardly mobile (44 percent) displayed status inconsistencies in the sense that their material and managerial statuses were higher than their educational–cultural statuses. Although men predominated, a non-trivial one-third of the upwardly mobile were women. More than half (55 percent) were still less than forty years of age in 1993, and fully 86 percent had not been members of the Communist Party, which was a significantly larger abstention from Party membership than in the population as a whole. Three-quarters of the upwardly mobile reported no religious affiliation, and in 1993 their political identification was primarily with the ODS. Their prestige self-placement was high, in spite of their inconsistent social statuses.

It must be doubted that all of those who maintained their statuses or who climbed to better ones constituted a real social elite in 1993. The main reason for doubting this is the widespread status inconsistencies. Many who remained in higher professional positions between 1988 and 1993 still had very modest incomes in the latter year, while many of those who climbed to higher positions during those five years had very modest educational and other cultural credentials. Let us ask what further changes took place in these categories after the spring of 1993.

ELITE PROFILES IN 1994

A survey of old and new Czech elites, carried out in 1994, was part of the aforementioned study of social stratification in Eastern Europe after 1989. One of the present authors, Milan Tucek, participated in this survey, which entailed the administration of a lengthy questionnaire to 1,509 members of the old state socialist and the new postsocialist economic, political, and cultural elites. Methodological problems of sample selection and representativeness were substantial. However, data for the economic elite can be judged reliable, data for the political elite provide much valuable information, while data for the cultural elite are not sufficiently comprehensive to provide more than suggestive and illustrative material. Let us consider each of the elites separately.

The Economic Elite

Of 867 respondents in the economic sphere, 495 belonged to the new economic elite, 290 were members of both the old and the new economic elite, while 82 had been members of the old elite who no longer occupied key positions in 1994. The fact that two-fifths of the economic elite in 1994 had held economic elite positions under state socialism (though not necessarily in the same position or same enterprise) is quite striking. The estimate of the number of people who left the economic elite shortly after November 1989 is 10–20 percent.

The proportion of males was high in 1994—around 90 percent—and there has since been no important change in this respect. The average age of economic leaders in 1994 did not suggest substantial inroads by a younger generation. Nor was there any major change in the political backgrounds of business leaders: 95 percent of the old leaders who had been displaced had been members of the Communist Party, but this was also true of 83.3 percent of those who retained elite positions despite the change of regime, and even 53.1 percent of the new managers and owners were former Communists. The proportion of business leaders with tertiary educational credentials appeared to have increased, to 85 percent; however, roughly half of those who had managed state enterprises and who in 1994 were managing private ones had achieved their highest educational credential through part-time study while they were employed. This implies that many of these managers began their careers during the "normalization" period after the Prague Spring's repression, hastily chosen to replace those who had been purged. Only later did they acquire something like the educational credentials normally expected of people in their positions.

The new economic leaders in 1994 were hardly inexperienced. Only about 14 percent of them were real newcomers in the sense that they had held no managerial positions during the 1980s. More than half had in fact been in higher managerial positions prior to 1989, and nearly a third of these had coordinated the activities of various departments in that period. In sum, more than 90 percent of the economic elite in 1994 consisted either of former state socialist managers or state socialist "cadres" who were already in line for top managerial positions. These patterns are consistent with our thesis that economic elite circulation was gradual and piecemeal between 1989 and 1994.

The Political Elite

Of the 131 political leaders sampled in 1994, 42 percent were members of the governing "power elite," one-third were members of opposition parties and organizations, and the remainder were high-ranking state bureaucrats or key trade union and other association leaders in political positions. Nearly half (47 percent) were less than forty-five years of age, and one-fifth had yet to reach their thirty-fifth birthday. There was no significant age difference between the governing and opposition sections of the political elite. Clearly, however, the new political elite was much younger than the state socialist elite it replaced, 27 percent of whom had been sixty years or older in 1989, whereas this advanced age had been reached by only 6 percent of the new political elite in 1994. As regards education, more than four-fifths of the new elite had tertiary credentials and, again, the governing and opposition segments did not differ greatly in this respect. A majority of the new elite had occupied higher professional positions before November 1989, and most of the rest had been in lower professional positions. Almost none had been manual or other routine workers, and this was probably the greatest difference between the 1994 political elite and its predecessor: a majority of the old state socialist political leaders had begun their work lives as members of the working class. These patterns conform to our claim that a near total circulation of the political elite had occurred by 1994.

The Cultural Elite

Of the 277 respondents who were located in leading cultural positions in 1994, a third had held the same or similar positions before November 1989. The main difference between the new and old cultural elites was the decrease in the number of persons from working-class backgrounds in the new elite. Interestingly, among those who survived the Velvet Revolution in elite positions, few were of working-class origin. When questioned about their families, the majority of respondents in the new cultural elite indicated that they came from highly educated and generally cultured backgrounds. On the other hand, the proportion of members whose fathers had been

Communist Party members, while not as high as in the old cultural elite, was significantly greater than in the population as a whole. More than 40 percent of the new elite had been members of the Party; in the old elite, of course, all cultural elite members had belonged to the Party. These data tend to support our hypothesis that cultural elite circulation has been both gradual and discrete.

ELITE ATTITUDES IN 1994

Also during 1994, the Center for Empirical Research (STEM) in Prague conducted a survey of "outlooks and attitudes of social elites in the Czech and Slovak Republics" (Konvicka, 1995). The sample consisted of 423 people selected from lists of occupants of elite positions in various social sectors. The center has kindly allowed us to summarize elite attitudes and value orientations as revealed by its studies. Probably the central finding was that fully 84 percent of the elite respondents evaluated the changes that had taken place since 1989 as positive. This was a far more upbeat assessment than that of the general Czech population in 1994. Political leaders and leaders of public sector institutions made the most positive evaluations, whereas military leaders were less uniformly positive. Moreover, three-quarters of all elite persons were optimistic about future prospects. Asked to choose between a state-paternalist and a liberal sociopolitical order, nine out of every ten elite respondents chose the latter, with military leaders again being less close to unanimous about this. It is safe to say that, in 1994, preferences for a liberal order were far less widespread in the Czech population as a whole.

Despite this strong elite endorsement of a liberal order, 35 percent of the respondents also endorsed or partly endorsed the idea that some political parties could nonetheless be banned, and this illiberal view was especially pronounced among elites in the public, cultural, scientific, and religious sectors. Clearly, that condition of a liberal order that protects dissenting minorities had yet to be fully accepted by Czech elites in 1994. Furthermore, a question about the need for a "strong leader" received affirmative responses from a significant number of top-level managers, entrepreneurs, and military leaders. It was evident that a fairly pronounced right-wing or, perhaps, neoliberal orientation prevailed among Czech elites five years after the Velvet Revolution.

The 1994 STEM data corroborated our own observation of the relatively high incidence of former Communist Party members among the elites: 37 percent of those sampled by STEM had been former Party members, compared with 23.9 percent of the population at large. Not surprisingly, former Party membership was especially frequent among military leaders, but it was also quite pronounced among high-level state administrative, economic, and, somewhat surprisingly, mass media leaders. Moreover, about half of all the respondents' fathers had been Party members. On the other hand, 40 percent of the respondents stated that they or their families had been persecuted by the old regime.

DEVELOPMENTS IN THE SECOND HALF OF THE 1990s

Signs of a slowdown in GDP growth and a less favorable balance of trade became apparent in 1995. Accordingly, a general social survey that we conducted during that summer recorded a substantial decline in popular satisfaction with the results of the postsocialist transformation. The population was divided into two large segments, one with positive and the other with negative evaluations of how their well-being had fared since 1989. This division was not related to people's assessment of democratization; a large majority still viewed their new liberties and possibilities for self-realization in highly positive ways. The main reason for the shift in public opinion was dissatisfaction of the "new middle class" (higher and especially lower professional employees) with their incomes and living standards. Political party preferences were, therefore, shifting toward the Social Democrats and away from the ODS and its allies. As a result, in the May 1996 parliamentary elections, support for the Social Democrats quadrupled, while support for the right-of-center governing coalition stagnated.

A political stalemate set in. Although an ODS-led coalition government was formed (with the help of two Social Democrat defectors) after the May elections, it was compelled to share key parliamentary positions with opposing parties. Thus, the Social Democrat leader, Milos Zeman, was elected chairman of the House of Representatives, and, following the senate elections in November, Petr Pithart, a member of the former dissident movement who had been prime minister of the Czech government until 1992 and who was unsympathetic to the ODS core of the coalition government formed in 1996, won the senate chairmanship. The approximately equal balance of government and opposition forces inside and outside parliament increased President Havel's political influence at the same time that it signaled the end of the right-wing ODS's monopolistic power position and of Václav Klaus's political primacy.

Economic difficulties, as well as social and political tensions, increased during 1997, and they were accompanied by a further shift of political preferences toward the Social Democrats. This made the ODS-led coalition government more fractious, so that several corruption scandals, coupled with mounting economic difficulties, led to Klaus's resignation as prime minister at the end of November 1997. The corruption scandals, which centered mostly on illicit financing of ODS political campaigns, were interesting because they bore out suspicions about how the privatization process had been carried out and because they revealed previously hidden linkages between the political and economic elites. An interim government, led by the former Central Bank president, Josef Tosovsky, was installed at the beginning of 1998 on the understanding that new parliamentary elections would take place later in the year. Pledging to continue most existing policies, the Tosovsky government nevertheless allocated cabinet positions to several former dissidents, as well as to a number of technocrats, and it stressed its openness to more diverse political and popular forces. All of these events reflected an underlying steady shift of popular support away from the right-of-center political elite camp, which seemed to be splintering into a number of factions, and toward the left-of-center camp, which displayed considerably more unity than in the early 1990s.

The changed political balance was concretized by the June 1998 parliamentary elections. Although no party emerged with a majority of seats, the Social Democrats greatly improved their position, the radical nationalist Republican Party failed to gain a single seat, while the ODS managed to contain breakaway tendencies in its ranks. The elections left the Social Democrats with a choice between forming a majority coalition government with small centrist parties or a minority government with sufficient tolerance from other parties that it would not easily be defeated in parliament. To nearly everyone's surprise, the outcome was a Social Democrat minority government based on an agreement with its principal opponent, the ODS, that the government would be tolerated. Although observers harbored doubts about the sincerity with which the two main political elite groups entered into this agreement, it was a clear signal that both wanted to move toward the center of the political spectrum and that, more important, each acknowledged the other's right to exercise government power according to its program and strategy. In short, developments during 1998 indicated that the political elite had become more pluralistic and open. The new internal relations within the political elite were a step toward what Field and Higley (1980: 37) call a "consensually unified" elite. This brought Czech politics much closer to the European democratic norm in which government power alternates peacefully between competing elite camps.

It was less clear, however, that radical forces at either end of the political spectrum, especially the Communist Party, were accepted, and incorporated into, the new political mode. Popular suspicion of the Communists remained widespread and it kept them from obtaining a place in government. At the same time, economic difficulties and the economic hardships that were borne disproportionately by lower social strata under the former ODS-led governments put wind in radical left-wing sails. This was noticeable in the advances that radical leftists made in local elections and in some regional constituencies, particularly where outmoded industrial enterprises and high unemployment rates were concentrated, in senate elections during 1998.

The revelations of corrupt practices that helped bring down the ODS-led coalition government in late 1997 may have important consequences for the economic elite's composition and functioning. The ability of "lumpen-bourgeoisie" members to retain key business positions and to engage in illicit practices has probably decreased. Economic slowdown has endangered many of the middle-sized enterprises and some large enterprises. A shortage of investment capital has forced the government to make more intensive efforts to attract foreign investments, and such investments are likely to alter the economic elite's makeup and actions.

Within the cultural elite, it seems probable that the recent political changes have contributed to a greater pluralism of attitudes and value orientations. Reduced infighting within the political elite is conducive to less ideological polarization among members of the cultural elite and to greater opportunities for advancement based on performance criteria rather than political affiliations. This probably benefits aspiring younger intellectuals and artists, especially women.

These are, however, guesses about the overall direction of change in the Czech Republic at the end of the 1990s. They are derived from various sets of official statistics, sociological surveys, economic analyses, direct observations, and information provided by the mass media. They are hypotheses rather than indisputable statements. Before concluding, let us summarize what systematic data there is that appears to support them.

A survey of political elite attitudes was conducted by STEM during February 1996 (Konvicka, 1997a). This was not long after our summer 1995 mass survey, mentioned above, detected increased popular dissatisfaction with the transformation process and shifts in political preferences toward the left-of-center parties. To what extent did the elite persons surveyed a few months later, in February 1996, perceive and share the changing popular appraisals? Surprisingly, the 1996 STEM survey showed no marked change in the optimistic elite outlooks that the earlier 1994 STEM survey had revealed. Four months before the May 1996 electoral shock, in which the ODS lost its unlimited power, the political elite did not notice or reflect any significant change in popular orientation.

Possibly the best explanation for this finding is that the political elite, surfeited by its own material success, was complacent (Konvicka, 1997a: 41). This explanation is consistent with the hypothesis that, down to 1996, the "winners" of the transition from state socialism were a relatively limited group of people who held key national, regional, and local positions. This elite segment was largely isolated from the wider stratum of upper-middle professional employees that experienced declining material conditions with the economic difficulties beginning in 1995, while the gap between the elite and the lower professional and working-class categories was even larger and still increasing. Elite complacency and isolation help to account for the stubbornly nonadaptive policies that the ODS government continued to pursue, the electoral setback it suffered in mid-1996, and its ouster from government at the start of 1998.

Findings from qualitative interview studies during 1996 and 1997 support this explanation. Specifically, a third and broader survey of elite attitudes and opinions was conducted by STEM during April 1997 (Konvicka, 1997b). It showed that the prevailing conservative orientation of political elites recorded a year earlier had still not changed. Although elite support for the Social Democrats had increased somewhat, it remained well below the support the Social Democrats were receiving in public opinion polls. However, whereas four-fifths of elite respondents had expressed satisfaction with the direction of change in Czech society in both the 1994 and 1996 surveys, by the spring of 1997 this proportion had declined to two-thirds, and only half of the respondents had optimistic expectations about developments over the next twelve months. Members of the economic elite, especially private entrepreneurs, were the least positive and optimistic in the April 1997 survey, whereas most political and cultural elites continued to hold quite rosy views. Overall, the majority of elite members who had proclaimed themselves satisfied with economic developments in February 1996 was replaced by a majority who said they were dissatisfied in April 1997, and half of all the latter respondents believed that more radical economic reforms were necessary.

If the self-confident and complacent outlooks of elite respondents affiliated with the ODS coalition government, together with the somewhat naïve attitudes of many respondents in the cultural elite, are put to one side, clear indications of elite disquiet could be seen in the April 1997 survey data. Many elite persons sensed that something was going wrong in the society, but they offered no coherent critique of previous policies and they could only opine that some eventual radicalization of the privatization process would be necessary. In other words, half a year after the ODS lost much of its governing capacity, half a year before the government crisis that led to the Tosovsky interim government, and a year before the Social Democrats' entrance into power, the elites were largely unresponsive to the needs, interests, and demands of most parts of the wider society, as these were registered in opinion polls. This helps to account for the evident de-legitimation of governing forces during this critical period of economic deterioration.

Taken together, the three elite surveys conducted between 1994 and 1997 show that the somewhat authoritarian, or, if one prefers, haughty attitudes and orientations of right-of-center leaders and their allies in the economic and cultural elites, as well as the increasing isolation of these elite groups from large segments of the society, led to their eventual political defeat.

From June 1998, this defeat gave previously excluded left-of-center elites access to power on the basis of an agreement that appeared to mitigate conflicts between the two main political elite camps. The democratic method of political elite alternation in government began to operate.

CONCLUSIONS

There are two competing explanations of elite change in former state socialist countries like the Czech Republic during the 1990s. One stresses the reproduction of elites, in which the old elites adapted quite easily to the transition from state socialism by converting their old political, social, and cultural capital into primarily economic, but also sometimes political, capital that could be used to hold power in the new conditions. The other explanation stresses a circulation of elites caused by blockages and other difficulties in the reproduction process, augmented by the conversion of some amounts of accumulated capital and by a resumption of interrupted mobility paths charted by parents or even grandparents before the imposition of state socialism after World War II. Our data do not unambiguously validate or invalidate either explanation in the Czech case; they show that social and political realities have been more complex than either implies.

Our data indicate substantial amounts of both reproduction and circulation, but the balance between the two processes varies significantly among the elites. Our data show that the political elite, following a stepwise but ultimately quite radical circulation path, was comprehensively transformed. To be sure, there are some significant cultural ties between the new political elite and the elites of interwar Czechoslovakia, but the half century separating the 1990s from the interwar period, as well as the wartime, postwar, and post-1968 upheavals (including the extensive emigration that occurred during "normalization" after 1968) prevented any recrudescence of the presocialist elite and their offspring. The disunity of the political elite caused by profound cleavages between the right-wing power elite and the democratic part of the opposition during the years 1992–96 has been replaced by more democratic patterns of restrained elite competition for government power. Elite reproduction has been more evident in the economic elite. It has been quite pronounced among leaders of the privatized state enterprises, but less so among leaders of the newly formed private enterprises and the subsidiaries of Western corporations. The cultural elite displays a combination of reproduction and circulation, of continuity and discontinuity. Political and ideological preferences, together with reduced state support for cultural institutions and activities, have worked against reproduction and continuity; the importance of accumulated, family-centered cultural capital has worked in favor of reproduction and continuity.

Whether these differences between Czech political, economic, and cultural elites are paralleled by differences between counterpart elites in other former state socialist countries is an interesting question. How many of the differences are peculiar to the Czech situation and how many are generic to postsocialist transformations? Finally, how much more elite change can we expect if, as seems quite likely at the end of the 1990s, the economic ground shifts even more substantially?

NOTES

1. The concrete historical aspects of Communist rule in Czechoslovakia have recently been described by Krejci and Machonin (1996).
2. Laws permitting restitution of properties confiscated after 1948 were quickly passed and led to one of the widest restitution programs of any undertaken in the postsocialist countries.
3. These estimates are derived by combining official workforce statistics with our social surveys during the first half of the 1990s.
4. Railroad workers, including lower-level professional as well as manual personnel, have also been vocal protestors. It is interesting that their protests received much greater ODS government attention than the protests of cultural workers.

BIBLIOGRAPHY

Adamski, Wladyslaw. 1990. *The Polish Conflict: Its Background and Systemic Challenges.* Amsterdam: European Cultural Foundation.

Bourdieu, Pierre. 1986. "The Forms of Capital." In *Handbook of Theory and Research for the Sociology of Education,* ed. J. G. Richardson. New York: Greenwood Press.

Field, G. Lowell, and John Higley. 1980. *Elitism.* Boston: Routledge & Kegan Paul.

Habermas, Jürgen. 1990. *Die nachholende Revolution.* Frankfurt am Main: Surhkamp Verlag.

Hankiss, Elemer. 1988. "'The Second Society': Is There an Alternative Social Model Emerging in Contemporary Hungary?" *Social Research* 55: 13–42.

Konvicka, Libor. 1995. *Elity 1994.* Prague: STEM.

———. 1997a. *Názory a postoje predstavitelu spolecenskych elit v Ceské republica a Slovenské republice* (Opinions and Attitudes of Social Elites' Representatives in the Czech and Slovak Republics). Prague: STEM.

———. 1997b. *Názory a postoje predstavitelu spolecenskych elit v Ceské republice a Slovenské republice: Zaverecna zprava 1997* (Opinions and Attitudes of Social Elites' Representatives in the Czech and Slovak Republics: Final Report 1997). Prague: STEM.

Krejci, Jaroslav, and Pavel Machonin. 1996. *Czechoslovakia 1918–1992. A Laboratory for Social Change.* London: Macmillan.

Lenski, Gerhard E. 1966. *Power and Privilege.* New York: McGraw-Hill.

Machonin, Pavel. 1993. "The Social Structure of the Soviet-Type Societies: Its Collapse and Legacy." *Czech Sociological Review* 1: 231–49.

————. 1994. "Social and Political Transformation in the Czech Republic." *Czech Sociological Review* 2: 71–87.

Machonin, Pavel, and Milan Tucek. 1994. "Structures et acteurs en République Tcheque depuis 1989." In *1989: Une révolution sociale? Revue d'Etudes Comparatives Est–Ouest* 25: 79–109.

————. 1996. *Ceská spolecnost v transformaci* (Czech Society in Transformation). Prague: SLON.

Mateju, Petr. 1995. "How Not to Make Historical Comparisons Empirically." *Czech Sociological Review* 3: 221–29.

————. 1997. "Elite Research in the Czech Republic." In *Elites in Transition,* ed. Heinrich Best and Ulrike Becker. Oppladen, Germany: Leske & Budrich.

Mateju, Petr, and Blanska Rehakova. 1994. "Une révolution pour qui? Analyse selective des modèles de mobilité intergénérationnelle entre 1989 et 1992." In *1989: Une révolution sociale? Revue d'Etudes Comparatives Est–Ouest* 25: 79–109.

Minck, Georges, and J. C. Szurek. 1992. *Adaptation and Conversion Strategies of Former Communist Elites.* Paris: RESPO/IRESCO.

Pareto, Vilfredo. 1935. *The Mind and Society: A Treatise on General Sociology.* New York: Dover Publications.

Slomcynski, Kasimierz. 1994. "Class and Status in East European Perspective." In *The Transformation of Europe: Social Conditions and Consequences,* ed. M. Alestalo. Warsaw: IfiS.

Szelényi, Ivan, and Donald Treiman. 1991. "Vyvoj socialni stratifikace a rekrutace elit ve vychodni Evrope po roce 1989" (The Development of Social Stratification and Elite Recruitment in Eastern Europe after 1989). *Sociologicky caspopis* 27: 276–98.

Touraine, Alain. 1991. "Zrod postkommunistickych spolecnosti" (The Birth of the Postcommunist Societies). *Sociologia* 23: 301–18.

Vecernik, Jeri. 1969. "Problémy prijmu a zivotni urovne v socialni diferenciaci" (The Problems of Income and Standard of Living in Social Differentiation). In *Czeskoslovenska spolecnost* (Czechoslovak Society), ed. P. Machonin. Bratislava: Epocha.

————. 1995. "Staré a nové ekonomické nerovnosti: pripad ceskych zemi" (Old and New Economic Inequalities: The Case of the Czech Lands). *Sociologicky casopis* 31: 321–34.

3

Slovakia

Elite Disunity and Convergence

John A. Gould and Soňa Szomolányi

Eight years after Czechoslovakia's Velvet Revolution and five years after Slovakia's "velvet divorce" from the Czech Republic, the European Commission in Brussels judged Slovak democracy to be seriously deficient. Recommending in July 1997 that Slovakia not be invited to begin negotiations for accession to the European Union (EU), the commission observed that "the institutional framework defined by the Slovak Constitution corresponds to that of a parliamentary democracy with free and fair elections; [however] the situation with regard to the stability of institutions and their integration into political life is unsatisfactory" (European Commission, 1997: 1.3).

That Slovakia has the basic trappings of democracy but has been unable to satisfy the political prerequisites for EU admission highlights the importance of political elites in transitions from state socialism (Simecka, 1997; Gould and Szomolányi, 1997). Until elites fundamentally agree that democratic norms and procedures constitute the "only game in town," the viability of democratic institutions remains in question (Higley and Pakulski, 1995; Linz and Stepan, 1996). Democratic competitions or institutions may threaten the basic interests of one or more elite groups. If this happens, attempts to protect those interests by nondemocratic means become a real possibility.

This, in a nutshell, explains the fragility of Slovak democracy during the 1990s. Although democratic institutions were in place, elite behavior and relations marred their effectiveness and undermined their integrity. The major reason was the division among Slovak elites over the controversial issues of national identity and sovereignty that have dominated Slovak political life for most of the twentieth century. Slovakia's achievement of independence on January 1, 1993, did not resolve these issues or eradicate long-standing elite divisions. Having succeeded in establishing a Slovak state, nationalist elites sought to use Slovak government offices to retain power by controlling the privatization process while claiming to defend national sovereignty against internal and external enemies, however they defined them. During his two terms as prime minister of the independent state, Vladimír Meciar and his Movement for a Democratic Slovakia (HZDS) presented the vision of a nation at risk in order to justify the exclusion of opponents from access to decision-making channels and institutional centers of authority that could be used to challenge HZDS control. The Meciar government's actions raised the stakes of political competitions. By making institutional functioning the end product, rather than the arbiter, of political conflict, the government weighted the rules of political competition against opposing groups. Even disputes over small issues came close to fights for political survival.

In the election campaign of 1998, however, a broad left–right coalition of opposition parties formed a single movement, the Slovak Democratic Coalition (SDK). Other opposition parties—notably the ex-communist Party of the Democratic Left (SDL)—pledged not to enter into a coalition with HZDS following the election. Although HZDS won a tiny plurality of 0.7 percent over the SDK coalition, it emerged virtually isolated on the political spectrum. The HZDS leaders admitted that theirs was at best a pyrrhic victory, and they stepped down from power. After lengthy negotiations, a broad SDK-led coalition government, with a parliamentary majority, took office.

The 1998 election and its aftermath provided Slovak elites with a unique opportunity to overcome many of their divisions. A remarkable 84.2 percent of the electorate voted, and the results appeared to reflect an underlying shift towards democratic values among citizens (Butorova, 1997). The broad elite coalition that won the election was possibly the first clear indication of a gradual elite convergence around democratic norms and procedures. This convergence was likely to continue if the new coalition government acted to ensure that government and opposition forces alike perceived democratic institutions and processes to be fair.

In this chapter, we analyze the dynamics of elite division and fledgling elite convergence in Slovakia. We first explain the division among Slovak elites following the 1989 democratic transition. We then analyze the elite configuration during the third Meciar government, which held office between 1994 and 1998. We conclude with an analysis of the 1998 election struggle and subsequent May 1999 presidential election and their implications about elites and democratic prospects in Slovakia.

ELITE DIVISION AFTER 1989

Slovakia was a puzzle to students of East European politics throughout the 1990s. Many of the patterns of social behavior and attitudes that characterized Slovakia also characterized neighboring Poland, Hungary, and the Czech Republic, yet the postsocialist political trajectories of those countries were quite different. Slovakia displayed a predisposition to populist and paternalistic politics similar to that of its neighbors, and its civic–political culture was, like theirs, weak (Lukas and Szomolányi, 1996; Mihalikova, 1997). After systematically reviewing Czech and Slovak polling data from 1990 to 1996, Kevin Krause (1998a) concluded that overwhelming proportions of the two populations held nearly identical political opinions. Systematic differences did exist, but they generally involved only small population segments. Such findings were repeated in other comparisons of the Czech Republic and Slovakia and in comparisons of all East Central European countries during the 1990s (Mihalikova, 1997). The puzzle was, therefore, why postsocialist political developments in Slovakia were far more rancorous and, as observed by the European Commission and others, conspicuously less democratic.

One explanation lies in Slovakia's long immersion in divisive issues of nationalism and state formation. Slovakia is the only country among the "Visegrad Four" Central European countries—the Czech Republic, Hungary, Poland, and Slovakia—without a sustained experience of statehood. Poland and Hungary had largely resolved the dual challenges of nationalism and state formation prior to the imposition of state socialism. Likewise, the Czechs were able to secure their national identity and language and develop a vibrant civic culture under Austro–Hungarian rule, so that, after independence in 1918, they constituted one of the most robust civil and political societies in Central Europe. Until the eve of World War I, by contrast, Slovaks were administered directly from Budapest so that their identity, language, and culture developed under the pressures of Hungarian policies of Magyarization. It is likely that some of the defensive and exclusionary aspects of Slovak nationalism reflect these early struggles for recognition and survival amid Magyar competition (Altermatt, 1996).

With the creation of the Czechoslovak Republic in 1918, Slovak elites disagreed over the creation of a single country consisting of the Czech and Slovak peoples. Concurrently, the elites disagreed about the appropriate political arrangement between the Czech and Slovak lands. These issues were never resolved and they contributed to deep divisions among Slovak elites. The divisions broke into the open following the Velvet Revolution in late 1989. Elites associated with the Slovak revolutionary movement, Public Against Violence (VPN), surprised and disappointed their Czech counterparts in Civic Forum by almost unanimously calling for a revision, first in the name, and then, after a few months, in the form of the Czechoslovak state. During the fall and winter of 1990–91, Slovak elites engaged in a competitive mobilization of Slovak voters over how best to restructure Czech–Slovak relations. As premier of the Slovak republic, Vladimír Meciar eventually came to dominate this mobilization, even though, or perhaps because, his initial position was a moderate one compared with that of some of his rivals. The latter included the radical nationalist and separatist, Vitoslav Moric, as well as the former religious dissident and leader of the Christian Democratic Movement, Jan Carnogursky, who initially dabbled in separatist ideas but later fell in line with VPN's profederalist stance. Unlike these nationalists and separatists, Meciar merely called for some form of power devolution from the federal government in Prague to the Slovak republic's government in Bratislava. During negotiations with his Czech counterpart and with the federal government, Meciar faced down separatist and chauvinist pressures from the radical nationalists, and he created the impression among Slovak voters that he championed their "reasonable" interests. However, Meciar kept himself in the limelight by constantly shifting and increasing his negotiating demands, thus preventing any timely settlement of the devolution question. He was also masterful in provoking Czech outrage and exploiting Czech elite insensitivity to his own advantage (Innes, 1997; Butora, Butorova, and Gyarfasova, 1994).

The political importance of Slovak nationalism and of Slovakia's place within the federal republic increased with the federal government's announcement of radical economic reforms on 1 January 1991. Declarations about the search for a Slovak national identity masked the vested interests of state managers of armaments-producing and other state-owned companies that were threatened by federal government programs for armaments conversion and voucher privatization. Meciar championed these industrial interests and won their support. The movement for Slovak secession, which until then had been confined to a small circle of intellectuals and politicians, acquired the strong economic backing of state enterprise managers, and this contributed greatly to Czechoslovakia's dissolution. At the same time, the managerial elite became a powerful pillar of support for Meciar's HZDS (Duleba, 1997b).

As unemployment mounted and production declined in Slovakia, elite factions competed to portray federal programs (designed largely by the Czech federal minister of finance, Václav Klaus) as inflexible "Czech inventions, created in the Czech environment for Czech conditions, and most importantly, inappropriate for Slovakia" (Miklos, 1997: 60). By early spring 1991, the Slovak Confederation of Industry, nationalists within the Christian Democratic Movement (KDH), the ex-communist SDL, and a newly formed association, called NEZES, led by Slovak economists-turned-politicians, were all demanding less price deregulation, easier credits for industry, a currency revaluation that would favor importers over exporters, and the halting or slowing of privatization.

Meciar was by then easily the most popular and trusted Slovak politician, and he used his popularity to engineer a split with the leadership of Public Against Violence. This occurred when VPN leaders refused to tolerate Meciar's populist tactics both in the movement and in the cabinet. They ousted him from the prime ministership in order to form a coalition government with KDH, whose leader, Carnogursky, became prime minister. As the new opposition leader, however, Meciar was free to intensify his populist outbidding. He artfully created and played on fears and resentments among less secure and sophisticated segments of the electorate, and he was aided in this by VPN and Czech political and media elite insensitivity toward Slovak attitudes and interests (Krivy, 1995; Butorova et al., 1993; Innes, 1997). Meciar also sought to build alliances with elites and social movements that VPN had been reluctant to exploit—especially the old Communist nomenklatura.

After ousting Meciar from the prime ministership, VPN leaders called increasingly for the adoption of rigorously anticommunist policies, and in the spring 1992 election campaign they ran on a platform that promised the intensified lustration of Slovak officials who had ties to the Communist-era secret police (Innes, 1997; Appel, 1997). Meciar, by contrast, took a stand against lustration, and most government officials and other nomenklatura members who had formerly been in the Communist Party's ranks supported him. By ousting Meciar and associating themselves increasingly with federal and Czech policies, VPN leaders became quite isolated politically. In the 1992 general election, the rump of VPN did not poll enough votes even to clear the 5 percent threshold for entering parliament. The national issue also hurt KDH, which suffered from the breakaway of its more nationalist and anti-radical reform wing and from poor campaign performances by its leaders (Innes, 1997: 429). HZDS emerged from the election as the strongest political force in parliament, and Meciar again became the head of government in Bratislava. Following the election, a pact between Meciar and the new Czech prime minister, Václav Klaus, led to Czechoslovakia's dissolution and the establishment of an independent Slovak Republic on January 1, 1993. This pact was reached and implemented without a referendum and despite polling data showing that a majority of Czechs and Slovaks opposed the dissolution (Butorova et al., 1993: 129–30).

By 1993, the bitter fights over national identity, secession, economic transformation, and Meciar's intolerant and somewhat undemocratic leadership style had greatly divided the Slovak political elites. After VPN's disastrous performance in the 1992 election, a self-styled "civic-democratic" opposition arose to counter the nationalist populism of Meciar's HZDS. Consisting originally of ex-federalists, this opposition eventually included former secessionists and a sprinkling of opportunists who had lost power struggles with Meciar.

Meciar and his group of state "founders" never elaborated a specific program for building the new Slovak state. It is possible that he did not expect that Czechoslovakia would dissolve so readily. Still, the concept of an "ethnic Slovak nation-state" was quite discernible in the Meciar government's actions following the break with the Czechs. The preamble of the Slovak Constitution, for example, begins with the phrase, "We, the Slovak nation . . ." Only later are ethnic minorities mentioned as "other citizens." Many at the time felt that this implied an exclusion of ethnic minorities from helping to build the new state. In particular, the preamble alienated the minority Hungarian community profoundly (Kusy, 1997). Formally, the principle of inclusive citizenship existed, but the nationalist–populist leaders frequently employed an informal rhetoric of exclusion, perhaps in an effort to maintain their base of political support. This was not the transparent exclusion that afflicted ethnic Russians in the Baltic countries. Rather, it rhetorically divided citizens into "good Slovaks" as opposed to those who were against the division of Czechoslovakia. This tactic continued right down to the 1998 electoral campaign, during which HZDS officials frequently asserted that their opponents had no right to govern "if they have declared openly that they disagreed with the establishment of the Slovak Republic" (CTV News, 3 December 1997). Meciar and his allies thus deepened elite divisions by their attempts to claim legitimacy as the Slovak state's only true founders.

Inter-elite antagonisms and the defection of HZDS members due to conflicts inside the party resulted in the HZDS government's loss of its narrow parliamentary majority in March 1994. However, HZDS won a plurality in the general election held on 30 September–1 October 1994. Significant financial support for the HZDS campaign came from the managers of state-owned industries. Later that fall, Meciar formed a coalition government with the far left-wing Association of the Workers of Slovakia (ZRS) and the far right-wing Slovak National Party (SNS). Electoral support for this new government was centered among rural, elderly, and less educated voters. In general, more educated and urban voters, as well as new entrepreneurs in the financial and service sectors, tended to reject Meciar's message, as did the minority Hungarian community. But there was no focal point around which Meciar's opponents could unite; consequently, their votes were dispersed ineffectually across a wide range of parties (Krivy, 1995).

ELITE UNITY AND DIFFERENTIATION, 1994–98

Although elite unity was never extensive in Slovakia, a momentary consensus about new rules of the political game followed the Communist collapse in November 1989. However, this consensus had largely unraveled by the time VPN leaders in the Slovak parliament ousted Meciar from the prime ministership in March 1991. What remained of elite consensus dissipated further in the wake of Slovak independence at the start of 1993. This was apparent in steps taken by the two post-independence Meciar-led governments—separated by only a six-month interim during 1994—to undermine centers of relatively autonomous institutional authority and power such as the presidency, the parliamentary opposition, the constitutional court, and the mass media. Nevertheless, Slovak elites remained quite differentiated, and this increased chances that one or more pacts establishing a new power balance between opposing political camps would be negotiated. Let us consider the extent of elite unity and differentiation in Slovakia during the mid-1990s.

Elite Unity

Some theorists maintain that elite unity has two components: normative agreement and mutual access to decision-making centers (see chapter 1; see also Field, Higley, and Burton, 1990). As we have noted, due to the contentious issues of nationalism and state formation, Slovak elites were never strongly unified, though this was masked by a surface ideological uniformity under state socialism. The more or less no-holds-barred competition among parties during most of the 1990s revealed the absence of elite unity quite clearly. Although this competition took place in several dimensions, prior to the 1998 election campaign Slovak political elites could easily be seen as constituting two opposing camps that were distinguished by their fundamentally antagonistic perceptions of democratic game rules and by their clashing rhetorics (Meseznikov, 1997; Krause, 1998a).

One camp consisted of the groups making up or associated with Meciar's former ruling coalition of HZDS, SNS, and ZRS. Elites in this camp often portrayed themselves as on the front lines of a defensive struggle for national survival against internal and external enemies of Slovakia's cultural and linguistic identity. They styled themselves as the founders and protectors of the independent Slovak state and they accused opponents of being naïve or actively complicit in efforts to grant Slovakia's Hungarian minority collective rights that would promote Hungary's eventual annexation of southern Slovakia. This camp also argued that various external forces were conspiring against Slovakia: the Hungarians and possibly the Czechs and Austrians, who were intent on compromising Slovakia's territorial integrity, as well as other "international interests" plotting to punish Slovakia for the Meciar government's refusal to let foreign capital dominate the privatization process. These views were regularly voiced in HZDS's daily newspaper, *Slovenska Republica,* where the most strident views were consistently articulated by HZDS commentators and parliamentarians such as Roman Hoffbauer and Dusan Slobodnik (see Simecka, 1997; Butora, Butorova, and Gyarfasova, 1994; Krause, 1998a).

Much of the Meciar-led camp's rhetoric portrayed the governing coalition as consisting of national patriots who were able to see the "real" threats to Slovak sovereignty and who were prepared to defend it. This portrayal had its greatest impact among older, less educated, rural voters. However, various actors who had more opportunistic aims also employed it. Of particular importance in this regard were Slovakia's reinvigorated industrialists—the loose networks of industrial managers and former nomenklatura members who did extraordinarily well in the privatization process. By aligning themselves with Meciar's ruling coalition—particularly during his third government—these individuals and groups gained insider access to state contracts, privatization opportunities, and other benefits flowing from the state–economy nexus (Gould, 1999).

The other, more loosely organized elite camp consisted of leaders of the anti-Meciar and anti-HZDS parties. Warily, often clumsily, these disparate leaders sought to pool enough resources to defeat their common foe. The camp was united, above all, by an acceptance of democratic game rules, and it was frequently referred to as Meciar's "civic democratic" opposition. This was not just an appealing label; several studies showed that the camp's members strongly held democratic values and were sharply critical of the Meciar camp's authoritarian tendencies (Kaldor and Vejvoda, 1997: 79; Krause, 1998a; Butorova et al., 1996: 51). Generally, they did not hold the alarmist view of external threats to Slovakia preached by Meciar and his allies, they favored integrating with Western Europe, they were generally less enthusiastic about Slovakia's independence, and they consequently voiced Slovak national identity less stridently (Krause, 1998a). There was, however, a significant amount of competition and division within the anti-Meciar camp. This occurred mainly between the subset of ethnic Hungarian parties and that of the mainstream parties arrayed along the standard left–right continuum. The former were distinguished by their unequivocal support for integration with Western Europe in order to protect their Hungarian communities, they had strongly opposed Slovak independence for this reason, and they were fervent advocates of minority rights.

Mutual elite access to decision-making centers is the other main component of elite unity mentioned above. Given the fearful and somewhat paranoid worldview put forth by the ruling coalition between late 1994 and 1998, and given its supporters' greater tolerance of authoritarian methods of rule, many elite members aligned with the Meciar government argued that it was necessary to come to some compromises with respect to the democratic rules of the game to achieve national goals. They claimed that some decisions and actions—especially those relating to privatization and internal security—had to be kept secret, and Meciar's third government went to great lengths to reduce its opponents' access to decision-making channels and processes. Some of the measures it took weakened democratic institutions.

A clear example was the all-night session of parliament on 3–4 November 1994. In this marathon sitting, Meciar's parliamentary majority excluded opposition members from meaningful participation on bodies set up to monitor and supervise a wide range of important state functions, including the Supreme Control Office, the Special Control Body (OKO), the General Prosecutor's Office, and the National Property Fund (NPF). This was done in spite of the fact that a new Meciar-led government had not even been formally constituted. Excluding the opposition from OKO was particularly crucial because that was the body that monitored the internal security service. The all-night parliamentary sitting also appointed from HZDS ranks the top executives for Slovak Radio and the Board of TV and Radio Broadcasting. This effectively turned the state-owned mass media into a partisan vehicle that devoted 75 percent of its news programming to the actions and statements of Meciar and his associates during the 1998 election campaign (RFE/RL Newsline 2: 192, 5 October 1998). The places allocated to opposition MPs on important parliamentary committees were cut to proportions far smaller than those to which their numbers in parliament entitled them, and the opposition was not allowed to choose its own representatives on those committees (Szomolányi, 1997).

Another exclusionary practice was the Meciar government's partisan application (or violation) of rules that should have been neutral. HZDS built a party–state apparatus that made an HZDS political orientation a requisite for obtaining favorable government decisions such as state budget allocations to a village or a municipality, awards of government purchasing contracts, and favorable privatization rulings by the Fund for National Property (Krivy, 1997: 119; Miklos 1997: 76–78). Furthermore, the ruling coalition violated the constitution by expelling one deputy, Frantisek Gaulieder, from parliament after he resigned from HZDS. It then refused to obey the constitutional court's ruling that he be reinstated. Finally, in May 1997, the Meciar government unilaterally canceled a potentially embarrassing referendum pertaining to the direct election of the president, despite a constitutional court ruling that the decision on whether to hold the referendum rested with an independent referendum commission, not with the government (Szomolányi, 1997: 19–20; Zavacka, 1997: 162–63).

These and other violations of equal access and fair play led Western diplomats to voice their displeasure repeatedly over Slovak political developments and to lodge numerous informal complaints and diplomatic protests with the government. Inadequate responses to these concerns and complaints led the governing bodies of the European Union and NATO to exclude Slovakia from the first wave of negotiations about the entry of Central and East European countries to both organizations (Duleba, 1997a). The inadequate responses reflected the Meciar government's fear that abiding by standard democratic game rules would undermine its rule (Snyder and Vachudova, 1997: 32).

Elite Differentiation

Elite differentiation is the other important dimension of elite configurations (see chapter 1). Wide differentiation, in which there are many distinct and relatively autonomous elite groups, requires the formation and re-formation of loose alliances based on short-term bargains. This prevents any one group from gaining the upper hand for a prolonged period. Narrow differentiation is more conducive to fixed and lasting alignments and divisions among a small number of groups. Although Slovak political elites were deeply divided during Meciar's third government, their political and economic alignments nevertheless displayed some flexibility. This flexibility was greater in the economic than the political sphere, however. In the political sphere, the successor to the old Communist Party, the Party of the Democratic Left (SDL), considered joining Meciar's coalition during the summer of 1996. But during the 1998 election campaign, as well as in the coalition talks that followed the election, SDL leaders stepped squarely into the anti-Meciar camp by refusing to discuss a coalition with HZDS and the right-wing SNS. Nearly a year before the 1998 election, the Party of Civic Understanding (SOP) tried to set itself up as an umbrella party. Its message was aimed at pragmatists who wished to overcome the demonizing of opponents, in which each of the main elite camps was engaged, in order to address national problems more directly and effectively. While SOP might have been attractive to HZDS voters during the 1998 election campaign, it became highly critical of HZDS once the latter began to attack it through the government-controlled state media. SOP leaders responded to these attacks by vowing not to join an HZDS-led coalition government after the election. They promised, moreover, to investigate alleged government crimes and abuses, and they called for opposition unity during and after the election in order to achieve an anti-Meciar parliamentary majority.

By mid-1998, political elite groups were still bunched in two opposing camps that were more divided over perceptions of basic democratic values and behaviors than over policy issues. Within each camp, however, there was muted competition along the left–right continuum. Meciar's governing coalition of 1994–98 depended for its parliamentary survival on a seemingly untenable "red–brown" alliance between the far right (SNS) and the far left (ZRS), which together gave the government its majority in parliament. The dominant opposition grouping, the Slovak Democratic Coalition (SDK), similarly encompassed the conservative Christian Democratic Movement (KDH), the Democratic Party (DS), and the Democratic Union (DU) on the right, and the Social Democratic Party of Slovakia (SDSS) and the Greens (SZS) on the left. This left–right spread was duplicated among the ethnic Hungarian parties, which came together in a single coalition prior to the election. It is worth noting that this complex political mosaic of left–right divisions, populist parties, and ethnic alignments was not peculiar to Slovakia and was, indeed, characteristic of much of postsocialist Eastern Europe during the 1990s (Tismaneanu, 1998).

In any event, during the negotiations to form a government after the 1998 election, SDL tried to build support from among the victorious parties for a left-leaning economic agenda. During those negotiations, the Hungarian minority coalition and Meciar's mainstream opponents were willing to put aside mutual suspicions in order to unite against a continuation of HZDS rule. All of this maneuvering indicated, in sum, that disparate parties and political elite groups were not bound to hard-and-fast policy positions; instead, the game among them was highly political.

Economic elite differentiation was also quite wide. Unlike the national-populist "patriots," who supported the HZDS-led ruling coalition out of a set of political beliefs and values, industrialists supported the Meciar government between 1994 and 1998 out of self-interested material considerations. Meciar cultivated this support by giving industrial leaders de facto control of the policies that affected their sectors and by making insider privatization available to them (Miklos, 1997: 64–66). Yet, this HZDS–industrialist alliance was not monolithic. Strains emerged in it during Meciar's third government and they increased greatly once the HZDS relinquished office after the 1998 election. A crucial conflict emerged from a latent fissure between industrialists, who were accustomed to benefiting from their close association with the Meciar government, and less politically aligned small- and medium-sized producers, who faced serious government-created obstacles in restructuring their enterprises. At the heart of this conflict was the government's inability to meet Slovak industry's needs for capital. Under Meciar, the government borrowed heavily on domestic and foreign capital markets to finance politicized but privatized industrial and infrastructure development. This "crowded out" private sector borrowing and dampened private sector investment. Firms that were barely surviving could not raise the capital needed to restructure their enterprises. Indeed, with Slovak banks paying as much as 20 percent interest on deposits, there was a strong and direct incentive for owners and managers to strip their companies of assets in order to earn the phenomenally high interest or to place money from their asset stripping in foreign currency accounts in expectation of a local currency devaluation.

Nor did Slovak firms frequently attract foreign partners that could inject new capital. Although a handful of Slovak manufacturers entered into high value-added joint ventures, overall, foreign business interest in Slovakia remained low. As of mid-1998, for example, Slovakia enjoyed a mere $US 1.4 billion in foreign investment, compared with the Czech Republic's $7.6 billion, Poland's $25.6 billion, and Hungary's $22.5 billion. In per capita terms, this amounted to $259 in Slovakia, $738 in the Czech Republic, $551 in Poland, and $2,228 in Hungary (The Economist Group, 1998). A major reason for the low absolute and relative levels of foreign investment was deep suspicion of the Meciar government among foreign investors and even among the government's industrial allies. Despite legal regulations and government statements that paid lip service to the encouragement of direct foreign investment, the dominant economic and political elites were ambivalent about, and sometimes downright hostile towards, foreign control of Slovak firms.

The problems of raising capital, both foreign and domestic, created a divergence between the Meciar government and the fundamental economic needs of many within the industrial elite. With a poorly functioning and heavily indebted economy, illiquid and nontransparent capital markets, and state-owned banks that often made loans based on political criteria, firms with sound management that could have performed reasonably well were unable to collect debts from deadbeat clients, obtain credits on loan markets, or find foreign buyers who would not seek an extra risk premium in any joint venture (Gould, 1996). With bank interest topping 20 percent and a political opposition that was promising to open the books on the government's privatization decisions, owners of firms were not disposed to put their spare cash into capital investments. In 1997, nonperforming, nonfinancial-sector liabilities increased by 25.4 percent from the previous year and amounted to 18.2 percent of GDP (M.E.S.A 10, 1998a: 1; 1998b: 2). By the 1998 election, Slovakia was effectively bankrupt.

Rampant clientelism in relations between Meciar's inner circle and his closest industrial allies was an additional strain. The tight bond between Meciar and Alexander Rezes, president of an important company, VSZ Holdings, was a case in point. Rezes served as Meciar's minister of transport until 1996, and then as his campaign chairman for the 1998 election. VZS Holdings was the parent company of Slovakia's largest firm, VSZ Steelworks, plus well over a hundred subsidiary and associated companies. It also had significant influence in the operations of two of the four largest financial institutions. Meciar's administration provided Rezes and his network of enterprises insider access to special privatization, taxation, and credit arrangements from state financial institutions and from almost every other area of intersection between the state and economic activities. Meciar did this, moreover, despite clear indications of corruption and mismanagement in VZS Holdings. The final cost to other corporations, taxpayers, and VSZ's more than twenty-five thousand employees was high. At the end of 1998, VSZ Holdings defaulted on its foreign obligations and faced bankruptcy (*Pravda*, 17 November 1998; cf. Miklos, 1997: 71–73).

The VSZ Holdings case illustrates how closely intertwined many political and economic interests became under the Meciar government. It is probably correct to say that patronage determined the privatization and shaped the political administration of firms accounting for more than half of all economic activity during the mid-1990s. Yet, the VSZ Holdings case also illustrates the conflicting interests among economic elites that arose from the Meciar government's clientelism. Preferential treatment for Meciar's clients greatly complicated the restructuring tasks other firms faced. Above all, clientelism blatantly diverted tax revenues and increased the costs of loans for most enterprises. Not surprisingly, therefore, by 1998 many industrialists formerly beholden to HZDS indicated that they were ready for a new government, provided it did not seriously challenge the means by which they had privatized their enterprises (*Pravda,* 10 October 1998).

THE 1998 ELECTION AND ELITE CONVERGENCE

Given the divisions among political and, to a lesser extent, economic elites, the freely contested 1998 election and the peaceful, relatively unimpeded transfer of power that followed it boded well for Slovak democracy. The election and its aftermath gave credence to the idea that Slovak elites might be converging toward a basic consensus on democratic norms and game rules. A year before the election, the present authors thought that a basic compromise amounting to a historically rare "elite settlement" between the opposing political camps was unlikely (Szomolányi and Gould, 1997: 7; cf. Higley and Burton, 1998: 48). The best hope for Slovak democracy, we guessed, lay in a gradual "elite convergence" that might be catalyzed by a decisive election (cf. Burton, Gunther, and Higley, 1992). But for this to occur, we thought three steps would have to be taken. First, a coalition of moderate, pro-democratic forces needed to win an election with convincing majority support. Second, such a victory would have to be followed by a stable governing coalition of the victorious parties. Finally, radical and extremist politicians would have to be marginalized so that, in order to regain government office sometime in the future, they would be forced to moderate their ideological positions.

Looking at the situation in the fall of 1997, we doubted that these steps were likely. In the event, however, the first step was accomplished with the SDK coalition's decisive victory in September 1998, and the second step came closer when an SDK coalition government consolidated itself during the following months. As regards the third step, some postelection fragmentation of HZDS, and the at least temporary willingness of SNS to moderate its ultranationalist rhetoric and parliamentary behavior, coupled with ZRS's self-destruction prior to the election, suggested that many political

leaders hostile to, or at least equivocal about, democratic game rules were
being pushed toward the margins of Slovak politics. While it is still too soon
to draw firm conclusions, a convergence between the parties that won the
1998 election and the more pragmatic groups in HZDS, as well as some leaders of SNS, is now conceivable.

Let us look more closely at what has happened. The first step necessary for
an elite convergence is a convincing election victory that forces defeated parties to reassess their political prospects and stances. In the September 1998 election, 84.2 percent of eligible voters cast ballots, and SDK-led forces won 93 of
the 150 seats in parliament. Even those who placed little stock in elections
could not fail to notice the clear repudiation of HZDS and its policies. To the
leaders of the Meciar camp, the overwhelming voter turnout was a warning
against plans, if any existed, to obstruct the election, ignore its outcome, or
complicate and retard the transfer of government power. For their part, the victorious parties interpreted the large turnout as a mandate to build a broad governing coalition. Neither of Meciar's two previous governments had received
support comparable to that won by the SDK coalition in 1998. In the 1994 elections, HZDS and its minor allies received 35.4 percent of the vote, and in the
1992 elections, HZDS's "mandate" to form a government (and create an independent Slovak state) came from only 30.4 percent of voters. By contrast, voter
support for the SDK-led government totaled 48.5 percent of voters in 1998.

The 1998 election outcome may have revealed a trend towards a more
tolerant and democratically oriented electorate. Domestic polls during the
preceding year recorded a steady increase in the proportion of individuals
valuing basic democratic principles and practices such as the rule of law,
negotiation and compromise, the acceptance of different opinions, respect
for minority rights, and the existence of a free media. Between 1994 and
1997, support for democratic principles among citizens grew from 47 percent to 59 percent, hybrid democratic–authoritarian views fell from 40 percent to 30 percent, and support for authoritarian practices dropped slightly
from 13 to 12 percent (Butorova, 1997). Hence, even before the 1998 vote,
a large and apparently growing majority of the public endorsed democratic
institutions and principles.

In this context, Meciar's government may have been its own worst enemy
(Krause, 1998b). The government's cancellation of the May 1997 referendum on direct presidential elections created widespread fears that it would
also obstruct or manipulate the 1998 election. These fears spurred the five
leading opposition parties to create the SDK coalition (Szomolányi, 1998a).
After the government passed a potentially discriminatory election law, the
SDK coalition transformed itself and registered as an electoral party.

SDK claims that the Meciar government alone was responsible for Slovakia's failure to meet the basic criteria for negotiating accession to the EU,
plus opposition anger with the government's authoritarian political style,

thus found an increasingly receptive audience beyond the coalition's hard-core supporters, who constituted perhaps 35 percent of voters. Indeed, in pre-election opinion polls roughly 60 percent of the public repeatedly expressed distrust of government actions and policies (Butorova, ed., 1998). The effects of citizens' rallies and other mobilizations in the last phase of the election campaign are difficult to estimate, but it is likely that the rallies and mobilizations contributed greatly to the large voter turnout and to the repudiation of the Meciar government. Most notable in this regard was the citizen campaign, OK'98, which was a nonpartisan initiative by nongovern-mental organizations aimed at ensuring a free and fair election. In particu-lar, OK'98 apparently persuaded large numbers of young people to vote.

While the referendum fiasco in May 1997 and discriminatory changes to the election law may have increased mass discontent with the Meciar gov-ernment, these events clearly galvanized Meciar's elite opponents and made the second step towards a convergence—the creation of a moderate, pro-democratic, and stable governing coalition—more likely. While the adjec-tive "democratic" is often bandied about, it clearly applies to the SDK coali-tion government that took office in October 1998. Polling data indicated that the coalition parties' members and supporters had in common strong commitments to democratic values and greater antipathies toward extrem-ist or authoritarian values and practices than did members and supporters of the former governing parties, HZDS, ZRS, and SNS (Butorova, ed., 1998: 87–96). In order to defeat Meciar, his opponents cooperated closely along democratic lines during the campaign. SDK coordinated the opposition effort, first by organizing a "democratic roundtable" in June 1998, in which other major opposition parties (SDL, SMK, and SOP), trade unions, the Association of Towns and Villages, the Gremium of the Third Sector (a peak organization representing independent NGOs), and the Council of Youth participated. The roundtable produced plans for a "grand coalition" gov-ernment that would include left and right parties and, importantly, the Hungarian Coalition. Common opposition to the Meciar government and the democratic orientations of the opposition parties' average supporters were the main factors that made this cooperation possible.

The government that was formed after the 1998 elections was a "coalition of coalitions" because two of its four components were themselves coali-tions: SDK, consisting of five parties; and the Party of the Hungarian Coali-tion (SMK), composed of three parties. Achieving agreement among cen-ter–right and center–left parties required a culture of compromise and cooperation among these parties' elites. The coalition agreement, as well as the new government program that was constructed by neoliberals, centrists, and social democrats (reformed Communists), indicated a relatively strong consensus among the several elite groups. It revealed significantly reduced fragmentation in the anti-Meciar elite camp.

Nevertheless, tensions in the new governing coalition remained strong. During the October 1998 negotiations that led to the new government, the coalition almost came apart over ethnonational issues when SDL balked at fulfilling its pledge to include the ethnic Hungarian parties in the government. SDL was pulled back into the coalition fold only after strong pressure from leaders of the nongovernmental organizations that had been so prominent in the election campaign (Butora, ed., 1998: 21). SDL's reluctant agreement overcame, at least temporarily, one of the greatest barriers to a lasting elite consensus in Slovakia, namely, the ethnonational question. The ethnic Hungarian parties received three cabinet posts and a vice-chair position in parliament. This went far toward addressing European Commission concerns about the insufficient protection of minority rights in Slovakia. Indeed, a representative of the European Parliament, Herbert Bosch, commented that the participation of ethnic Hungarians in the new coalition government was a "sensation" not sufficiently appreciated by the European Commission (*SME*, 4 November 1998).

While it is still too soon to tell if the second step toward an elite convergence—a stable coalition government—has been fully achieved, the third step—the marginalization of radical and extremist politicians—has also begun to be taken. In the words of Juan Linz and Alfred Stepan (1996: 6), democratic consolidation requires that "no significant national, social, economic, political, or institutional actors spend significant resources attempting to achieve their objectives by creating a nondemocratic regime." Marginalizing extremist actors who are disloyal toward a democratic regime is a sine qua non of democratic consolidation. In the history of other European countries, accomplishing this step has most often involved democratic parties repeatedly winning elections so that extremist groups conclude that they can gain power only by competing effectively in the existing electoral game (Burton, Gunther, and Higley, 1992).

Some marginalization of extremist, nondemocratic actors has occurred in Slovakia. As noted earlier, the Meciar government regularly excluded opponents from decision-making channels and bodies. This was justified by questioning opponents' fidelity to Slovak interests. Despite the repeated exclusions its component parts suffered at Meciar's hands, the SKD-led government has since 1998 taken steps to restore democratic principles and procedures to parliamentary life. Ironically, this has meant being much more generous to HZDS and SNS than these two parties had been toward their opponents (Krause and Gould, 1998). Hence, HZDS and SNS have been offered opportunities to participate fully in parliamentary committees and in the parliamentary leadership group. The vice-chairman of SNS became one vice-chairman of parliament. He was elected to this post after HZDS deputies refused to put forward a candidate. SNS also received the chairmanships of two important parliamentary committees, and Jan Slota, chairman of SNS, became chair of the Special Control Body (OKO) that monitors the internal security service. Also in contrast to previous practices, the new coalition government accepted for parliamentary committee positions any deputies that a party nominated. The single exception was Ivan Lexa, Meciar's former director of internal security, who was suspected of involvement in the 1995 abduction of the ex-president's son, Michal Kovac, Jr., and in the related murder of an alleged witness to the kidnapping. Following the 1998 election, Meciar himself surrendered his parliamentary seat to Lexa and in so doing gave Lexa parliamentary immunity against criminal prosecution, but in early 1999 this immunity was revoked by a special act of parliament and Lexa was arraigned.

At the end of 1998, HZDS still had an opportunity to propose its deputies for the chairmanships of four parliamentary committees. However, the HZDS stance was that, since it won 0.7 percent more votes than SDK in the September 1998 election, it could legitimately claim the chairmanship of parliament as a whole as the party with the largest number of votes had previously done in Slovakia and other European countries. Ignoring their own practice when they were in power, HZDS leaders also argued that the principle of proportional party representation on parliamentary committees was not being observed. The EU's observer, Herbert Bosch, countered, however, that the opposition parties did in fact enjoy adequate representation in parliament (*SME*, 14 November 1998).

The willingness of the new government to share some power with its opponents probably helped to undercut and marginalize political extremism in Slovakia. By including opponents in decision-making, the new government assured its opponents that policies harmful to their interests would not be undertaken without warning. Additionally, this power sharing had the potential to exacerbate divisions between moderates and extremists within and among the opposition parties, and to this extent it could isolate extremists. As 1998 ended, a widening gap between HZDS and SNS was evident. In contrast to HZDS, SNS donned the mantle of a "constructive opposition" that would not obstruct parliament's functioning. Further, though HZDS leaders refused to engage in media exchanges with leaders of the new governing parties, SNS leaders entered into spirited media debates with government representatives. SNS leaders refused, however, to accept the Hungarian minority parties' participation in the cabinet, claiming that leaders of those parties were dangerously irredentist. Nevertheless, though they remained intolerant toward the Hungarian minority, most of the SNS parliamentary group appeared to respect democratic institutions and game rules.

Despite HZDS's refusal to be a "constructive opposition," there were some signs of change in its stance, too. The fact that the September 1998 election and subsequent transfer of government power occurred peacefully and according to constitutionally prescribed procedures showed some

HZDS inclination toward political accommodation. To be sure, it had been dragged to this kicking and screaming. A month before the election, for example, HZDS induced the courts to review SDK's eligibility to participate in the election. Following the election, HZDS held on to power until the last possible minute in order to arrange as many protections for its members and allies, especially in the economic sphere, as it could. And it was largely unwilling to work with its victorious opponents to coordinate the transfer of government power.

HZDS policy still seemed to be dominated by its most outspoken and radical deputies. More pragmatic elements in the party—mainly those associated with the industrial lobby—were largely silent. But three somewhat distinct and competing HZDS factions appeared to be emerging: one faction of pragmatists, a second of ideologues, and a third centered on the most discredited HZDS leaders such as former Interior Minister Gustav Krajci, Ivan Lexa, and some others. How relations between these factions develop depends heavily on what Meciar chooses to do. At the least, there is potential for increased HZDS fragmentation, particularly if pragmatists in the party conclude that they can best pursue their interests by reaching accommodations with the new government. In the waning weeks of 1998, Meciar announced that he was leaving public life. But his departure was brief because, little more than three months later, he announced his candidacy for the May–June 1999 presidential election.

It is too early to say whether these trends will add up to an elite convergence. They may be stopped or reversed as the coalition government grapples with the severe economic problems that the Meciar government left behind. During 1998 it became apparent that the "economic miracle" of the mid-1990s was short-lived and based on unsustainable government borrowing. Among the consequences are schools without money, an impending collapse of the health care system, illiquidity and widespread business insolvencies, and high unemployment rates. The government is pledged to encourage foreign investment, restructure and then privatize the banks— possibly with the help of foreign capital—and revive the illiquid and depressed equity market. It expects economic growth to slow appreciably during the first half of its four-year term (*SME*, 26 November 1998).

The government's success in dealing with economic hardships will naturally help determine its stability. In late 1998, Slovakia had the highest unemployment rate in East Central Europe (13.9 percent). The records of other countries indicate that democratic government is more likely to survive economic crisis if there are no political actors offering a "painless" but system-destroying solution. Slovakia had some experience of such a situation in 1991–1992, when HZDS and its allies promised "national [that is, Slovak] and less painful economic reforms." That formula helped them win the 1992 election, which presaged the breakup of Czechoslovakia.

CONCLUSIONS

A basic principle of democracy is that governments relinquish power when they lose elections. Counting the government alternation that followed the 1998 election, power in Slovakia has changed hands twice without severe impediments. The first turnover occurred when the six-month coalition government in 1994 surrendered power to the coalition led by Meciar after losing that autumn's election. Despite fears that HZDS would employ unconstitutional means to hold onto power after its electoral defeat in 1998, the second peaceful turnover demonstrated that the two main political elite coalitions in Slovakia are "sufficiently committed to democracy to surrender office and power after losing an election" (Huntington, 1991: 267). Slovakia has, in other words, passed the "two turnover test" that is the minimum indicator of democratic consolidation.

The commitment of Meciar's HZDS to democracy remained in doubt, however. It is difficult to determine if Meciar's government surrendered power in 1998 out of respect for democratic game rules or because the enormous voter turnout against it led HZDS leaders to conclude that negating or obstructing the election result would be counter-productive for their longer-term interests. It is also possible that fears about the Meciar government's refusal to relinquish power were largely unwarranted and reflected the ingrained distrust of Meciar among elites who had long opposed him. In any event, civic actions aimed at securing a fair election, the neutral position taken by the army and police, and the presence of international observers from countries of the HZDS's choosing all contributed to a peaceful power transfer.

There remained the problem of a vacant presidency. Despite eleven rounds of voting over a period of five months during 1998, parliament had been unable to agree on a new president. This constituted a serious deficiency in the political system, one that was seen as indicating that the transition to democracy was still not completed. In early 1999 the new coalition government pushed through parliament a constitutional amendment that prescribed direct presidential elections, and an election was promptly scheduled for May 1999. Surmounting its internal ethnic, class, and regional cleavages, the ruling coalition agreed on a candidate, Rudolf Schuster, chairman of the Party of Civic Reconciliation (SOP). To the consternation of many, however, Meciar announced that he was returning from his short sojourn in private life to stand for the presidency. No candidate won a majority of votes in the election's first round, and this left Schuster and Meciar to contest the second round. On 30 May 1999, Schuster soundly defeated Meciar, 57 to 43 percent. This outcome was widely viewed as demonstrating the existence of a clear majority of voters who wished to put a definitive end to the Meciar era. By demonstrating the electoral futility of

Meciar's confrontational political style, the presidential election augured well for further elite convergence.

Although many of the events we have discussed are recent and of uncertain import, we conclude that a gradual, albeit fragile, convergence toward an elite unity propitious for a stable democratic regime was underway during the second half of the 1990s. First, it appeared that elites were developing a stronger normative consensus on democratic values, institutions, and procedures. The SDK-led coalition government contributed to this by allowing its opponents greater access to decision-making channels than the Meciar governments allowed. At the same time, the 1998 parliamentary and 1999 presidential elections registered shifts in the electorate toward democratic orientations and values. Second, elite differentiation was widening, and this made it steadily harder for any group to entrench itself in government power. The industrial elite was becoming more autonomous vis-à-vis its previous patron, HZDS. At the same time, and as the case of VSZ Holdings suggested, many industrialists had little choice but to cooperate with the new coalition government in order to cope with their economic difficulties. The new opposition parties, HZDS and SNS, were also increasingly differentiated. SNS demonstrated pragmatism and a readiness to promote its interests through parliamentary cooperation, while HZDS remained obstinate and petulant in the aftermath of its defeat. Yet, HZDS was no longer the monolithic party it once was; strains were mounting between its three main factions, and defections by some HZDS pragmatists became quite conceivable. If they occur, HZDS extremists will lose some of their influence and be pushed toward the political periphery.

In sum, during the last years of the 1990s Slovak elites showed clear signs of converging gradually toward a consensual configuration. Consequently, the Slovak political regime was becoming more reliably democratic. The dangers that arose from sharp elite fragmentation during and after Slovakia's democratic transition were receding.

BIBLIOGRAPHY

Altermatt, Urs. 1996. *Das Fanal von Sarajevo: Ethonationalismus in Europa.* Zurich: Verlag Neue Zarcher Zeitung.

Appel, Hilary. 1997. "Politico–Ideological Determinants of Liberal Economic Reform: The Case of Privatization." Paper presented to the Annual Conference of the Northeastern Political Science Association, Philadelphia, Pa., 15 November.

Burton, Michael G., Richard Gunther, and John Higley. 1992. "Introduction: Elite Transformation and Democratic Regimes." In *Elites and Democratic Consolidation in Latin America and Southern Europe,* ed. John Higley and Richard Gunther. New York: Cambridge University Press.

Burton, Michael G., and John Higley. 1998. "Political Crises and Elite Settlements."

In *Elites, Crises, and the Origins of Regimes*, ed. M. Dogan and J. Higley. Lanham, Md.: Rowman & Littlefield Publishers.

Butora, Martin, Zora Butorova, and Olga Gyarfasova. 1994. "From Velvet Revolution to Velvet Divorce? (Reflections on Slovakia's Independence)." In *Transition to Capitalism? The Communist Legacy in Eastern Europe*, ed. Janos Matyas Kovacs. New Brunswick, N.J.: Transaction Publishers.

————. 1998. "Obcianske organiz'cie vo volb'ch '98." *OS* 11 (November): 20–22.

Butorova, Zora. 1997. "Public Opinion in Slovakia: Continuity and Change." In *Slovakia: Problems of Democratic Consolidation and the Struggle for the Rules of the Game*, ed. Soňa Szomolanyi and John Gould. New York: Columbia International Affairs Online; and Bratislava: Slovak Political Science Association/Friedrich Ebert Stiftung.

Butorova, Zora, et al. 1993. *Current Problems of Slovakia after the Split of the CSFR*. Bratislava: Center for Social Analysis.

————. 1996. *Current Problems of Slovakia on the Verge of 1995–1996*. Bratislava: Center for Social Analysis.

Butorova, Zora, ed. 1998. *Democracy and Discontent in Slovakia: A Public Opinion Profile of a Country in Transition*. Bratislava: IPA.

Duleba, Alexander. 1997a. "Democratic Consolidation and the Conflict over Slovakia's International Alignment." In *Slovakia: Problems of Democratic Consolidation and the Struggle for the Rules of the Game*, ed. Soňa Szomolanyi and John Gould. New York: Columbia International Affairs Online; and Bratislava: Slovak Political Science Association/Friedrich Ebert Stiftung.

————. 1997b. "Foreign Policy of the Slovak Republic." Paper presented at the Conference on the Slovak Republic Five Years after the Dissolution of the Czechoslovak Federation, East–Central European Forum, Warsaw, 28–29 November.

The Economist Group. 1998. "Statistics." Business Central Europe Online.

European Commission. 1997. *Agenda 2000—Commission Opinion on Slovakia's Application for Membership of the European Union*. Brussels. I.3.

Field, Lowell, John Higley, and Michael G. Burton. 1990. "A New Elite Framework for Political Sociology." *Revue Européenne des Sciences Sociales* 28, no. 88 (November): 149–79.

Gould, John. 1999. "Winners, Losers and the Institutional Effects of Privatization in the Czech and Slovak Republics: The Case of the Eastward Enlargement of the European Union: The Case of the Slovak and Czech Republics," Robert Schuman Centre, Working Paper Series, European University Institute.

Gould, John, and Soňa Szomolanyi. 1997. "Bridging the Chasm in Slovakia." *Transitions* 4 (November): 70–76.

Higley, John, and Jan Pakulski. 1995. "Elite Transformation in Central and Eastern Europe." *Australian Journal of Political Science* 30 (October): 415–35.

Huntington, Samuel. 1991. *The Third Wave: Democratization in the Late Twentieth Century*. Norman: University of Oklahoma Press.

Innes, Abby. 1997. "The Breakup of Czechoslovakia: The Impact of Party Development on the Separation of the State." *East European Politics and Societies* 11 (Fall): 393–435.

Kaldor, M., and I. Vejvoda. 1997. "Democratization in Central and East European Countries." *International Affairs* 73 (January): 59–82.

Krause, Kevin. 1988a. "National Issues and Institutional Encroachment in Slovakia." Paper presented to the national conference of the American Association for the Advancement of Slavic Studies, Boca Raton, Florida, 25 September.

————. 1998b. ". . . Their Own Worst Enemies . . . National Issues and Party System Polarization in Slovakia." Paper presented to the national conference of the American Political Science Association, Boston, Mass., 6 September.

Krause, Kevin, and John Gould. 1998. "Velkorysost vo vlastnom zaujme—zasada demokracie medzi volbami." *SME.* 14 November.

Krivy, Vladimir. 1995. "The Parliamentary Elections, 1994: The Profile of Supporters of the Political Parties, the Profile of Regions." In *Slovakia Parliamentary Elections, 1994,* ed. Soňa Szomolányi and Grigorij Meseznikov. Bratislava: Slovak Political Science Association/Friedrich Ebert Stiftung.

————. 1997. "Slovakia's Regions and the Struggle for Power." In *Slovakia: Problems of Democratic Consolidation and the Struggle for the Rules of the Game,* ed. Soňa Szomolányi and John Gould. New York: Columbia International Affairs Online; and Bratislava: Slovak Political Science Association/Friedrich Ebert Stiftung.

Kusy, Miroslav. 1997. "The State of Human and Minority Rights in Slovakia." In *Slovakia: Problems of Democratic Consolidation and the Struggle for the Rules of the Game,* ed. Soňa Szomolányi and John Gould. New York: Columbia International Affairs Online; and Bratislava: Slovak Political Science Association/Friedrich Ebert Stiftung.

Linz, Juan, and Alfred Stepan. 1996. *Problems of Democratic Transition and Consolidation.* Baltimore: Johns Hopkins University Press.

Lukas, Zdenek, and Soňa Szomolányi, 1996. "Slovakia." In *Central and Eastern Europe on the Way into the European Union: Problems and Prospects of Integration in 1996. Strategies for Europe,* ed. W. Weidenfeld. Gutersloch: Bertelsman Foundation Publishers.

M.E.S.A 10 (Bratislava), 1998a. Slovak Monthly Report no. 5 (May).

M.E.S.A 10 (Bratislava), 1998b. Slovak Monthly Report no. 7 (July).

Meseznikov, Grigorij. 1997. "The Open Ended Formation of Slovakia's Political Party System." In *Slovakia: Problems of Democratic Consolidation and the Struggle for the Rules of the Game,* ed. Soňa Szomolányi and John Gould. New York: Columbia International Affairs Online; and Bratislava: Slovak Political Science Association/Friedrich Ebert Stiftung.

Mihalikova, Silvia. 1997. "Socio-Political, Economic, and Axiological Orientation and Changes in Central European Societies," *Report on International Sociological Research,* ed. Z. Strimska. Paris: C.N.R.S.

Miklos, Ivan. 1997. "Economic Transition and the Emergence of Clientelist Structures in Slovakia." In *Slovakia: Problems of Democratic Consolidation and the Struggle for the Rules of the Game,* ed. Soňa Szomolányi and John Gould. New York: Columbia International Affairs Online; and Bratislava: Slovak Political Science Association/Friedrich Ebert Stiftung.

Simecka, Martin. 1997. "Slovakia's Lonely Independence." *Transitions* 3 (August).

Snyder, Tim, and Milada Vachudova. 1997. "Are Transitions Transitory? Two Types of Political Change in Eastern Europe Since 1989." *East European Politics and Societies* 11 (Spring): 1–35.

Szomolányi, Soňa. 1995. "Does Slovakia Deviate from the Central European Transition?" *Slovakia Parliamentary Elections, 1994,* ed. Soňa Szomolányi and Grigorij Meseznikov. Bratislava: Slovak Political Science Association/Friedrich Ebert Stiftung.

————. 1997. "Identifying Slovakia's Emerging Regime." In *Slovakia: Problems of Democratic Consolidation and the Struggle for the Rules of the Game,* ed. Soňa Szomolányi and John Gould. New York: Columbia International Affairs Online; and Bratislava: Slovak Political Science Association/Friedrich Ebert Stiftung.

————. 1998. "Bez z'pasu a kompromisov to nepojde ani na Slovensku," *OS* 4 (April): 42–44.

Szomolányi, Soňa, and John Gould. 1997. "Elity: V'taz neberie vsetko." *Domino-Forum* 6, no. 37 (November 7–14): 7–8.

Tismaneanu, Vladimir. 1998. *Fantasies of Salvation: Democracy, Nationalism, and Myth in Post-Communist Europe.* Princeton, N.J.: Princeton University Press.

Zavacka, Katarina. 1997. "The Development of Constitutionalism in Slovakia." In *Slovakia: Problems of Democratic Consolidation and the Struggle for the Rules of the Game,* ed. Soňa Szomolányi and John Gould. New York: Columbia International Affairs Online; and Bratislava: Slovak Political Science Association/Friedrich Ebert Stiftung.

4

Hungary

Elites and the Use and Abuse Democratic Institutions

Rudolf L. Tökés

The birth of Hungary's new democracy was a peaceful, yet complex, process. Depending on one's perspective, its gestation can be viewed as extending over the nation's centuries-long struggle for freedom and independence, or as occurring in less than a year—between June 1989 and April 1990. In those ten months, the outgoing and incoming political elites created and delivered a comprehensive package consisting of the National Roundtable Agreement (NRTA), a revised constitution, and the first free parliamentary elections. Although the NRTA was later amended by political pacts, the essential elements of the new institutional architecture were in place before the formal launching of parliamentary democracy in May 1990.

Hungary has since held three national elections and 1999 was the second year of its third freely elected government's term in office. By now, the country's political institutions are firmly embedded in a social and economic context that is encapsulated by the terms democracy, rule of law, market economy, and emerging civil society. It seems that the National Roundtable's elite negotiators were either extremely prescient or just plain lucky in finding the right formulae for political stability and socioeconomic progress (see Tökés, 1996).

The accuracy of either diagnosis is open to debate, and the purpose of this chapter is to rethink and reflect on the institutional outcomes of the National Roundtable process and subsequent political agreements. My discussion rests on three propositions. First, that the substantive legal and institutional products of the NRTA and later pacts, though intended as improvised solutions to policy dilemmas at the time they were agreed on, had by the late 1990s become core elements of Hungary's new political architecture. Second, that the agreements, unwritten understandings, and personal expectations of the elite negotiators and pact makers of 1989–90 laid the foundations for a new, and in some ways sui generis, political model. Third, that this model is more than the sum of its gradually evolving institutional parts; it is neither "Eastern" nor "Western" but a new Hungarian model for the early twenty-first century. As such, it offers an agenda for economic modernization, social progress, a new national and an emerging European identity.

A full discussion of these propositions would require reexamining Hungary's road to the NRTA under state socialism, and it would also entail an extended consideration of the political changes and institutional designs that accompanied the 1989–90 democratic transition. Here, however, I focus only on how the new elites and institutions of Hungarian democracy have functioned since the transition.

THE INSTITUTIONAL TERRAIN

How have democratic institutions been working in Hungary, and for whose benefit? More specifically, what is the fit, and how good is it, between formal rules and regulations that are embodied in various institutions and the actual behavior of elite actors elected or appointed to govern Hungary during the 1990s? Is it enough to use the Western academic transitologists' favorite cliché and say that when democracy becomes "the only game in town" a democratic regime is consolidated, so that its institutions are likely to perform in a self-sustaining fashion? Or is there something missing from this formula?

Contrary to textbook-spawned axioms, there are many kinds of democracies and many kinds of political games that are played on the tolerant turf of a democratic polity. So how is the game being played in Hungary? What are the rules and how closely do the players (and the spectators) abide by them? In a thought-provoking essay on "Illusions about Consolidation," Guillermo O'Donnell offers sensible guidance on these matters:

> When the fit [between formal rules and actual behavior] is loose or practically nonexistent, we are confronted with the doable task of discussing actual behavior and discovering the (usually informal) rules that behavior and expectations do follow. Actors are as rational in these settings as in highly formalized ones, but the contours of their rationality cannot be traced without knowing the actual rules, and the common knowledge of these rules, that they follow. (O'Donnell, 1997: 46)

Political institutions are man-made artifacts, and laws and other rules are tools with which to secure compliance with institutional goals and to satisfy the interests that created the institutions in the first place. Yet, for institutions to work and laws to be obeyed, provisions must be made to foster consonance between the rules and the cultural context in which they are embedded. The latter shapes public judgments about the legitimacy of the ends and the means of politics. Perceptions of legitimacy hinge on the degree to which the rule makers and those affected by the rules have shared beliefs in the public good that is meant to be achieved by the exercise of institutional power.

In democratic and nondemocratic systems alike, political legitimacy is derived from a written or unwritten social contract between the regime and the citizen. The written contract is most often incorporated in constitutions, in political manifestos, or in the (authoritarian) leader's ideological and policy statements. The U.S. Constitution speaks of "life, liberty, and the pursuit of happiness" and thereby specifies cardinal principles while leaving their implementation to the institutions of government. By contrast, continental European constitutions tend to codify, at times in considerable detail, both the purposes and the modus operandi of governmental institutions. In either case, the state's exclusive possession of administrative power and its enforcement by coercive means are legitimated by trade-offs between the state's entitlements and the citizens' "inalienable" negative and (often opaquely formulated) positive rights.

In its evolving configurations, the Hungarian constitution (in the form of a new "basic law," redesigned old laws, and newly created institutions and regulatory mechanisms, all enacted in 1989) may be perceived as replacing the state socialist regime's unwritten social contract. The latter had been an amalgam of programs and aspirations that were codified as positive rights in the constitution of 1949 (amended in 1972). The new basic law and associated laws and institutions put in place during 1989 also enshrined legitimacy-generating positive rights. The difficulty has been that these positive rights are fundamentally incompatible with the policy imperatives of a resource-scarce economy like Hungary's during the 1990s. The new political elites' principal task has thus been to overcome the disjunction between codified rights and scarce resources while at the same time trying to implement the nation's threefold agenda of democratization, marketization, and laying the foundations of a law-governed state.

The institutional products of the transition period were fruits of elite compromise and consensus on the minimal requisites for peaceful systemic change. Naturally, the signatories of the political agreements in 1989–90 also harbored personal values, ideological commitments, and partisan policy preferences that were not or could not be fully articulated at that time. In one way or another, such *ex ante* beliefs were, in their best sense, rooted in visions of a good society, lawful governance, and enhanced personal autonomy in a democratic and sovereign state. With the onset of freedom, however, the facade of elite consensus on the rules of the political game and the missions of political institutions promptly collapsed. A more complex spectrum of beliefs about game rules and institutional missions has replaced it.

According to Andras Korosenyi's penetrating classification of competing elite conceptions of institutional legitimacy in Hungary, "the public good" might best be realized by (1) parliament, the political parties, and institutions of popular sovereignty; (2) "nonpolitical" institutions, such as the president of the republic, the ombudsmen, the regular courts, and the constitutional court; (3) neocorporatist "expert" agencies of public administration; (4) political movements (including those oriented toward direct democracy) and active minorities within civil society; or (5) none of the above (Korosenyi, 1998: 197–201). In my view, these diverging elite conceptions of how to achieve the public good may be reformulated as modal elite orientations toward politics in general and institutions in particular.

This reformulation should begin with the observation that Hungarian elite discourse on the public good is shaped by two seemingly incompatible propensities within the political class as regards ideological thinking and consensus-seeking behavior. Both are rooted in strong traditions. Ideological thinking pervades the mindsets of politicized humanistic intellectuals, while consensus-seeking behavior is characteristic of the elites' survivalist culture (Tökés, 1996: 3–13). The ideological thinking of intellectuals is informed by inflexible norms, monocausal explanations, and mental constructs that attribute hostility to, and see malign conspiracies in, ideas and outcomes that fail to conform to a priori truths. "Structural paranoia" is one label for this process of cognition. Clashes among proponents of imported orthodoxies advocated by radical monetarists, born-again supply-siders, populist–socialist redistributionists, "Euro-integrationists," and native culturalists are examples of nonnegotiable ideological postures, and they serve to explain suboptimal policy outcomes.

In the Hungarian context, however, this "clash of creeds" (*hitvitak*) among intellectuals is attenuated by unwritten rules of elite solidarity that call for closing ranks and presenting a facade of unity to ensure the survival of the political class and the nation it claims to represent. The pragmatic objective of arriving at consensual outcomes may yield durable solutions; on the other hand, by "agreeing to disagree," decision makers may succeed only in rolling over intractable problems and generating a policy stalemate. In this latter situation, an inability to sustain cooperative–competitive political relations through deal making, compromise, and effective teamwork may set elites on diverging paths that lead to barren disputes.

Korosenyi's analysis implies that conceptions of how the public good may be embodied in political institutions can be classified as "modified majoritarian instrumental-pragmatic" or as "contra-majoritarian consensual" (see Korosenyi, 1998). Each conception spawns modal orientations toward the requisites of good government, institutional efficacy, and societal autonomy. Those who are positioned in the broadly defined center and right-of-center of the ideological spectrum share the "instrumental–pragmatic" conception and they are oriented toward parliamentary sovereignty and the accountability to parliament of elected and appointed public officials, most especially government ministers and state bureaucrats. They support the principle of the separation of powers together with a transparent system of checks and balances among branches of government, and they endorse traditional principles of Hungarian public law as regards lawful governance and a legally bounded societal autonomy.

The "contra-majoritarian consensual" conception of how institutions embody the public good is shared by left-of-center and left-wing members of the political class, practitioners in the media, and much of the politicized intelligentsia. This spawns three more specific orientations. The first may be labeled "normative–emancipatory." It privileges citizens' personal liberties, enshrined as constitutionally protected negative rights, and it views both parliament and government as posing a potential majoritarian threat to societal autonomy. A variant of the normative–emancipatory orientation affirms institutions of direct democracy, such as plebiscites and referenda, or the superior values of an antipolitical civil society (a right-wing version speaks of the superior values of ethnicity and indigenous culture); it thus denies the legitimacy of all elite-operated political institutions. A second, "autonomist–corporatist" variant also disputes the importance of parliamentary sovereignty but sees the public good embodied in nonpolitical corporatist institutions of administrative, technocratic, scientific, and cultural expertise. Finally, a "legal-emancipatory" variant applauds anti-republican and contra-majoritarian decisions by an activist constitutional court, which ostensibly protects society from abuses of legislative and executive power by parliament and the government.

POLITICAL ACTORS

According to Adam Przeworski, "All societies facing the task of constructing democracy face three generic issues: substance versus procedure, agreement versus cooperation, and majoritarianism versus constitutionalism" (Przeworski, 1995: 40). I want to sort out the ways in which Hungarian institution builders addressed these issues during the 1990s. Let me begin by stating the obvious, namely, that the Hungarian democratic regime, although "consolidated" to a remarkable extent, is still evolving—as is the society in which the regime is embedded. Still, the evidence at hand permits some general assessments of how the tasks Przeworski lists are being performed.

The designated key players of the political game are the political parties, parliament, the government, the president of the republic, and the constitutional court. These players share the playing field with nongovernmental institutions, such as the media, corporatist interest groups, and the business community. In my view, the rules that govern and define the complex pattern of interactions among the key players and between them and nongovernmental entities may be conceived as one or more of three—written, unwritten, and invisible—"constitutions." As I will try to show, each of these "constitutions" has a role in shaping public policies, allocating values and resources, and building (and reconstructing) institutions in Hungary today.

The written constitution consists of Act XX of 1949 as amended, of "basic laws" that can only be enacted or amended with parliamentary super majorities, and of other laws, statutes, ratified international treaties, and decrees that are in force. The modus operandi of key institutions—particularly the standing rules, resolutions, and declarations of principles of parliament—may also be viewed as part of the written constitution, as may documents of judicial review, that is, landmark decisions of the constitutional court. In one way or another, all of these elements of the written constitution register visions of lawful governance, affirm core values, set norms, structure behavior, generate expectations, allocate space and authorize spheres of competence for institutions, and define citizens' rights and duties in a law-governed state.

In Giovanni Sartori's view, "Constitutions are required to be content neutral . . . [they ought to] establish how norms are to be created; they do not, and should not, decide what is to be established by the norms," and he cautions that "we must be aware of 'aspirational constitutions' " (Sartori, 1997: 200). The Hungarian constitution may or may not have been written by ideologues, but its text reflects crucial ambiguities with respect to aspirational and programmatic aspects. If there can be more than one reading of the jurisdiction of institutions of popular sovereignty, of the entitlements of the president of the republic, of the respective spheres of competency of the regular court system and the constitutional court, of the degree of operational autonomy of stand-alone institutions of public administration, and, above all, of the basic, especially positive, rights of citizens, the written constitution remains vulnerable to ideological passions, political exigencies, and judicial activism.

Is the constitution a temporary shelter or a permanent roof over the house of democracy? The Hungarian political class is of two minds about this. On the one hand, in 1994 and 1995 there was enough parliamentary concern about widely perceived flaws in the constitution to elect an all-party drafting commission to produce a new text that would see the nation into the next century. On the other hand, party elites saw to it that the drafting process required near-unanimity of two government and four opposition parties and made the passage of a new text conditional on an affirmative vote by four-fifths of MPs (Bihari, 1998). The inevitable failure of this effort—valiantly championed by legal scholars from both sides of the parliamentary aisle—left the broader political and cognitive issue of closing the books on the process of systemic change, and hence the legitimacy of this process, unresolved.

The unwritten constitution is about the way actors "get things done" in Hungarian politics. It consists of mindsets, embedded and acquired habits, pragmatism and idealism, corruption and rectitude, the style and idiom of public and private discourse, pathologies of conflict resolution and interest reconciliation, and other culturally conditioned patterns of behavior. The unwritten constitution is eminently political—it is about power and the capacity to effect desired outcomes. Virtually all key political players perform as decision makers or as executors of decisions in institutional settings. According to the new institutionalists in political science, "Institutions affect the way in which individuals and groups become activated within and outside established institutions, the level of trust among citizens and leaders . . . and the meaning of concepts like democracy, justice, liberty and equality" (March and Olsen, 1989: 164). Probably so, but how long does (or should) it take for political actors to fully internalize the "spirit," such as it is, of post-communist institutions?

At issue is the way in which political elites reconcile their individual and collective interests with the letter and the spirit of the law. As individuals—and if they happen to be democrats—they may wish to follow the dictates of their democratic conscience and abide by the laws. However, as team players in the party executive, as parliamentary MPs, as senior government officials, or as board members of institutions, they are captives to the logic of the country's elite-brokered democratic transition and the ethical ambiguities of the state's constitutional norms. Although not living in a consociational democracy, they, in Sartori's words, function "in a cross-pressured system held together by countervailing solidaristic elites bent upon neutralizing the centrifugal pull of their [society]" (Sartori, 1997: 72). As members of the politically active minority, they have a vested interest in collective survival, as well as in keeping the demobilized public at bay.

Political elites are active in at least one, and usually more than one, institutional setting. Let me briefly consider the modus operandi of elites in three such settings in Hungary today: the political parties, parliament, and the government bureaucracy.

Political Parties

With the exception of the socially well-embedded Socialist Party (HSP), the political parties are electoral mechanisms with periodically mobilized local organizations and rank-and-file supporters (Tökés, 1997). They operate in two sets of circumstances, each of which generates a distinctive party configuration. First, when parties belong to a government coalition, their members' fortunes are linked with the strongest party, or, as between 1994 and 1998, with the party whose leader is both prime minister and party chairman. Second, when parties make up the opposition, their members are in the hands of a "hard core" leadership of professional politicians. In both configurations, the incumbent leadership controls the ranking of candidates on the party's national and territorial lists, as well as (lucrative) legislative committee assignments. Although Michels' "iron law of oligarchy" is a given, the individual MP's "free mandate" leaves the door open to his or her internal dissent or defection to another party.

In Hungary, opposition parties make ends meet from budgetary allocations that are made in proportion to the seats they captured at the last national election. This is not entirely true of the Socialist Party because, both in and out of government, HSP has vast resources in terms of tangible assets and intangible network capital. By the latter, I refer not merely to the capability of "old comrades' networks" to trade favors with other nomenklatura veterans in parliament, the state bureaucracy, and the state-controlled economic sector, but to the perpetuation by holdover elites of the old regime's profoundly corrupt—what Edward Banfield termed "amoral familist"—administrative culture (Banfield, 1958; see also Putnam, 1993: 173–76). "Conflicts of interest" are, of course, an all-party affair. More variable are party elites' declared and—through family members—undeclared involvements in lucrative business activities and in legislative and government lobbying on behalf of such interests.

Most Hungarian parties, but especially HSP, have discretionary links with banks, state-owned firms, and multinational corporations. Kickbacks, for the benefit of party treasuries, from recipients of government contracts and consultancy and management fees have been parts of a scandal-ridden picture. (Alleged ties with organized crime are another part of the picture that, due to space limitations, cannot be discussed here.) Much of this is reminiscent of the regional party bosses' intimate ties with state enterprises in industry and agriculture under the old state socialist regime. The main difference between the old and the new regime lies in the magnitude of resources—mainly real estate and intangible perquisites, but also liquid assets such as stocks, dividends, and unearned fees—that are involved in illegal transactions. In any case, the survival and resurfacing, even in the liberal and right-of-center parties, of pathologies of the old Hungarian Socialist Workers Party methods of internal conflict resolution and decision making by small clientelist networks has lessened the parties' accountability to their membership and the general public.

Parliament

From the public's viewpoint, parliament is in part political theater and in part an impenetrable venue of decision making. The theater part pertains mainly to the televised proceedings of the "Esteemed House." Although political rhetoric and provocative parliamentary questions have important public educational functions, the real legislative work takes place in committees and at meetings of the parties' parliamentary caucuses. This is as it should be in a working parliamentary democracy. However, for want of staff support and independent legislative research capabilities, the parliamentary parties are at the mercy of the government bureaucracy when it comes to producing alternative drafts of bills. The MPs have the right, either in the committees or on the house floor, to amend any and all government drafts, but for desired outcomes they must lobby extra-parliamentary institutions directly. Failing this, the MPs can hope for the best and, if still in doubt, vote the party line. At any rate, the MPs individually and collectively immunize themselves from accountability and political liability for legislative malpractice. If worse comes to worst, the constitutional court will fix up the law by declaring it unconstitutional and returning it to the chastised solons for modification.

If not as a body, and not always for the public good, then, the MPs in their individual capacity are preoccupied with advancing their constituents' as well as their own personal interests. Whereas the former is an appropriate activity, the latter is fraught with ethical dilemmas. At issue is the conflict of public and personal interests for party bosses and backbenchers alike. Although the number of lawyers and professional politicians in parliament has increased significantly during the 1990s, the majority of MPs—especially when caught in the midst of interparty disputes about modifying the contentious laws that require a two-thirds super majority for passage—lack the professional competence to cast their votes "in the spirit" of parliamentary sovereignty, as well as for the public good. One would suppose that the (infrequent) use of secret ballots would permit the lawmakers to "vote their conscience" and their unfettered understanding of their institutional mandate. However, the outcome of votes, like those on the draft constitution in the summer of 1996 and on the election of justices of the constitutional court, reveals profound confusion with respect to the role and mission of these core institutions. In such cases, the settling of scores with party bosses and the venting of ideological passions seem to take precedence over institutional priorities of improved governance.

Government Bureaucracy

A nonpolitical civil service and its administrative autonomy are essential requisites of good government. It is civil servants who translate a regime's political will into administrative action. What happens, however, when the key bureaucrats, whether for political or economic reasons, desert their posts for greener pastures in banking, business, and industry? The large-scale migration of administrative talent from government to the private sector typically followed the collapse of state socialism in Eastern Europe. It is axiomatic that the postsocialist regimes have functioned and survived thus far largely at the sufferance of holdover administrative elites. The question is "At what cost?"

The challenge of having experts implement the new Hungarian regime's immense legislative output was a crucial test of the viability, especially the legitimacy, of new and old institutions. As a unanimous gesture to the bureaucrats' indispensability for effective political steering, all three cabinets during the 1990s—in the Antall-Boross, Horn, and Orban governments—treated the bureaucratic establishment with kid gloves. In doing so, the postsocialist regime gave a new lease on life to what Tamas Sarkozy (1996: 16–18) calls a "semi-state" (versus a "liberal-decentralized") model of public administration.

Public administration in Hungary involves not only the delivery of traditional state services of central and regional governments to the public, but also direct managerial and indirect control over a vast range of state-owned assets and over citizens' economic, social, and cultural activities. As designated agencies of mandated and discretionary state redistributions, the top bureaucrats have been given a free hand in setting rules that, in one way or another, deeply intrude into the lives of both citizens and nongovernmental institutions. The "regulatory rage" of bureaucrats, to borrow a term from Sarkozy (1996:20), has preempted and distorted legislative intent, and skewed the constitutional division of powers among the branches of government.

Top administrative positions—to an extent well beyond the German civil service model—have (again) become political spoils. Although the Civil Service Law, Act XXIII of 1993, and Act CI of 1997 seek to define activities deemed "incompatible" with civil service status, this has not deterred top executives from occupying lucrative positions in business firms that are under their agency's direct control or regulatory oversight. Thus, emerging phoenix-like from the constitutional lacunae left by the National Roundtable process and largely unfilled under the étatist thrust of four successive governments, the state bureaucracy has become an autonomous and, by all indications, a runaway branch of government. Instead of being closely associated with parliament as its natural partner, the bureaucracy is closely associated with semiautonomous public institutions, rent-seeking political parties, business lobbies, neocorporatist interest groups, and the murky world of public foundations. It is said that Hungary is a "country without consequences," and this will be so until today's *Lumpenbeamter* is transformed into tomorrow's Weberian law-abiding civil servant of personal integrity and political neutrality. Exogenous pressures, such as the demands of Brussels for "Euro-conform" delivery of public services in member states, will be essential to making this transformation happen.

A NEW HUNGARIAN MODEL

I have sketched the interaction between elites and institutions since Hungary's democratic transition. My aim has been to capture the ways in which elite actors have conceived and developed institutions with which to structure policy making, shape political behavior, and enhance the legitimacy of political outcomes. I have juxtaposed elite intentions with the way that the institutions themselves influence behaviors, expectations, and legitimacy perceptions. My main conclusion is that, despite many shortcomings, the Hungarian institution-and legitimacy-building process has yielded positive results. It has embedded democratic institutions and gained more or less supportive public responses to the new democratic regime's values and policy goals. Still, the new and restructured political and economic institutions are tolerated rather than fully accepted and valued for themselves. The political system's overloaded policy agenda, the large-scale socioeconomic dislocations, and the widespread pathologies of cognitive dissonance cause ambivalent citizen orientations toward institutions of all kinds. Given the magnitude of the changes since 1989–90, contingent consent to the institutional status quo is probably the most that can be expected of Hungarian citizens. From this it follows that, on balance, it is still the elite political actors and their ideological preferences that shape and manipulate institutions, rather than the institutions or their "spirit" structuring elite and mass behavior.

Professional politicians in charge of the polity's five institutional pillars—the political parties, the parliament, the government, the president of the republic, and the constitutional court—are the key players in the democratic game. The rules of the game are set in the constitution, which is constantly interpreted and revised by the players. The spectators keep the score, the spectators being the three-fifths of eligible citizens who turn up at voting booths every four years and cast their ballots for parties and candidates of their choice. It is not certain whether the players and the spectators have the same objectives in mind and, if so, whether they are willing to abide by the same rules to achieve their respective goals. Simply put, almost a decade after the transition, a very substantial number of citizens are still not convinced that a change of system has in fact taken place in Hungary. Judging by polls measuring citizens' trust and distrust in institutions, the jury is still out.

I speculated at the outset that we may be witnessing in Hungary the emergence of a hybrid, "neither Eastern nor Western" model as a new national agenda, and I will conclude with some comments about this possibility. I am thinking of the still unfolding scenarios of institution building and institutional change in Hungary. I submit that during the next ten to fifteen years these scenarios will merge into a complex agenda of economic modernization and social progress, together with a new national and an emerging

European identity. To make my case, a brief "then and now" overview of institutional change is in order.

In 1989–90 a new party system was born. Although sensibly crafted electoral laws yielded six rather than ten or more parliamentary parties after the first contested election in May-June 1990, all but HSP were cut from the same cloth. That is, most new MPs and their party leaders were inexperienced, disoriented, and ideologically driven intellectuals brought to power on the strength of the voters' one-time anticommunist temper tantrum at that first election. Moreover, each of the parties was a catchall electoral coalition with a strong potential for splintering and losing its political identity. Starting from the original six, by 1994 there were eighteen parties and policy caucuses in parliament. However, together with party fragmentation there was another process—that of the party system's polarization along the left–right continuum.

The coalescence of like-minded parties at the opposite ends of the ideological spectrum began with the HSP–Free Democrats coalition in 1994, and it was completed four years later with the electoral victory of the center–right coalition led by the Federation of Young Democrats–Hungarian Civic Party (Fidesz). Thus, by 1998 there had developed what could be seen as a nascent two-party system—with the nuisance factor of the small ultranationalist Hungarian Justice and Life Party (MIEP) added for good measure. Both Fidesz and its satellite parties and the HSP–Free Democrats opposition bloc are German- and Austrian-style *Volkspartei* electoral coalitions. Should the present voting blocs survive intact in the 2002 election, Hungary will have moved toward a German-type Christian Democrat versus Social Democrat two-party system, with the addition of one or two mainly single-issue parties. Analysts will differ over the import (and the likelihood) of this outcome, but I would view it as an extremely positive development for Hungary's future political stability.

Hungary is a small country with an oversized (and very expensive) parliament. Although the National Roundtable negotiators agreed on 350 seats, 36 more were slipped in after the NRTA for a total of 386. The main advantage of this number was that it rescued many aspiring intellectuals from unemployment and kept the size of the individual parliamentary districts small enough to permit "native sons" (and a few daughters) to represent their small communities. On the other hand, this oversized assembly of loquacious solons has turned out to be a great deal less professional and less productive than the Fidesz-proposed alternative of 200 to 250 MPs would be. The excessive number of parliamentary committees (in which membership—usually multiple—entails handsome financial compensation) is also responsible for the low productivity and legislative gridlock.

These built-in constraints are further aggravated in cases where one of the numerous laws requiring a two-thirds super majority comes to the floor of parliament for passage. Majorities of this kind are difficult to come by in the best of times, yet the reduction in the number of such laws itself requires affirmative votes of the same magnitude. In any case, the present house rules providing for balanced representation of government and opposition interests at internal consultative forums do not seem to work when it comes to accommodating new entrants not bound by the NRTA understandings. A case in point is the Istvan Csurka–led Hungarian Justice and Life Party (MIEP). Although sitting on the opposition side of the aisle, MIEP is more likely to vote in favor of the Fidesz government than either HSP or the Free Democrats, who were dug in for trench warfare during the life of the parliament that was elected in early 1998. Csurka's party was positioned to cast the decisive vote in house committees consisting of equal numbers of government and opposition MPs.

Compounding these difficulties has been the generic problem of relentless anti-republican pressures from many quarters—the constitutional court and various semiautonomous institutions in particular—that seek to thwart parliament's authority, as well as its legislative efficacy. Repeated instances of attempted political end runs, either in the form of threatened plebiscites or as efforts to "balance" the house by adding a corporatist second chamber, have attracted incumbent MPs' attentions and, more to the point, their political survival instincts. Although no radical changes can be expected immediately, these end runs are likely to be successful—perhaps as part of a pre–European Union entry crash program—sometime in the next ten years.

The German model of *Kanzlerdemokratie*, specifically the provision for a prime minister who is de facto irremovable, has been the key to Hungary's political stability since 1990. On the other hand, the chief executive's positional stability has yet to be translated into effective governance. The records of Jozsef Antall and Gyula Horn as party chairmen and prime ministers revealed the woeful lack of a cadre of highly skilled and genuinely nonpartisan senior civil servants able to coordinate and execute government policies competently. Antall's ideological soulmates in Democratic Forum and Horn's old party cronies in HSP proved to be only marginally competent administrators and poor team players. Consequently, both prime ministers became prisoners of competing ministerial fiefdoms, party pressures, and unhindered backdoor access by policy lobbies. Neither was particularly anxious to let go of state assets or to stamp out the endemic corruption associated with the privatization process. Moreover, neither had the political courage to tolerate a strong minister of finance, let alone an assertive coalition partner, in his cabinet.

In mid-1998, the Fidesz government, with Viktor Orban as prime minister, undertook a purposeful reorganization of the executive branch, starting with the Office of the Prime Minister. The reassertion of state control over maladministered corporatist pension funds, the disbanding of spurious bodies of interest reconciliation, the (possible) revamping of the over-sized and unaccountable security services, and the strengthened oversight of the banking sector were all steps in the right direction. However, the goals of a well-administered state, a downsized bureaucracy under the management of competent civil servants, and balanced budgets are not yet in sight. How Hungary's double-digit inflation and large budget deficits can be reconciled with "Euro-conform" governance remains anyone's guess.

The office of the president of the republic has thus far been tailored to fit the present incumbent, Arpad Goncz. The legal lacunae in the president's constitutional job description were of concern during the Antall era when the prime minister's political style and ideological preferences were at odds with those of the president. In a country where there are dozens of self-styled "above politics" intellectuals with presidential ambitions, a successor to Goncz will not be difficult to find. On the other hand, the declared candidacy of Jozsef Torgyan—a two-fisted country lawyer whose Smallholders' Party is essential to the viability of the Fidesz-led coalition—for the office of president in 2000 raises all kinds of intriguing possibilities. As a certified anti-leftist intellectual, Torgyan's chances of prompt parliamentary approval may be likened to that of the proverbial snowball in the netherworld. Meanwhile, the art of walking without leaving political or ideological footprints is being practiced by many presidential hopefuls—with no certainty about who will be chosen for the much-coveted office. In sum, the office of president seems to be moving from a "semi-strong" toward a ceremonial–symbolic institution that will better "fit" the model of a consolidated democracy.

During the 1990s the constitutional court became the self-appointed guardian of Hungarian democracy, albeit as something of a throwback to the earlier state socialist era of what might be called "paternalistic-emancipatory" politics. The court's judicial activism, unless kept in bounds by an assertive parliament, could impede the country's progress toward full-fledged parliamentary democracy. The justices' visceral anticapitalist proclivities, disdain for institutions of popular sovereignty, legal grandstanding on behalf of demonstrably bankrupt egalitarian policies of state redistribution, and ill-conceived intrusions into the proper domain of other state institutions could, if left unchecked, compromise the nation's progress on many fronts. Although the court's virtually untrammeled powers of judicial review have been a decisive component of the "Hungarian model" of transition politics, some of these powers, like the transition itself, ought to be removed for the sake of a truly law-governed state.

Answers to the first questions of politics—"Who governs and for whose benefit?"—are gradually emerging from the still less than transparent record of institution building in Hungary. For the public to believe that there was a change of system, the books must be closed on the still open-ended National Roundtable process. This may or may not call for the writing of a new constitution, but it definitely requires coming to terms with the past. When the senior holdover personnel of the state's five (!) security services are put out to pasture and sent to well-deserved oblivion, and when the lustration of all key government personnel by independent jurists (rather than by the incumbent security apparatus) is completed, the public will respond and accept democratic institutions as their own.

In sum, Hungary's new national and emerging European identity will come into being as a consequence of the state's and the community's progress toward embracing European norms of governance and democratic citizenship. Institutions are said to structure and modify political behavior and personal values. Hungary's membership in NATO and its prospective membership in the European Union will be the ultimate tests of the nation's institutional achievements and the commitments of its elites and citizens to the institutions and values of political democracy. With luck, the next two decades will see this happen.

BIBLIOGRAPHY

Banfield, Edward. 1958. *The Moral Basis of a Backward Society*. Glencoe, Ill.: Free Press.

Bihari, Mihaly. 1998. "1997: The Year of the Constitutional Court." In *Hungarian Political Yearbook*. Budapest: R-Forma Kiado.

Korosenyi, Andras. 1998. *A Magyar Politikai Rendszer* (The Hungarian Political System). Budapest: Osiris.

March, James G., and Johan P. Olsen. 1989. *Rediscovering Institutions: The Organizational Basis of Politics*. New York: Free Press.

O'Donnell, Guillermo. 1997. "Illusions about Consolidation." In *Consolidating Third-Wave Democracies: Themes and Perspectives*, ed. Larry Diamond and Marc Plattner. Baltimore: Johns Hopkins University Press.

Przeworski, Adam. 1995. *Sustainable Democracy*. Cambridge: Cambridge University Press.

Putnam, Robert D. 1993. *Making Democracy Work: Civic Traditions in Modern Italy*. Princeton, N.J.: Princeton University Press.

Sarkozy, Tamas. 1996. *A hatekonvyabb kormanyzasert* (For More Effective Governance). Budapest: Magveto.

Sartori, Giovanni. 1997. *Comparative Constitutional Engineering*. New York: New York University Press, 2nd ed.

Tökés, Rudolf L. 1996. *Hungary's Negotiated Revolution: Economic Reform, Social Change, and Political Succession, 1957–1990*. Cambridge: Cambridge University Press.

———. 1997. "Party Politics and Political Participation in Postcommunist Hungary." In *Democratization and Political Participation in Post-Communist States*, ed. Karen Dawisha and Bruce Parrott. New York: Cambridge University Press.

5

Poland

The Political Elite's Transformational Correctness

Bogdan Mach and Wlodzimierz Wesolowski

How did the Polish political elite view politics and democracy a half dozen years after state socialism? The study we draw on was conducted in the spring of 1996, and it was motivated by the apparent disorganization of politics following Poland's democratic transition in 1989. The large political parties seated in parliament were fragmented internally in their ideologies and programs. Outside parliament, there were several parties and political blocs *in statu nascendi* that were conspicuous for their radical rhetoric and readiness to offer voters slogans rather than programs (Wesolowski, 1997). Politics also seemed to lack a set of generally accepted rules of fair play. It was perhaps only in February and March 1997, during the debate over a new constitution, that movement toward a clear set of political game rules could be observed.

A distinctive feature of the transition from state socialism in Poland and neighboring countries was that politics could no longer be defined abstractly, according to some textbook formula or some officially approved theorist. However, when there is no prescribed conception of politics and no clear-cut pattern to follow, dissonance and inconsistency in understanding and practicing politics are likely. After state socialism in East Central Europe, politics have become what the majority of politicians, or at least the dominant politicians, do. This warrants examining how they perceive and think about politics.

In the longer run, the weakness of Poland's party system may hamper the overall process of systemic change, which includes transforming the economy and stabilizing new democratic institutions. During the 1990s, however, the economic and political transformation was going forward—Poland's gross national product grew faster than in other countries of the region, and its new democratic regime was functioning reasonably well. We explain the paradox of an unconsolidated political party system, on the one hand, and the relatively "normal" performance of the new regime, on the other, by hypothesizing the existence of a "transformational correctness" or even a "transformational compulsion" among the elites that guided the transformation. Specifically, we hypothesize that the Polish political elite believed it was obligated to pursue market and democratic reforms. To see this elite belief as a form of political correctness is doubtless unjust as regards some sophisticated and strongly motivated political leaders; nonetheless, there are grounds for thinking that it is a fitting characterization of the semiconscious assumptions of many, perhaps even the majority, of politicians involved in the day-to-day business of formulating and implementing laws.

Political elite understandings may be compared in at least five areas:

- Opinions about who should be versus who actually is involved in politics, that is, about the desirable as against the real characteristics of politicians;
- Conceptions of politics that politicians believe to be prevalent among their peers versus conceptions the individual politicians actually hold;
- Visions of a "good state" and the features believed to make it good;
- Visions of democracy as embodied in ideas about what is most important in a democratic system and the extent to which this exists;
- Characteristics of "right" and "left" orientations and the factors that facilitate or hinder political agreements between those who hold these differing orientations.

We hope to shed light on political elite perceptions of how politics were being played and what the elite's own roles were in Poland during the mid-1990s. Our analysis is based on three assumptions. First, we assume that postsocialist elite attitudes and orientations were not yet fully crystallized (cf. Weber, 1958). Because of this, we assume, second, that elite understandings were manifested indirectly in politicians' perceptions of each other and their evaluations of recent and current political developments. Finally, we assume that these evaluations, as well as more general expectations about political life, can be used to chart the political elite's emerging attitudes and orientations.

THE POLITICAL ELITE

Our study involves 215 parliamentary deputies representing four parties, plus 61 politicians who aspired to be deputies but who were not elected to the Sejm (the lower house of parliament) in 1993.[1] Why focus on both actual and aspiring parliamentarians? The scarcity of political leaders and the weakness of most parties made the Sejm the body in which the most important party leaders, including most cabinet members, were located, the most important political debates took place, and the process of transforming Poland was most clearly unfolding. Each Sejm that was elected after 1989 contained many new members. These new members, together with deputies reelected for a second or even a third time, described their parliamentary service as amounting to a "crash course in politics." Through parliamentary activities, they were gradually becoming professional politicians, and they viewed themselves in this way. Serving in the Sejm was an intense experience that greatly altered and broadened former political outlooks. This is why studying Polish politics and the political elite during the 1990s has required a focus on those persons making up the Sejm.

But why the additional focus on would-be deputies who failed to win Sejm election in 1993? In fact, these failed candidates received the largest shares of votes in their electoral districts. In this respect, they were really electoral winners, and most of them were prominent in national politics. They failed to gain election only because, on the national level, their parties failed to cross the threshold of 5 percent of the nationwide vote (8 percent for party coalitions) necessary to obtain a share of Sejm seats. Although financial and organizational constraints on our research made it difficult to include would-be parliamentarians who belonged to the two most important right-wing and center-right parties and blocs outside parliament—the Christian National Union and the Center Alliance—we finally managed to reach and interview them.

It was also important to study center-right politicians outside parliament because the composition of the Sejm was sharply skewed toward the left between 1993 and 1997. It was dominated by the Democratic Left Alliance (SLD), which is the composite successor to the Polish United Workers Party and which consists of the Social Democratic party (SdRP) and its allies such as the All Poland Trade Unions Alliance (OPZZ) and various women's, youth, and other organizations. Second in the number of Sejm deputies between 1993 and 1997 was the Polish Peasant Party (PSL), which was a "satellite" of the Polish United Workers Party under the state socialist regime. Between 1993 and 1997, the SLD and the PSL together held two-thirds of the Sejm seats. The remaining parliamentary parties were the liberal-democratic Freedom Union (UW), the social-democratic Labor Union (UP), the nationalist Confederation for Independent Poland (KPN), and the Non-Party Bloc for Reforms (BBWR), which portrayed itself as right-wing by virtue of its free market orientation, but which was also moderately nationalist in stance. By including in our study right-wing politicians who failed to gain election we offset the Sejm's strong left-of-center coloration.

These extraparliamentary politicians were affiliated with the Christian National Union (ZChN), a party of lay Catholics with mostly traditionalist leaders, and the Center Alliance (PC), a party that is strongly anticommunist and stands for Poland's modernization and its economic integration with Western Europe.

DESIRABLE VERSUS ACTUAL POLITICIANS

Let us first consider the political elite's views of who should be involved in politics (see table 5.1). Responses to our question about this allow us to conclude that there was substantial elite consensus about who were and were not desirable actors on the political stage. Respondents from all parliamentary parties, as well as from the two parties not represented in the Sejm, shared the belief that those most fitted for the job of politician were "leaders who are able to gain social support for their programs" and (slightly less frequently) those who already were "respected civic leaders." Least acceptable to all groups of respondents was the idea that politicians should be experts. Another unpopular view, except in the Democratic Left Alliance (SLD), was the notion that politics should be left to "experts" or to "party leaders."

This basic elite consensus about the most and least acceptable profiles of politicians did not mean, of course, that there were no differences between party groups. However, these differences were all located within what might be thought of as the transformational path of politics leading away from state socialism. Politics were overwhelmingly seen as the arena in which prosocial and pro-state "leaders," "authorities," and others were guiding Poland through the unfamiliar terrain of "transformation" (a popular expression). This conception of politicians as guides was especially widespread among

Table 5.1   Profiles of Politicians: "Who *Should Be* Involved in Politics?" (Percentage) (N=232)

Party Affiliation	N	Experts	Party Leaders	Civic Leaders	All Who Are Interested	Leaders Able to Gain Support
Labor Union	33	6.3	9.4	25.0	28.1	31.3
Democratic Left Alliance	50	6.0	26.0	22.0	4.0	42.0
Peasant Party	50	6.0	10.0	34.0	8.0	42.0
Freedom Union	50	6.0	8.0	10.0	20.0	56.0
Center Alliance	30	3.3	6.7	13.3	16.7	60.0
Christian National Union	30	3.3	10.0	6.7	13.3	66.7
Extra-parliamentary (BBWR & KPN)	32	3.1	6.3	25.0	12.5	50.0

right-wing politicians, especially right-wing politicians who were not in the Sejm: two-thirds of the members of the Christian National Union and 60 percent of the Center Alliance respondents articulated it. By contrast, only a third of the Labor Union (UP) parliamentarians thought that politicians should be reliable guides. The most widespread view among UP leaders was that politics consisted of the activities of all citizens. Twenty-eight percent of UP politicians held this view, which distinguished this most left-wing of parties from the other left-oriented parties—the Democratic Left Alliance and the Polish Peasant Party—none of whose leaders embraced the idea that politics should be equated with civic activities. On the contrary, a quarter of the Democratic Left Alliance leaders saw politics as the activities of party leaders like themselves (no more than 10 percent of the other parties' leaders held this rather elitist view).

Although the different party elites had slightly differing conceptions of who should be a politician, on the whole they strongly or very strongly thought that desirable political leaders were those who acted on behalf of the common good, be it of the state or the society. Conversely, all party elites (except for the 26 percent of SLD leaders just mentioned) believed that politics should not be the domain of experts or party leaders.

If we next examine responses to a question about the kinds of people actually involved in Polish politics during the mid-1990s (see table 5.2), we again find significant similarities in political elite assessments. Thus, all the party elites strongly believed that party leaders were those who were actually involved in politics. When we compare conceptions of who should be and who actually was in politics, we see that, except for the few who conceived politics as the "rule of experts," what was thought to be most desirable was perceived to be nonexistent in reality, and vice versa. In other words, virtually all elite members, irrespective of party affiliation, wanted politics to be a job for active and socially conscientious leaders. However, the proportion of each party elite who thought this was actually the case was small. It is important to note that this disjunction between the ideal and the real was especially pronounced among right-wing politicians.

CONCEPTIONS OF POLITICS

When asking political leaders how they conceived of politics, we gave them ten typical definitions of politics that are widely used in political science, and we requested that they rank-order the three that corresponded most closely with their personal conception. The party elites were strikingly similar in their choices. The most popular definition of politics in all groups was "an activity aimed at strengthening the state." The second most popular was "an activity for the benefit of society." Differences between the party elites only

**Table 5.2   Profiles of Politicians: "Who *Is* Involved in Politics?"
(Percentage) (N=232)**

Party Affiliation	N	Experts	Party Leaders	Civic Leaders	All Who Are Interested	Leaders Able to Gain Support
Labor Union	33	—	45.5	3.0	39.4	12.1
Democratic Left Alliance	50	—	40.0	14.0	26.0	20.0
Peasant Party	50	2.0	56.0	—	28.0	14.0
Freedom Union	50	—	42.0	2.0	48.0	4.0
Center Alliance	30	—	63.3	—	26.7	10.0
Christian National Union	30	—	66.7	3.3	26.7	3.3
Extra-parliamentary (BBWR & KPN)	32	6.3	43.8	—	7.5	9.4

began to emerge in respondents' third choices. Depending on the party
group, politics as "a struggle for power," "a struggle for social influence," or
"a representation of group interests" was the third definition most frequently
chosen. Only a few leaders opted for any of the other seven definitions we
provided. Especially as regards defining politics as "providing people with
leadership," the silence of respondents was surprising because all groups
agreed, as noted above, that politics was mainly a job for socially conscientious leaders and they all complained that such leaders were in short supply.

All party elites thus held roughly the same conceptions of politics, and they
differed mainly in the frequency with which they chose one or another of the
two or three most popular definitions (see table 5.3). Although the most popular definition in all groups was politics as "an activity aimed at strengthening the state," this was more frequently chosen by Christian National Union
leaders than by Labor Union and Democratic Left Alliance leaders. Similarly,
though no party elite prioritized politics as "a struggle for social influence,"
this conception was significantly more widespread among Democratic Left
Alliance politicians than among right-wing ones. However, such differences
were too small to undermine the fundamental similarity of conceptions
among all party elites. As groups, they all preferred social–collective definitions of politics emphasizing activity on behalf of the state or society at large.
Conceptions of politics as a struggle for power and influence or as a representation of particular interests were much less popular among all groups.

Let us look more closely at how conceptions varied between the party
elites. If all the socially and collectively oriented conceptions (that is, working to strengthen the state, working for the benefit of society, providing
leadership, and mediating between interests) and all the remaining definitions, which referred to particularistic aspects of politics (that is, struggling for power, struggling for influence, working for the benefit of one's

Table 5.3 Definitions of Politics Chosen by Party Elites (Mean Index of First Three Selections)* (Percentage) (N=232)

Party Affiliation	Struggle for Power	Struggle for Social Influence	Represent Group Interests	Activity to Strengthen the State	Mediate Group Interests	Represent Local Demands	Activity for Sake of Own Party	Activity for Benefit of Society	Provide People with Leadership	Other
				Mean Values of the Index for the Indicated Meaning of Politics						
Labor Union	.30	.55		1.79	.30	.15	.39	1.46		.15
Democratic Left Alliance	.58	1.02	.56	1.74	.24	.30	.40	1.08	.04	—
Peasant Party	.46	.62	.62	2.12	.30	.30	.26	1.22	.08	—
Freedom Union	.40	.80	.30	2.26	.32	.28	.24	1.18	.18	—
Center Alliance	.40	.40	.47	2.07	.20	.30	.07	1.57	.23	.30
Christian National Union	.74	.35	.42	2.61	.42	.19	.19	.97	.07	.03
Extra-parliamentary (BBWR & KPN)	.28	.19	.50	2.16	.09	.50	.44	1.56	.13	.09

*Index has the value of 3 if a given characteristic was chosen as the most important (rank 1); 2 if chosen as next important; 1 if chosen in third place; 0 if not chosen at all.

own party or selected group interests), are aggregated into two categories, clear differences between the Democratic Left Alliance, on the one hand, and the Freedom Party and right-wing parties, on the other, emerge. About 80 percent of the leaders of the Freedom Party and the right wing parties chose "collectivist" or, we might say, "communitarian" conceptions. By contrast, only a slim majority (52 percent) of Democratic Left leaders chose such collectivist-communitarian definitions; 48 percent of them opted, instead, for the more particularistic conceptions. Peasant Party and Labor Union leaders fell in between, with seven out of every ten choosing collectivist conceptions, and the remaining three choosing particularistic ones. In short, Democratic Left Alliance leaders were split into more or less equal-sized groups of collectivists and particularists, whereas in the remaining parties either collectivists or communitarians formed the clear majority. This difference is important and we shall return to it when we assess the party elites overall.

We also asked respondents to estimate "the percentage of politicians" who actually understood politics according to each of the ten definitions we supplied. Once again, there was a striking convergence of answers. All party elites indicated that, in reality, Polish politicians define politics as an "activity for the sake of their own party." This widespread perception was consistent with the earlier perception (see tables 5.1 and 5.2) that, in reality, it is mainly party leaders who are involved in politics, though no large number in any party group (except the Democratic Left Alliance) thought this a good thing. Ironically, though only 3 of the 276 politicians interviewed said that they personally thought "activity for the sake of their own party" was what politics was all about, more than two-thirds of all party elites (except for Freedom Union, where the proportion was three-fifths) believed that this was how politics were in reality as typically defined by politicians across the political arena. Definitions of politics as "a struggle for power" and "a struggle for social influence" were also frequently attributed to other politicians, though few admitted to themselves accepting such definitions. The great majority of our respondents, irrespective of party, assigned these two definitions, plus the definition of politics as "activity for the sake of one's own party" to at least 60 percent of all other Polish politicians.

In sum, members of the political elite overwhelmingly saw Polish politics as, in practice, a job for party leaders aimed at strengthening one's own political party or at procuring power or influence. At the same time, they regarded this as inconsistent with their visions of the ideal politician and their own definitions of politics. The clear conclusions to be drawn are that in all party elites the conceptions of politics attributed to the majority of politicians were (1) largely consistent with the dominant opinion in each group about who in fact was involved in politics, (2) largely inconsistent with personally held definitions of politicians, and (3) poor reflections of the politicians' normative visions of the desirable politician.

A "GOOD STATE"—WHAT DOES IT MEAN?

What aspects of the political system would have had to be present in order for the political elite to conclude that the system was "good"? When we asked about this we again obtained very similar responses. All visions of a "good state" were consistent with the general notion of a transition to democracy, and this was the case in all party elites. Moreover, the various elites did not differ in their opinions about what is most and least important for a "good" state; they differed only somewhat as regards specific features of "a good state's power structure," and all respondents located these specific features somewhere between an "upper" and a "lower" limit of desirability.

To illustrate this, between two-thirds and nine-tenths of all the party elites declared that if state authorities were to be perceived as "good," officials must first of all respect the law. Conversely, less than a fifth of the parliamentarians and less than a quarter of the right-wing politicians outside parliament thought that a "prominent leader who attracts support" was important for a good state, while less than half thought that "political leaders who are effective organizers of socioeconomic life" were important. There was, in other words, a widespread aversion to equating a good state with populist features and tendencies.

The party elites did differ in the extent to which they thought civic activity ("citizen activity co-shapes the state's tasks") was a crucial feature of the good state. Leaders of the right-wing parties, as well as of the Labor Union and the Freedom Union, twice as frequently thought civic activity important as did leaders of the Democratic Left Alliance and the Peasant Party. Majorities or near majorities of the latter instead emphasized "leaders who are effective as organizers of socioeconomic life" and "leaders with the ability to understand society." Only about a third of Labor Union, Freedom Union, and Center Alliance respondents thought these two leadership conditions important for a good state. Members of the right-wing parties inside and outside parliament (the Non-Party Bloc and the Confederation for an Independent Poland inside it, and the Christian National Union outside it) cited one or the other of the two leadership conditions with some frequency, but they seldom chose both. Of all the party groups, Freedom Union members least frequently cited the two leadership conditions as components of a good state.

In sum, all the elite groups clearly regarded upholding the law as the most important feature of a good state, and they thought that having prominent leaders who attracted support was the least important feature.

The main difference between them was over the importance of civic activity, which Democratic Left Alliance and Peasant Party leaders much less frequently prioritized.

ATTRIBUTES OF DEMOCRACY

In all elite groups, "rule of law," "protections of personal freedom," and "freedom of expression" were viewed as the most important features of a smoothly functioning democracy. Asked to prioritize many desirable features of democracy on a seven-point scale that ranged from "very important" to "not at all important," respondents gave lower average priorities to "government concern for social well-being," "guaranteeing minority rights," and "citizen activity." Nevertheless, nearly all viewed these aspects of democracy as "important." One difference between the party elites is interesting because it presumably reflected distinct ideological positions. This was the marked tendency among leaders of the right-wing parties to assign their lowest priority to "guaranteeing minority rights." When respondents were further asked to use the same seven-point scale to indicate which aspects of democracy were already well established in Poland, "freedom of expression" and "free choice between parties" were given the highest average rankings. Strikingly, the "rule of law" was given a low ranking, despite the fact that this had earlier been regarded by large majorities of all groups as one of the most important features of democracy. Obviously, many members of the political elite did not think that the rule of law was as yet firm in Poland, and this view was common among all party groups.

To uncover more systematic differences between the party elites' views of democracy's attributes, we subjected their assessments to a factor analysis. We omitted those democratic features whose assessments were most skewed (that is, those that the majority of respondents rated as "very important") and we aggregated responses rated as "not at all important" and "very unimportant" because their frequencies were low. We then factor-analyzed the responses in each political group in order to check whether the factor structures of the different parties were similar. The results for right-wing parties—the Non-Party Block for the Support of the Reforms (BBWR), the Confederation for an Independent Poland (KPN), the Center Alliance (PC), and the Christian-National Union (ZChN)—were slightly different from the results for the other groups. The first factor, which we labeled democracy as "civic participation," included items stressing citizen activity, citizen control of power structures, free choice between parties, a large measure of autonomy for local government, and protection of minorities. Among the right-wing parties, autonomy for local government and protection of minorities constituted a separate factor. A second main factor, which we labeled democracy as "government by good leadership" ("stewardship" for short), was found in all groups and included "caring for the well-being of citizens" and "selecting the best people to govern the country."

The results of our factor analysis were straightforward. Participatory and civic aspects of democracy were significantly more important for Freedom Union and Center Alliance leaders than for leaders of the Peasant Party, Christian National Union, or Democratic Left Alliance. However, the Christian National Union leaders' stance on "civic participation" was fully explained by the low importance they assigned to the protection of minorities and by the high importance they assigned to local government autonomy. When these two items were excluded from "civic participation," the attitude of Christian National Union leaders toward democracy did not differ significantly from that of all other party groups, including the other right-wing party groups—the BBWR and KPN—which both moderately favored "civic participation." The assessments labeled "stewardship" formed an equally clear pattern: the Democratic Left Alliance, Peasant Party, and right-wing groups believed this to be an important attribute of effective democracy, whereas the Freedom Union, Christian National Union, and, to a lesser extent, Labor Union viewed stewardship as relatively less important.

Our factor analysis warrants classifying the leaders of the Labor Union as simultaneously, though moderately, in favor of both civic participation and stewardship. By contrast, Democratic Left Alliance and Peasant Party leaders strongly favored stewardship while downgrading civic participation. Freedom Union leaders had a distinctive profile in that they strongly opposed stewardship and moderately favored civic participation. Center Alliance leaders moderately favored civic participation but showed no strong preference for or against stewardship. Finally, because of their hostile stance toward protecting minorities while wanting to give local government greater autonomy, Christian National Union leaders moderately opposed civic participation and strongly opposed stewardship.

These patterns require three comments. First, as already mentioned, all party elites viewed all of the features of democracy presented to them as very important or important. To say, therefore, that one group favored or opposed civic participation or stewardship does not imply some absolute orientation toward democracy; it merely indicates a certain distance from the mean evaluation, which consisted of a strong positive evaluation of both civic participation and government by good stewards. Second, locating the groups according to their distance from the mean evaluation accords well with the proclivities of each group on the other dimensions we have discussed: visions of the "good politician," ways of understanding politics, and conceptions of the "good state." Third, differences over the importance of civic participation as against stewardship should be seen as falling within the general orbit of ideas about Poland's democratic transition. As we hypothesized initially, virtually all political elite assessments about how things should go and how they were actually going in Poland had a strong whiff of "transformational correctness."

POLITICAL SYMMETRIES AND ASYMMETRIES

During the nineteenth century, "politically correct" orientations characteristically emphasized the need to protect religious rights in public life, to protect national identity, and to operate a laissez-faire economy based on private ownership. Nearly everywhere today, such ideas have given way to more complex ideological and policy orientations. These orientations seem even more complex in Poland in the aftermath of state socialism (Jasinska-Kania, 1996). It would be wrong, however, to say that the nineteenth-century doctrines have become obsolete. What we have today is a greater individualization of beliefs and, accordingly, a combination of quite different ideas within each political party.

We asked politicians about the characteristic features of "left" and "right" political orientations (see tables 5.4 and 5.5). The question was open ended because we wanted respondents to express their own views. The attributes of left and right orientations mentioned most frequently were no surprise: a positive evaluation of private property had its counterpart in a positive evaluation of state intervention; an appreciation of religion had its counterpart in the demand for a secular state. It is noteworthy, however, that "an appreciation of the nation" had no counterpart. Nor did anyone mention "internationalism" as characteristic of the left political orientation. Though conspicuous in Polish political discourse under state socialism, "internationalism" has now disappeared. It is also noteworthy that the "responsiveness of politicians to public opinion," which is part of the left orientation, had no counterpart in the form of an elitist component in the right orientation. Elitism was not verbalized by politicians on either the right or the left of the political stage.

Measured by the frequency with which their various features were expressed, the strength of left and right orientations among the several party elites can easily be seen in tables 5.4 and 5.5. Once again, the similarities were striking, though there were, of course, some differences. One difference was the frequency with which "egalitarianism and concern for social justice" was mentioned; nearly half (47.1 percent) of the Labor Union deputies mentioned this, but only 5 percent of the Freedom Union deputies and little more than 3 percent of the Center Alliance deputies mentioned this. Perhaps the only really counter-intuitive pattern was that "responsiveness to public opinion," which is customarily associated with a left orientation, was mentioned by nearly half (48.1 percent) of the Democratic Left

Table 5.4 The Most Often Mentioned Features of the Right Political Orientation (Percentage) (N=232)

Party Affiliation	Positive toward Private Property	Positive toward Religion & Church	Positive toward Nation & Tradition	Critical of Left	Critical of Social Welfare
Labor Union	58.8	64.7	47.1	0.0	29.4
Democratic Left Alliance	34.6	42.3	34.6	15.4	15.4
Peasant Party	75.0	41.7	16.7	—	8.3
Freedom Union	68.2	40.9	36.4	4.5	4.5
Center Alliance	73.3	46.7	66.7	—	—
Christian National Union	79.3	65.5	69.0	—	—
Extra-parliamentary (BBWR & KPN)	58.8	29.4	70.6	—	—

Table 5.5 The Most Often Mentioned Features of the Left Political Orientation (Percentage) (N=232)

Party Affiliation	Positive toward State Intervention	Positive toward Social Welfare	Positive toward Egalitarianism and Social Justice	Strongly in Favor of Secular State	Responsive to Public Opinion
Labor Union	39.4	58.8	47.1	52.9	23.5
Democratic Left Alliance	3.7	40.7	11.1	33.3	48.1
Peasant Party	20.0	72.0	8.0	44.0	20.0
Freedom Union	60.0	65.0	5.0	30.0	5.0
Center Alliance	56.7	43.3	3.3	40.0	—
Christian National Union	51.7	34.5	10.3	34.5	6.9
Extra-parliamentary (BBWR & KPN)	18.8	18.8	18.8	18.8	—

Alliance deputies, but only 5 percent of the left-wing Labor Union deputies thought to mention it. Conceivably, the latter took responsiveness to public opinion for granted, whereas Democratic Left respondents, who formed the main part of the government and who were frequently accused of inheriting an authoritarian legacy from state socialism, were assiduous in proclaiming the importance of responsiveness.

PERCEPTIONS OF POLITICAL ADVERSARIES

The features of right and left orientations revealed in tables 5.4 and 5.5 stimulate another observation. This is that the various party elites tended to articulate features that they thought their opponents harbored privately but concealed in their public rhetoric. For example, compared with other party groups the leaders of the Labor Union, which is a staunchly secular party, said that a "positive approach to the Catholic Church" was a distinguishing feature of the right orientation more frequently than did right-wing leaders themselves. By the same token, Center Alliance, Christian National Union, and Freedom Union leaders, all of whom headed pro-market parties, named a "positive approach to state intervention" as a key component of the left orientation much more frequently than did SLD or Labor Union leaders. These selections were intended to portray adversaries in a rather negative light, and they indicated that doctrinal differences between the party elites were perceived as real.

More evidence of this tendency emerged when respondents were asked about the factors that hinder political agreements. Most often mentioned was "different opinions about the communist past" or some similar response. Both the strongly anticommunist party groups outside parliament and the postcommunist Democratic Left Alliance voiced this with equal frequency. It testified to a real sense of division between the two elite camps. Similarly, when respondents were asked to discuss the "characteristics of the political elite," they frequently pointed to "negative" relations between individuals and groups making up the elite: personal conflicts and antagonisms, personal ambitions, the inability of some groups to cooperate, and political envy. Also quite frequently mentioned were "different ideologies and outlooks." At the same time, however, the overriding need to continue with reforms was frequently cited as a factor facilitating political agreement within the elite. An agenda in which continuing reform was at the forefront, regardless of doctrinal and other differences, appeared to be the principal basis for elite cooperation.

The division between a "postcommunist bloc" and a "former opposition bloc" that is the legacy of state socialism was reflected in responses to another open-ended question about who or what constituted "the most important part of the political elite." Sizable majorities of leaders in all but the small right-wing parties inside and outside parliament considered parliamentary deputies and party leaders to constitute the elite's most important part, and this suggested a substantially homogeneous perception of how post-transition politics were organized. But divisive residues of the state socialist experience were also articulated. Thus, sizable numbers of Freedom Union, Non-Party Bloc, Confederation for an Independent Poland, Center Alliance, and Christian National Union leaders insisted that the postcommunist "nomenklatura" was the most important part of the elite. In short, the Communist versus anticommunist schism endured. It is noteworthy that in all parties few leaders gave primacy to business, media, or Catholic Church forces within the political elite. It appeared that politicians regarded their sphere of activity as relatively autonomous from other spheres, and to this extent they registered the ongoing process of elite differentiation in Poland.

CONCLUSIONS

Our principal finding is that party elites with conflicting ideologies and programs were, on the whole, surprisingly similar in their views of how politics should, and actually did, function in Poland during the mid-1990s. We interpret this to mean that among Polish politicians there was a fundamentally common perception of the tasks confronting them during a period of continuing system transformation. We label this common perception transformational correctness.

Despite this "correct" view of the political landscape, patterned differences between the party elites did exist. Diverging perceptions of right and left orientations and of how political influence was "really" structured (for example, whether the "nomenklatura" remained the most important part of the elite) revealed these patterned differences. To the extent that the several parts of the political elite think differently about how Polish politics are and should be structured, explosive political conflicts remain possible. They are not probable, however. This is because conflicting elite perceptions and, consequently, conflicting actions are substantially undercut by the common conviction that emerged in our study about the overriding importance of continuing market reform and keeping democracy stable.

NOTES

1. We sampled 50 deputies from each larger political grouping present in parliament and we included all the deputies from the smaller groups there: 33 Labor

Union, 16 BBWR, and 16 KPN. From parties outside parliament we sampled 30 would-be deputies from the ZChN and 30 from the PC. The sampling procedures are described in Wesolowski and Post (1997).

BIBLIOGRAPHY

Jasinska-Kania, Alexandra. 1996. "Miàdzy neo-liberalizmem a neo-socjalizmem: problem krystalizacji prawicowych i lewicowych ideologii i wartosci w Polsce." In *Oswajanie rzeczywistosci: Miàdzy realnym socjalizmem a realna demokracja,* ed. M. Marody. Warsaw: Instytut Studi¢w Spolecznych.
Weber, Max. 1958, "Politics As Vocation." In *From Max Weber,* ed. H. Gerth and C. W. Mills. New York: Oxford University Press.
Wesolowski, Wlodzimierz. 1997. "Political Actors and Democracy: Poland 1990–97." *Polish Sociological Review:* 4.
Wesolowski, Wlodzimierz, and Barbara Post, eds. 1997. *Polityka I Sejm.* Warsaw: Wydawnictwo Sejmowe.

6

East Germany

Elite Change and Democracy's "Instant Success"

Christian Welzel

It is conventional wisdom that democratic transitions and democratic consolidations depend upon quite different kinds of regime support.[1] For transitions it is sufficient that elites agree to adopt democratic institutions and procedures, even if they do so for short-term tactical reasons. Accordingly, democratic transitions are often described as rational processes of deliberate regime choice driven by negotiated elite pacts and settlements (O'Donnell and Schmitter, 1986; Burton, Gunther, and Higley, 1992). For the consolidation of democracy, however, it is necessary that elite support broadens into mass support and that the tactical agreements of elites deepen into normative commitments to democratic institutions among elites and citizens alike. In the mainstream understanding of democratic consolidation, this broadening and deepening of support occurs during a habituation phase in which elites and citizens become accustomed to democratic practices (Rustow, 1970; Barry, 1978; Schmitter and Karl, 1991). Normative support for democracy among elites and citizens is, therefore, a possible consequence of, not a precondition for, the existence of democracy. History offers striking examples of this habituation model. To take but one, it has often been claimed that support for democracy was limited and weak during the first years of the West German democratic regime after World War II, but that support broadened and deepened together with rapid socioeconomic development and the democratic practices it facilitated during the 1950s and 1960s (see, for example, Conradt, 1989; Baker, Dalton, and Hildebrandt, 1981).

There is a second, quite different way in which democratic consolidation can be achieved, however. This occurs when democracy has the normative support of elites and citizens from its very outset—when democracy is consolidated at the same time it is adopted. Huntington (1991), Diamond (1992), and Linz and Stepan (1996) show that several third wave democratizations corresponded to this "instant success" model. Modernization under predemocratic regimes is said to be the major reason for them. Thus, Diamond (1992) argues that modernization (that is, socioeconomic development) promotes the spread of democratic values (that is, a civic culture) and the formation of collective actors (that is, a robust civil society) that demand democracy.[2] Modernization is, therefore, a process favoring the evolution of democracy's attitudinal and associational bases. If this evolution takes place under an authoritarian regime, the democratic regime that follows is likely to be consolidated from its start.

My thesis is that democratization in East Germany adhered to the instant success model. Modernization under Communist rule in the German Democratic Republic (GDR) created attitudinal and associational bases for democracy sufficient to guarantee democratic consolidation as soon as the GDR regime was replaced. At first glance, my thesis may seem vulnerable to two counter arguments. First, that it was the *failure to modernize* that brought about the GDR regime's downfall. Second, that democratic consolidation has, in any event, occurred through German reunification, not through processes internal to East Germany itself. Although these counter arguments are credible, I will show that all the features and consequences of modernization necessary for democratization's instant success had, in fact, developed under the GDR regime. Accordingly, democratic consolidation in East Germany should be dated from the first free parliamentary elections in March 1990, not from German reunification more than half a year later, in October 1990. Reunification meant national unity for all German citizens, but democratic consolidation in East Germany was achieved by the efforts of the citizens living there and it existed before reunification. It is, therefore, factually incorrect to regard East German democratization as part and parcel of reunification; in reality, democratization and reunification occurred sequentially.

THE "INSTANT SUCCESS" MODEL OF DEMOCRATIZATION

In the instant success model, modernization triggers a causal chain that results in a consolidated democracy. Democracy is consolidated when elites are "consensually unified" in their normative support for democracy and when this elite support is shared by a large majority of citizens (Burton, Gunther, and Higley, 1992). So we know the beginning and the end of the causal chain. But what are the links, or stages, that constitute it? By drawing on some general insights in political sociology, we can deduce these stages and describe the whole sequence in ideal–typical form.

Modernization, conceived broadly as socioeconomic development, is a syndrome of interrelated changes. Two of the most striking changes are rising education levels and an expanding service sector (Bell, 1973). Together, these changes create a large and ever-growing *educated service class* consisting of "knowledge workers"—scientists, teachers, journalists, writers, and artists, as well as technical, managerial, administrative, and public relations specialists (Gouldner, 1979). Hence, the first stage of modernization is the emergence of an educated service class.

Research on value change shows that members of the educated service class possess "civic competence" in extraordinarily high degrees (Inkeles, 1983; Brint, 1984; Lamont, 1987; Scarbrough, 1995). Civic competence is a set of value orientations, among which tolerance, interpersonal trust, ideological moderation, feelings of efficacy, and demands for democratic liberties are the most prominent. Civic competence is relevant to politics in two ways. First, it motivates and enables citizens to organize political movements and criticize political authorities. Where modernization occurs, the politically active part of a citizenry consists disproportionately of members of the educated service class. Second, civic competence is inherently compatible with the workings of democracy, and those who possess civic competence strongly favor democracy normatively. Putting all this together, one can maintain that the growth of an educated service class means increased numbers of politically interested and democratically oriented citizens. The advent of this attitudinal basis for democracy is thus the second stage in the instant success model.

If normative support for democracy evolves under an authoritarian regime, it necessarily produces political dissatisfaction. According to Albert Hirschman (1992), dissatisfaction can be expressed by "voice" or "exit," though strong threats of repression can force citizens to abstain from these options and abide an authoritarian regime—a process that Kuran (1992) has termed "preference suppression" under Communist regimes. However, even the most repressive regime cannot prevent all dissatisfied citizens from opting for "voice" or "exit." This is particularly true for members of the educated service class whose strong civic competence enables them to organize political opposition, even if it is only a small part of the educated service class that does so. If the educated service class has become large, even a small part of it constitutes a significant opposition to the repressive regime. Embryonic democratic opposition networks emerge outside regime organizations in the form of civil or human rights movements ("outside opposition"). Such opposition networks may also evolve inside regime organizations in the guise of reformist factions ("inside opposition"). The instant success model's third stage is, thus, the creation of an embryonic associational basis for democracy.

Under an entrenched authoritarian regime it is very risky for both the inside and the outside opposition to challenge ruling elites directly through public actions. Sometimes, however, opportunity structures switch suddenly to favor the opposition groups. There are at least two circumstances in which this switch may occur. First, an internal split or a loss of external support may paralyze ruling elites. Second, opposition groups may be inspired by "demonstration effects" in neighboring countries to challenge the ruling elites. If one or both circumstances occur, opposition groups are likely to agitate for legalization of their embryonic organizations and for free elections. In the course of this agitation, previously passive members of the educated service class join the ranks of inside and outside opposition groups. Public agitation for democratic reforms and the growth of the inside and outside opposition groups are, thus, a fourth stage in the instant success model.

In order for a democratic transition to occur, however, the ruling elites must be unwilling or unable to suppress the agitations. If this happens, electoral mobilizations and elections become the major mechanism for regime change. An essential element of this change is the circulation of elites. In this respect, electoral mobilizations are important because they bring inside opposition groups (that is, reformers) to prominence in the authoritarian regime's organizations. The first free elections then effect the transfer of state power from authoritarian organizations to the newly legalized organizations of the outside opposition groups, although some inside opposition leaders also succeed in the free elections. In the fifth and final stage of the instant success model, in other words, state power comes to be held by an amalgam of new elites heading both outside and inside opposition groups. This is the moment when democracy is simultaneously adopted and consolidated. Table 6.1 summarizes the instant success model of democratization.

Stage 1: The Growth of the Educated Service Class

During forty years of state socialism, East Germany experienced a remarkable increase in the size of the educated service class. The proportion of the employed population with a university degree increased from 2 percent in 1961 to 9 percent in 1989 (*Statistisches Jahrbuch der DDR*, 1974, 1990). During the same period, the comparable proportion in West Germany reached only 7 percent (Geißler, 1991). Moreover, by the end of the 1980s the proportion of East Germans aged twenty to twenty-four years who were enrolled in tertiary education amounted to 33.5 percent (the proportion of West Germans was almost identical: 33.3 percent), and people twenty-five years or older had, on average, ten years of schooling (in West Germany the average was

Table 6.1 The "Instant Success" Model of Democratization

Meta-Stages	Stages		Elements Constituting the Stages
Preparing the bases for democracy	Stage 1: Emerging social basis of demands for democracy		Modernization:
			Rising levels of education
		+	Expansion of the service sector
		−	Growth of the educated service class
	Stage 2: Spreading demands for democracy (i.e., attitudinal basis for democracy)		Growth of the educated service class
		−	Spread of civic competence:
			Spread of political interests and skills
		+	Spread of demands for democratic liberties (liberty orientations)
Undermining autocracy	Stage 3: Emerging embryos of a democratic opposition (i.e., associational basis for democracy)		Spreading liberty orientations
		+	Spreading political interests and skills
		+	Authoritarian rule
		−	Political dissatisfaction, predisposition to form democratic opposition
			Predisposition to form democratic opposition
		+	Repressive threat of the regime elite
		−	Majority of dissenters remaining passive
		+	Minority of dissenters forming an embryonic democratic opposition
	Stage 4: Enlarging the democratic opposition to mass level		Embryonic democratic opposition
		+	Switch of opportunity structure
		−	Mobilization of passive dissenters for the democratic opposition
		+	Unwillingness or inability of the regime elite to suppress opposition
		−	Pact between the regime elite and the opposition concerning the preparation of free and general elections
Implementing and consolidating democracy	Stage 5: Elite circulation through elections		Pre-electoral mobilization
		+	Elections
		−	Elite circulation in favor of the (inside and outside) opposition

eleven years). Thus, under state socialism East Germany reached education
levels comparable to those of advanced industrial countries.

Some 87 percent of university graduates in the GDR were employed as
professionals in work that involved high degrees of cognitive skills (GDR
Biographies Survey 1991–92).[3] Their per capita incomes were 20 percent
above the average (Geißler, 1991). Although the GDR's gross domestic
product per capita was only about half that of West Germany's, it was comparable to the per capita GDPs of Spain and Ireland by the end of the 1980s.
Clearly, there was remarkable growth of an educated service class whose
members were economically established, with secure jobs that yielded
above-average incomes in a relatively prosperous society. The question is
whether this educated service class was becoming the bastion of demands
for democratic liberties and thus moving the GDR into the instant success
model's second stage.

Stage 2: Spreading Orientations toward Liberty

The model teaches that as the educated service class expands, demands
for greater liberty spread. This happens in two ways. First, the growth of the
educated service class enlarges the proportion of people oriented toward
greater liberty (that is, the educated service class itself). Second, it increases
the proportion of people in the general population who are similarly oriented once embryonic agitation within the educated service class becomes
more widely known. Both trends can be seen in data from the World Values
Survey 1990–91, which are charted in figures 6.1 and 6.2[4] The y-axis in figure 6.1 represents the *general* proportion of liberty-oriented people in a society, while the y-axis in figure 6.2 represents their *specific* proportion in the
educated service class, defined as respondents who reported completing
their full-time education at twenty years of age or later.[5] In the World Values Survey, demands for greater liberty are operationalized by the postmaterialism items of "giving people more say in important government decisions" and "protecting freedom of speech." Where respondents gave their
first priority to either of these items they were classified as oriented toward
greater liberty.[6] The x-axes in figures 6.1 and 6.2 represent an important
aspect in the growth of the educated service class as reported in the 1992
UNESCO Statistical Yearbook, namely, national education levels in terms of
the relative number of students in universities.

Figures 6.1 and 6.2 reveal a strong correlation between national education levels and the proportions of persons with liberty orientations. In particular, it is obvious from figure 6.2 that rising education levels enlarge the
specific proportions of liberty-oriented persons in the educated service class
at *increasing* rates. This presumably reflects collective interactions: the liberty orientations of educated persons are strengthened the more they come

Figure 6.1 Education and the Proportion of Liberty-Oriented People in Society

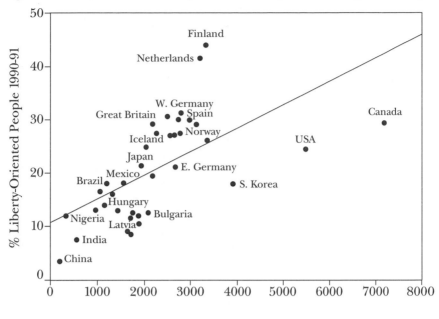

Number of Students per 100,000 Inhabitants 1990

R = .62

Source: World Values Survey 1991

into contact with other educated people. It appears that this socially cat-alyzing process has occurred in capitalist and socialist societies alike.

Given that this process appears to be universal, it presumably occurred in East Germany under state socialism. Unfortunately, no representative surveys of the GDR population exist with which to determine whether the educated service class was characterized by stronger liberty orientations than those of average citizens. One must rely, instead, on retrospective views of former GDR citizens. In the so-called Baseline Social Survey taken after German reunifi-cation in 1991, East Germans were asked about the defects of state socialism that they most disliked.[7] The items they were asked to rank were "low standard of living," "lack of opportunities for democratic participation," "absence of the right to travel abroad," and "suppression of political opposition." Among university graduates, fully 66 percent gave either their first or second priority to the lack of democratic participation and the suppression of political oppo-sition: 31 percent gave both items their first and second priorities, and 35 per-cent gave their first priority to one of the two items while giving second pri-ority to some other item. These proportions compare with 15 and 28 percent, respectively, among the 43 percent of persons without university degrees who

Figure 6.2   Education and the Proportion of Liberty-Oriented People in the Educated Service Class

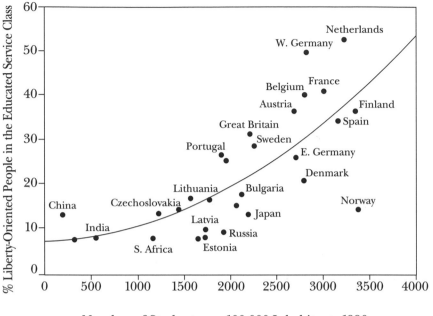

Number of Students per 100,000 Inhabitants 1990

R = .74

Source: World Values Survey 1991

assigned their first or second priority to lack of democratic participation and the suppression of political opposition. A similar pattern emerged in responses to a parallel set of items about orientations toward liberty taken from the standard postmaterialism battery. Sixty percent of university graduates gave their first and second priorities to wanting "more say" and more "freedom of speech": 28 percent of them prioritized both items, and 32 percent prioritized one of the two items. The proportions among nongraduates were again much smaller: 12 and 23 percent, respectively.

Although the attitudes recorded in the 1991 Baseline Study were retrospective in nature, the data indicate that liberty orientations were significantly more widespread among the GDR's educated service class than among the general population. It is interesting to note, moreover, that differences between the extent of these orientations among educated service class members and among average citizens were similar in eastern and western Germany: in eastern Germany in 1991 it was 60 as against 35 percent, and in western Germany it was 78 as against 54 percent.[8]

It is worth asking, however, if the mix of liberty orientations differed greatly between former citizens of the GDR and former citizens of West Germany. To assess this, I divided respondents into those who assigned their first priority to wanting "more say" and those who assigned wanting more "free speech." This is an important distinction because wanting "more say" pertains to the citizenry collectively, while wanting more "free speech" relates to citizens as individuals. The distinction mirrors the contrasting ideological thrusts of the GDR and the Federal Republic: socialism's emphasis on collective goods and capitalism's emphasis on individual goods. One would thus expect to find a larger proportion of former GDR citizens prioritizing "more say" and a larger proportion of West Germans emphasizing "free speech." Indeed, in the 1991 Baseline Study, "collectivists" who wanted more say outnumbered "individualists" who wanted more free speech by 76 to 24 percent among former GDR citizens, but only by 60 to 40 percent among former West German citizens.

This east–west difference was not peculiar to Germany and was, in fact, characteristic of Europe in general by about 1991. This can be seen in data from the second World Values Survey. If all "individualist" and "collectivist" respondents from the former state socialist regimes of Eastern Europe and all respondents from the capitalist democracies of Western Europe are aggregated and compared, collectivists outnumbered individualists by 75 to 25 percent among the East Europeans but only by 59 to 41 percent among the West Europeans.[9] These differences were nearly identical to those observed between eastern and western Germans. Hence, we can with some confidence conclude that the more collectivist liberty orientation of former GDR citizens was a legacy of state socialism and its collectivist thrust.

Regardless of its citizens' more collectivist orientation, the GDR passed through and beyond the second stage in the instant success model, in which liberty orientations become significantly more widespread and more strongly held by the educated service class than among average citizens.

Stage 3: Embryos of Democratic Opposition

By repressing anti-regime riots in 1953 and by building the Berlin Wall in 1961, the GDR showed itself to be one of the most repressive regimes in the Soviet bloc. Accordingly, GDR citizens expected to incur very high costs if they chose "voice" or "exit" to manifest dissatisfaction with the regime. In fact, down to the autumn of 1989 there were only marginal public manifestations of political dissatisfaction and opposition in the GDR. However, there is evidence that members of the educated service class used exit and voice options more often than the average citizen. Surveys of refugees from the GDR, for instance, regularly showed that younger and middle-aged members of the educated service class were much more numerous than others among those who decided to go to the West (Hilmer and Köhler, 1989). Studies in 1984 and 1989 found that "lack of freedom of speech" rather than "bad economic conditions" was the prime motivation that refugees cited for their flight from the GDR (71 percent in 1984, and 74 percent in 1989).

By the end of the 1970s, an embryonic but significant outside opposition network made up of peace and civil rights groups had emerged in the GDR, with tacit support from the Protestant Church. Though there are no exact data that measure this network's size and density, scholars describe the activists who formed it as predominantly young and middle-aged members of the educated service class (see, for example, Knabe, 1988). This social profile was common to outside opposition networks in all East European state socialist regimes (Joppke, 1994). Inside opposition networks also emerged within the ruling East German Socialist Unity Party (SED). Though less strongly than in the Hungarian Socialist Workers Party, SED dissidents began calling for democratic reforms in 1987. As was the case with the outside opposition groups, the dissidents inside the SED consisted mainly of educated service class members (Bortfeldt, 1992). In short, embryonic structures of democratic opposition and a civil society were centered in the educated service class. Until 1987–88, however, the chance that public protests would succeed seemed very low, while their costs were so high that not many people risked open dissent. Opposition networks and, thus, the associational basis for democracy had not yet acquired a large size.

Stage 4: Enlarging Democratic Opposition to the Mass Level

Between 1987 and spring 1989 the cost–benefit calculation changed dramatically in favor of mass opposition to the regime. Beginning in 1987, Mikhail Gorbachev distanced the Soviet regime more and more openly from the Brezhnev doctrine, and this gave rise to doubts about the repressive capacity of regimes in the Soviet bloc. Anticipated costs of public protests declined as the East European socialist regimes lost their vital external support. In Poland and Hungary, ruling elites split quite openly into hard- and soft-liners, with the latter wanting to initiate negotiations with opposition groups about democratic reforms. The Polish and Hungarian reforms quickly nourished expectations for democratic change in East Germany and Czechoslovakia. But no ruling elite split occurred in those two countries. Accordingly, if they were to realize their heightened expectations for democratic reforms, the only option open to Czechoslovak and East German opposition groups was public agitation and mobilization (Welzel, 1995). However, the situation was increasingly ripe for events that would trigger this.

In the GDR, the triggering event occurred on 11 September 1989, when thousands of ostensibly vacationing GDR citizens crossed the dismantled Hungarian border into Austria. In the wake of this mass flight, many more citizens who were prepared to stay in a democratized GDR began to join protests in Leipzig, Dresden, East Berlin, and other cities (Opp, 1991). These mass protests evolved from small weekly meetings that had begun during the preceding months. Labeled "vigils" and "peace prayers," those initial meetings were a response to the manipulated results of elections to local councils during May 1989, and they were also a backlash against the GDR parliament's official approval of the Tiananmen Square massacre in China during early June. The meetings took place in church squares, and mainly members of the dissident networks of the embryonic civil society attended them.

When mass public demonstrations proliferated during autumn 1989, members of the educated service class participated in disproportionate numbers. As a series of surveys of the "Monday protestors" in Leipzig discovered, the proportion of the "intelligentsia" among the initial demonstrators amounted to more than one-third, which was a participation rate nearly three times the educated service class's proportion in the population (Mühler and Wilsdorf, 1991).[10] Only during the democratic transition's next phase did the proportion of educated service class members among demonstrators decline to approximately 15 percent. This decline followed a shift in the demonstrations' goals. While democratization of the GDR was the initial goal, that of German reunification rapidly came to the fore as 1989 neared its end.[11] It is obvious that many educated service class members were more strongly attracted to GDR democratization, which was attainable without reunification. The reason is simple. Compared with large parts of the population, members of the educated service class suffered relatively little economic deprivation. Their dissatisfactions were primarily political, not economic, and a majority of educated service class members were therefore more interested in democratic reforms than in the economic improvements that German reunification would probably entail.

Despite their reservations about reunification, however, members of the educated service class joined both inside and outside opposition groups, and they began to stand for offices in the established and emerging parties. In short, some of them moved rapidly toward positions in the new political elite, and this inaugurated the instant success model's fifth and final stage.

Stage 5: Elite Circulation

An extensive 1995 survey (the "Potsdam Elite Study") of 2,341 German elites holding top positions in politics, business, trade unions, state administration, the media, and cultural and other organizations produced data with which to ascertain the extent to which educated service class members in the former GDR became elite members in reunified Germany.[12] Of the elites who participated in the survey, 272 (12 percent) reported growing up and living in the GDR. It is these persons that we will call "east German elites," that is, persons of east German origin who held elite positions in 1995, as distinct from the west Germans who held elite positions located in the five eastern states of Germany in that year.[13]

The data show that the overwhelming number of the east German political elite held their first political office during the 1990s. Although 28 percent of them had been members of the old Socialist Unity Party, and though 17 percent had belonged to one or another "democratic bloc" party in the GDR, the number who had held a position in those parties was negligible, amounting to little more than a dozen persons. Most of those who had been members of the GDR's official parties began to seek political positions only when dissidents inside those parties began to mobilize for democratic reform during the autumn of 1989. In other words, this portion of the east German political elite in 1995 consisted of persons who had been latecomers to the ranks of those opposing the GDR regime from inside its own organizations. There were no significant differences in this respect between east German political elite members who belonged to the Democratic Socialists (PDS), Christian Democrats (CDU), or Liberal Democrats (FDP) in 1995.

On the other hand, 55 percent of the new east German political elite had had no party affiliation in the old GDR. They instead moved directly from outside opposition groups to elite positions once the GDR regime fell, and this happened via new parties that did not exist under Communist rule—principally the Social Democrats (SPD) and the Bündnis 90 party. About 40 percent of these former nonparty persons had been engaged in the civil rights or peace movements before 1989. In short, they had been part of the outside opposition at a time when the GDR regime still had a significant repressive capacity. Because the outside opposition comprised no more than 0.3 percent of the GDR's adult population prior to the last year or so of Communist rule, those who pioneered the outside opposition were grossly overrepresented in east German political elite positions in 1995.[14] The remaining 60 percent of former nonparty persons had joined the outside opposition to the GDR regime when mass protests began in the 1989 autumn.

The extent of political elite circulation in eastern Germany can also be seen in the changed age, occupational, and educational profiles of elite position-holders. The average age of the GDR's top elite was about sixty-three years, while that of the new east German political elite was about forty-seven years in 1995. In occupational terms, 66 percent of the new elite had held professional positions in the GDR workforce and were typically knowledge workers with relatively great autonomy in their jobs. Thus, 41 percent of the new elite in 1995 had been employed in community services, that is, educational, scientific, cultural, and human services (including churches). Another 18 percent had been employed in the economic sector (most often as engineers, not managers), while the remainder had been scattered across other sectors. But perhaps the most remarkable feature of the new elite in 1995 was its education profile. Nearly 80 percent held a degree from one of the main GDR universities, as distinct from the special academies that had been operated for SED members. A large proportion, 45 percent, consisted of persons trained in the natural sciences (including medicine) or engineering, though 8 percent had been educated as Protestant theologians. In terms of both occupation and education, it is evident that the east German political elite in 1995 stemmed heavily from the GDR's educated service class—particularly those parts of it that entered the inside and outside opposition groups before or during the 1989 mass mobilization.

ELITE SUPPORT FOR DEMOCRACY

If the elite transformation that accompanied the East German democratic transition can usefully be thought of as passing through the five stages I have summarized, it remains necessary to ask about the extent to which the new east German political elite is unified by a normative, rather than a tactical, commitment to democracy. I showed earlier that, by a difference of two to one, members of the educated service class in eastern Germany—as in western Germany—held strong liberty orientations more often than the average citizen. Among the new east German elite these orientations were still more pronounced: 81 percent gave one or another item about democratic liberties his or her highest priority in the 1995 survey of elites. This proportion compared favorably with west German elite respondents, among whom—after forty-five years of democratic experience—the corresponding proportion was 77 percent. Thus, not only did educated service class members constitute most of the new east German political elite, but one can also infer that it was those members of the service class who were most oriented toward liberty that did so. The data suggest that there is sufficient normative support for democracy among the new east German elite to prevent any weakening of the democratic consensus in the reunified national elite as a whole.

Yet, there remains a question about whether the two geographic segments of the German elite have different specific understandings of democracy and whether their understandings are the same as those found in the east and west portions of the German citizenry. It will be recalled that in the early 1990s, surveys showed a disjunction between east Germans, who placed greater emphasis on the collectivist dimension of liberty ("having more say") and west Germans, who more frequently stressed the individualist dimension ("more freedom of speech"). It can be seen in table 6.2 that the same disjunction existed at the elite level in 1995: 71 percent of the eastern political elite emphasized the collectivist dimension, as compared with only 41 percent of the western elite.

Table 6.2   "Individualist" and "Collectivist" Views of Democratic Liberties among German and European Citizens, 1991, and among German Elites, 1995

		% *"Individualists" among Liberty- Oriented People*	% *"Collectivists" among Liberty- Oriented People*	N
German citizens	East	24	76	221
	West	40	60	462

Cramer's V: .15 (p _ .001)
Source: Baseline Survey, 1991.

European citizens	East	25	75	1,288
	West	41	59	7,014

Cramer's V: .15 (p _ .001)
Source: World Values Survey, 1990–91.

German elites	East	29	71	220
	West	59	41	1,551

Cramer's V: .19 (p _ .001)
Source: Potsdam Elite Study, 1995.

Drawing any firm conclusion about such elite differences on the basis of only two survey items is unwarranted. Fortunately, the 1995 elite study queried democratic precepts more specifically. When subjected to factor analysis, six of these items constituted a single dimension, whose one pole represented a "citizen-guided" understanding of democracy, and whose other pole constituted an "elite-guided" understanding (cf. Inglehart, 1990). The attitudes of eastern and western elites towards the items are presented in table 6.3, where the items are loaded on the citizen-guided pole and on the elite-guided pole.

One can see that eastern elites were located closer to the citizen-guided pole than western elites. From an ideological standpoint, however, it is probably mistaken to view the easterners' proclivity toward citizen-guided democracy as a residue of state socialism. This is because the preference for citizen-guided democracy is anchored in broader leftist traditions, especially those of the New Left, as represented by the Greens and the more radical wing of the Social Democrats. Hence, the proclivity of eastern elite persons toward citizen-guided democracy may stem entirely or mainly from their support of left-of-center parties. Indeed, eastern elites much more frequently support the Social Democrats, Greens, and Democratic Socialists than do western elites (55 to 32 percent).[15]

A factor analysis showed that, when controlled for variables such as age, career sector, and 1995 party affiliation, the possible effect of prior regime

Table 6.3   German Elites' Agreement with Six Democratic Precepts, 1995 (Percentage) (N=2,300)

	% Partly Agree and Fully Agree	
Items	West German Elites	East German Elites
Introducing referenda is a necessary completion of representative democracy.	53	81
Democracy should not be limited to the political arena but should be implemented in as many arenas as possible.	72	89
Citizens' political participation should be limited to voting in elections.	14	5
In the long run democracy requires strong leadership capable of resisting special interests.	26	16
Citizens should lose the right to strike or demonstrate if they disturb public order.	35	25
Too much media criticism of political leaders damages democracy.	31	25
N	2,030	270

Source: Potsdam Elite Study, 1995.

experience (that is, living under the GDR or West German regime) on respondents' locations on the continuum between citizen-guided and elite-guided democracy was small (adjusted beta coefficient of .03), especially compared to the influence of party affiliation (adjusted beta coefficient of .53). With respect to democratic precepts, in other words, there was less east–west difference within party groups than between easterners and westerners in different parties. Put differently, because they more frequently supported left-of-center parties, eastern elite persons located themselves closer to citizen-guided democracy. It is, therefore, not surprising that in all the constitutions of the new eastern *lander* there are provisions for referenda at both local and state levels. This amounts to saying that reunification has strengthened in the whole of Germany a secular trend that is apparent in nearly all Western democracies, namely, an increasing preference for citizen-guided politics. It is interesting to note that, inspired by the east German example and probably also reflecting the wider secular trend, west German states have now begun to introduce constitutional provisions for referenda.

CONCLUSION: DID MODERNIZATION WORK DIFFERENTLY IN STATE SOCIALISM?

The population of the German Democratic Republic passed through all the stages of the instant success model of democratization. Four of the five stages were completed before reunification, while the fifth had at least begun before reunification in late 1990. The basis of democratic consolidation in eastern Germany was the modernization sequence, not west German influence through reunification. Without that modernization sequence, it would have been impossible to achieve democratic consolidation so rapidly, even with the massive aid and influence that the reunified Germany expended on eastern Germany during the 1990s. The crucial condition was the level of modernization that the GDR had attained by the late 1970s and early 1980s. Without that, no liberty-oriented educated service class and thus no social basis for democratic elite circulation would have existed. Hence, despite the unique circumstance of reunification, East Germany is best seen as a paradigmatic instance of how consolidation can be achieved without a lengthy habituation to democracy.

The data presented in this chapter indicate that, in one aspect, modernization had similar effects, but in another aspect it had quite different effects, in state socialist and capitalist societies. The effects of modernization were similar in so far as it enlarged the educated service class—and, thereby, the general and specific proportions of liberty-oriented persons in state socialist and capitalist societies alike. This is important evidence of modernization's universal democratic impact on political culture regardless of the type of regime that exists. On the other hand, modernization's effects differed in so far as the mix of collectivist and individualist views of democratic liberties were distributed differently between the two kinds of societies—individualist views being more pronounced in the capitalist societies, and collectivist views more prominent in the state socialist ones. In this regard, the western and eastern parts of Germany today are a microcosm of Europe as a whole.

NOTES

1. The term "democracy" is used here to characterize regimes in which (1) the legislative body is constituted periodically by free (competitive) and general (inclusive) elections; (2) the legislative body holds effective legislative power; (3) the head

of government is elected periodically in free and general elections either by the legislative body or by the citizenry.

2. Scholars might argue that democratic values do not derive from a country's modernization but are the result of value diffusion involving "outside learning" about other countries. However, I would stress that modernization and outside learning are not incompatible. On the contrary, outside learning depends heavily on extensive education and communication facilities, which are primary features of modernization.

3. The GDR-Biographies Survey was conducted in 1991–92 under the direction of Karl-Ulrich Mayer at the Max Planck Institute for Educational Research in Berlin, Germany. I am grateful to Karl-Ulrich Mayer for his permission to use these data and to Heike Solga for technical support.

4. The principal investigator in the World Values Survey 1990–91 was Ronald Inglehart of the University of Michigan, Ann Arbor. The data cover representative surveys in more than forty nations. The data set is available at the Inter University Consortium on Political Research (ICPSR) at the University of Michigan, Ann Arbor.

5. People finishing full-time education when they are more than twenty years of age have usually acquired a tertiary degree. Thus, they share an essential characteristic of the educated service class.

6. The other items were "maintaining order in the nation" and "fighting rising prices." Compared to these items, "more say" and "free speech" represent liberty items because they imply more possibilities and therefore more liberties for citizens to act in society. As outlined by Welzel and Inglehart (1998), liberty orientation in this sense is not the same as postmaterialism. Liberty orientation is one of two components that are distinguished from each other in postmaterialism. The other component is represented by life-quality items referring to esthetic–ecological ("beautiful cities and countryside") and ethical ("more humane society") orientations.

7. The principal investigators in the Baseline Survey 1991 were Peter Mohler, Erwin K. Scheuch, Michael Braun, and Michael Häder. The survey covered a random sample of 3,058 Germans who were at least eighteen years of age. The data set is available at the Zentralarchiv für Empirische Sozialforschung (ZA) in Cologne, Germany.

8. Regression analysis shows that the proportion of liberty-oriented persons in society depends on (1) national education levels and (2) national income levels (in terms of GNP/capita). The proportion of liberty-oriented people in east Germany is lower than in west Germany because of east Germany's lower income level.

9. The East European countries in the survey were Belarus, Bulgaria, Czechoslovakia, Estonia, Hungary, Latvia, Lithuania, Poland, and Russia. The West European countries were Austria, Belgium, Britain, Denmark, Finland, France, Iceland, Ireland, Italy, the Netherlands, Norway, Portugal, Spain, and Sweden.

10. The project's investigators joined "Monday demonstrations" in Leipzig on 13 November and 11 December 1989, and on 15 January and 12 February 1990. At each of these demonstrations they randomly distributed questionnaires enclosed in stamped envelopes. The response rate was about 80 percent.

11. The major demands were to delete the Socialist Unity Party's leading role in the constitution (Article 1), legalize the outside opposition's organizations (of which the New Forum and the newly founded Social Democratic Party were the most important), and prepare for free, competitive parliamentary elections. Beginning in

November, the public demonstrations were augmented by demonstrations mounted by the inside opposition, that is, by members of the Socialist Unity Party. The insiders demanded the dissolution of the Politburo and the Central Committee, as well as free, competitive intraparty elections to create legitimate leadership. At the beginning of December, the Politburo and the Central Committee were dissolved and free, competitive elections for a national congress of the Socialist Unity Party were announced. This congress took place later in the month. The electoral campaign for the congress and further intraparty elections allowed for a thorough renewal of the party elite by the inside opposition. The new leadership of the renamed Party of Democratic Socialism (PSD) then met regularly with leading members of the outside opposition at a national roundtable.

12. The Potsdam Elite Study was directed by Wilhelm Bürklin at the University of Potsdam. It initially identified a sample of 4,100 elite positions. This was a sectoral quota sample of top position holders in politics, administration, associations, the economy, the mass media, culture, justice, and the military. The selection criteria are described in Bürklin, Rebenstorf, et al. (1997). The data set is available at the Zentralarchiv für Empirische Sozialforschung (ZA) in Cologne. The present author participated in the study's planning, field research, and analysis.

13. Of these 272 east German elite members, 89 percent can be classified as political elite members holding leading positions in federal or state parliaments, governments, parties, large associations, and the mass media. Twelve percent of the east German elite members held top positions in western Germany and 88 percent in eastern Germany. Of all elite members holding hold top positions in eastern Germany, east Germans constituted 60 percent. The remaining 40 percent were west Germans. For more detailed analyses of the following figures see Welzel (1997; Welzel and Inglehart, 1998).

14. Blattert, Rink, and Rucht (1995) estimated that some forty-one thousand citizens had been active in the opposition movement before fall 1989. This figure corresponds to 0.3 percent of the adult GDR citizenry.

15. Western elite members' support for leftist parties is limited to the Social Democrats and the Greens, whereas 20 percent of the eastern elite members support the Democratic Socialists (postcommunists).

BIBLIOGRAPHY

Baker, Kendall L., Russell J. Dalton, and Kai Hildebrandt. 1981. *Germany Transformed*. Cambridge: Harvard University Press.

Barry, Brian. 1978. *Sociologists, Economists, and Democracy*. Chicago: University of Chicago Press.

Bell, Daniel. 1973. *The Coming of Postindustrial Society*. New York: Basic Books.

Blattert, Barbara, D. Rink, and Dieter Rucht. 1995. "Von den Oppositionsgruppen der DDR zu den neuen sozialen Bewegungen in Ostdeutschland." *Politische Vierteljahresschrift* 36, no. 2: 397–422.

Bortfeldt, Heinrich. 1992. *Von der SED zur PDS: Wandlung zur Demokratie?* Bonn: Bouvier.

Brint, Steven, 1984. "'New Class' and Cumulative Trend Explanations of the Liberal Political Attitudes of Professionals." *American Journal of Sociology* 90 (July): 30–31.

Bürklin, Wilhelm, Hilke Rebenstorf, et al. 1997. *Eliten in Deutschland: Integration und Zirkulation.* Opladen: Leske& Budrich.

Burton, Michael, Richard Gunther, and John Higley. 1992. "Introduction" In *Elites and Democratic Consolidation in Southern Europe and Latin America,* ed. J. Higley and R. Gunther. Cambridge: Cambridge University Press.

Conradt, David P. 1989. "Changing German Political Culture." In *The Civic Culture Revisited,* ed. G. Almond and S. Verba, 212–72. Princeton: Princeton University Press.

Dalton, Russell J. 1996: *Citizen Politics in Advanced Western Democracies.* Chatham, N.J.: Chatham Press.

Geißler, Rainer. 1991: "Transformationsprozesse in der Sozialstruktur der neuen Bundesländer." *Berliner Journal für Soziologie* 2: 177–94.

Gouldner, Alvin W. 1979. *The Future of Intellectuals and the Rise of the New Class.* New York: Seabury.

Hilmer, R., and A. Köhler. 1989. "Der DDR läuft die Zukunft davon." *Deutschland Archiv* 6: 1383–87.

Hirschman, Albert O. 1992. "Abwanderung, Widerspruch und das Schicksal der deutschen Demokratischen Republik." In *Selbstbefragung und Erkenntnis,* ed. A. O. Hirschman. Hamburg: Carl Hanser.

Huntington, Samuel P. 1991. *The Third Wage: Democratization in the Late Twentieth Century.* Norman, Okla.: University of Oklahoma Press.

Inglehart, Ronald. 1990. "Values, Ideology, and Cognitive Mobilization in New Social Movements." In *Challenging the Political Order: New Social and Political Movements in Western Democracies,* ed. Russell J. Dalton and Manfred Kuechler. Cambridge, Mass.: Polity Press.

Inkeles, Alex. 1983. *Exploring Individual Modernity.* New York: Columbia University Press.

Joppke, Christian. 1994. "Revisionism, Dissidence, Nationalism: Opposition in Leninist Regimes." *British Journal of Sociology* 45 (December): 543–61.

Kleßmann, Christoph. 1991. "Opposition und Dissidenz inn der Geschichte der DDR." *Aus Politik und Zeitgeschichte* B41/91: 52–62.

Knabe, Hubertus. 1988. "Neue Soziale Bewegungen im Sozialismus: Zur Genesis alternativer politischer Gruppen in der DDR." *Kölner Zeitschrift für Soziologie und Sozialpsychologie* 40: 551–69.

Kuran, Timur. 1992. "Now Out of Never: The Element of Surprise in the East European Revolutions of 1989." *World Politics* 44 (April): 7–48.

Lamont, Michele. 1987. "Cultural Capital and the Liberal Political Attitudes of Professionals." *American Journal of Sociology* 92 (May): 1501–5.

Linz, Juan J., and Alfred Stepan. 1996. *Problems of Democratic Transition and Consolidation.* Baltimore: Johns Hopkins University Press.

Mühler, Kurt, and Stefan Wilsdorf. 1991: "Die Leipziger Montagsdemonstration." *Berliner Journal für Soziologie* 1: 37–45.

O'Donnell, Guillermo, and Philippe C. Schmitter. 1986. "Tentative Conclusions about Uncertain Democracies." In *Transitions from Authoritarian Rule,* ed. G.

O'Donnell, P. C. Schmitter, and L. Whitehead, vol. 4. Baltimore: Johns Hopkins University Press.

Opp, Karl-Dieter. 1991. "DDR '89: Zu den Ursachen einer spontanen Revolution." *Kölner Zeitschrift für Soziologie und Sozialpsychologie* 43, no. 2: 302–21.

Pareto, Vilfredo. 1968: *The Rise and the Fall of Elites.* Totowa, N.J.: Bedminster Press.

Rohrschneider, Robert. 1994. "Report from The Laboratory: The Influence of Institutions on Political Elites' Democratic Values in Germany." *American Political Science Review* 88: 927–37.

Rustow, Dankwart A. 1970. "Transitions in Democracy: Toward a Dynamic Model." *Comparative Politics* 2 (April): 337–63.

Scarbrough, Elinor. 1995. "Materialist–Postmaterialist Value Orientations." In *The Impact of Values,* ed. E. Scarbrough and J. van Deth. Oxford: Oxford University Press.

Schmitter, Philippe C., and Terry L. Karl. 1991. "What Democracy Is . . . and Is Not." *Journal of Democracy* 2 (March): 75–88.

Statistisches Jahrbuch der Deutschen Demokratischen Republik. 1974, 1990, ed. Zentralamt für Statistik der DDR. Berlin (East): Dietz Verlag.

Tarrow, Sidney. 1991. "Kollektives Handeln und politische Gelegenheitsstruktur in Mobiliserungswellen." *Kölner Zeitschrift für Soziologie und Sozialpsychologie* 43: 647–70.

Welzel, Christian. 1995. "Der DDR-Regimewechsel im Lichte genereller Transitionsmechanismen." *Politische Vierteljahresschrift* 36 (March): 67–90.

———. 1997. *Demokratischer Elitenwandel: Die Erneuerung der ostdeutschen Elite aus demokratie-soziologischer Sicht.* Opladen: Leske & Budrich.

Welzel, Christian, and Ronald Inglehart. 1998. "The 'Trinity' Structure of Human Development and the Role of Democracy in 41 Nations." Unpublished paper. Wissenschaftzentrum, Berlin: WZB.

7

Serbia

The Adaptive Reconstruction of Elites

Mladen Lazić

The transformation from state socialism has given new theoretical and empirical impetus to the study of elites. Many surveys of elites in Central and East European countries were undertaken during the 1990s, and they were embedded in theoretical discussions of elites in postsocialist conditions. While this research produced much important data, the theoretical discussions underscored the ambiguities that have dogged the study of elites since its beginning. These ambiguities concern the elite concept itself, the locations and roles of elites in the process of social structuration, the relationship between elites and classes, and much else. Basic, unresolved questions have led to unproductive discussions, clearly illustrated by the debate over the extent of elite circulation as against elite reproduction in postsocialist countries. It is not possible to resolve such questions in a chapter, but it is necessary to sketch some answers in order to make my study of elites in Serbia more meaningful.

CLASS AND ELITE THEORIES

In the history of elite theory, two general approaches can be distinguished. The first approach, which was characteristic of the classical elite theorists, is individualistic in its thrust. Pareto, Mosca, and their followers defined elites according to individual capabilities: entrepreneurial talent, ability to organize, and so on. Because this approach leads inevitably to a psychologistic interpretation of social life, I ignore it here. The second approach is positional and it has generally taken two tracks. On one track, the holding of top institutional positions has been used to separate elites from the rest of society. On the other track, accumulated power and, very often, the readiness or capacity to act has been the basis for identifying elites.

A problem with the first, institutional track is that it is empirical rather than theoretical. Nothing is wrong with defining elites in terms of their institutional positions so long as one stays at the descriptive level. Difficulties appear, however, when such a definition is extended to the analytical level. I will mention two difficulties. First, proponents of the institutional approach—following the practice of elite theorists—as a rule investigate only the top of the social hierarchy (economic, political, military, and other "power" elites); consequently, they relegate the rest of society to an undifferentiated "mass." In this way, relations within social hierarchies are blurred because the "mass" cannot be understood as other than a mere object of elite actions. Therefore, instead of the relations between elites and masses, only the shaping of the masses by elites is analyzed. This gives rise to a second and more important difficulty, namely, that the institutional approach may be useful for describing the concrete recruitment, behavior, attitudes, and interrelations of institutionally based elite groups, but it cannot deal with the problem of how institutions are themselves constituted and reproduced because they are a product of complex relations throughout social hierarchies.

Scholars who employ the positional approach in elite studies often use a too general or, in Max Weber's phrase, a too "empty" conception of power. For example, Eva Etzioni-Halevy initially adopts a standard definition of elites as persons and groups who may be "differentiated from non-elites by the extent of their power and influence" (1993: 13). Later, however, she becomes more specific: "[Elites] may be those who—even within their own classes—have a greater share of active control over organizational/administrative resources of power. Or they may be those who have a greater share of resources of knowledge, ambition, charisma, time, motivation and energy. In any case, they are the men and women within each social class who, on the basis of these resources, have the ability and willingness to engage in certain actions which are of wider significance and have an impact on society" (Etzioni-Halevy, 1993: 44).

Three elements stand out in Etzioni-Halevy's definition. First, power is specified as "control over resources": physical coercion, organizational-administrative, symbolic, material-economic, psycho-personal. Because she begins with a very general conception of power, it is not surprising that in her definition she combines the individualistic ("ambition," "motivation," "charisma") and positional approaches to studying elites. I would say, by contrast, that in social and political analysis a stress on the *systemic origin* of elite positions is crucial. Therefore, it is more appropriate to interpret "resources" in Pierre Bourdieu's sense of "capital"—economic, social, political, cultural—as something that may be accumulated, reproduced in expanded form, acquired and lost, or converted (cf. Bourdieu, 1986).

The second element that stands out in Etzioni-Halevy's definition is her use of action as a specific attribute of elite persons. Elite theorists have, implicitly or explicitly, always pointed to action as the crucial aspect of elites. Etzioni-Halevy confuses matters, however. Action is not, primarily, the result of a person's "willingness" but is, rather, a necessary consequence of the positions that elites hold because their "resources" cannot be reproduced, accumulated, and so on, without action. Etzioni-Halevy claims that "for action to occur a decision has to be reached and, at the very least, an attempt has to be made to implement it" (1993: 35). For this reason, she argues, classes cannot act; only elites can act. But she employs a surprisingly narrow and tautological conception of action: implementing or attempting to implement decisions is perforce action. To posit decision-making as the fundamental indicator of action seems more appropriate to a theory of organization than to a general theory of the social system and social change.

We are coming to a third, equally problematic element of Etzioni-Halevy's definition that is particularly important for my study. Etzioni-Halevy understands elites as the upper parts of social classes, and it seems that in this way she seeks to solve the old problem of reducing the rest of society to a "mass." The result of her maneuver, however, is to join two traditionally competing approaches—class and elite theories. In order to achieve this fusion, Etzioni-Halevy consistently defines classes in a very general way, as groups "differentiated from each other by the extent to which they own and control various resources and, most prominently, material resources" (1993: 13). The problem with this definition is that it is gradational ("extent" implies a quantitative gradation of inequality), so that it misses the key point of class theory, namely, the interpretation of interclass relations as basically conflictual.

Etzioni-Halevy's maneuver requires some general remarks about the relation between class and elite theories. The historical development of both theories, as well as their internal logic, conceptual apparatuses, and so on, make it clear that their protagonists have been trying to analyze two different sets of problems. The fundamental question for class theorists is how social systems—or, more generally, modes of production of social life—have been inaugurated and dissolved, the "laws" governing their rise and fall, the conditions for their reproduction, and so on. By contrast, elite theorists are concerned with a different set of questions, to wit, who are the most active participants in inaugurating, reproducing, and dissolving dominant social relations in various historical circumstances. Class theorists, in other words, have been dealing with general system dynamics, while elite theorists have been concentrating on concrete mechanisms of social change. That is why class theory has been elaborated at a more abstract analytical level than elite theory, even if many inconsistencies and a change in theoretical stand-points, such as the shift to functionalist theory in order to avoid "unrealis-tic" presuppositions, can be found in studies of large-scale historical processes. By contrast, elite theory has been trivial, descriptive, and nonan-alytical at the abstract level, although it has often spawned compelling empirical research. In short, class and elite theories are complementary, not mutually exclusive, in so far as they both try to answer important questions in social science. However, merging class and elite theories leads to incon-sistencies because class and elite positions often do not match. To take the most obvious example, the political or cultural elite in a worker movement may not belong to the working class. Therefore, class and elite theories have to be kept separate and used selectively according to the problem that is being analyzed.

I prefer to define elites as groups who (1) possess concentrated control over accumulated resources that are necessary for reproducing the basic conditions upon which a given (or potential) social mode of production rests, and who (2) play an active role in reproducing these conditions. Let me briefly elaborate this definition. First, it is structural *and* historical. Accu-mulated resources such as capital are the foundation upon which a specific social mode of production is built. Resources are always economic, political, and cultural in nature, though the specific order of determination among them is what shapes a particular form of society: the accumulation of capi-tal is the foundation of a capitalist society; the monopolistic merger of polit-ical, economic, and cultural resources is the foundation of a state socialist society. Therefore, elites must be defined differently (historically) in differ-ent societies, and this holds true for studying their relations with classes. In addition, it is necessary to distinguish between elite groups according to the accumulated resources each commands and also according to each group's relation with an existing social order: some elites may be its guardians, while others may be the bearers of an alternative but not a new social order. Note that in my definition the accumulation of resources and the actions of elites are interdependent: accumulation is the key precondition for action, while action is necessary for accumulation.

CLASS AND ELITE IN TRANSFORMATIONS
FROM STATE SOCIALISM

I want to show how class and elite theoretical perspectives may be used in research on the breakdown of state socialism and the resulting process of social transformation. Theoretical and empirical studies (cf. Feher, 1984; Lazić, 1987; Lazić, 1994) have shown that state socialism was a particular type of class society. The specific form of its reproduction, in which the ruling class monopolized control over all subsystems of society, made this class the only active social subject. This meant that there was a concurrence between the top layer of the ruling class and the one and only elite in state socialist societies. The lower layers of the ruling class, plus the people—mostly intellectuals—who organized dissident movements, could be called subelites, following the terminology of Etzioni-Halevy (1993: 44). The other social categories in state socialist societies—intermediate strata, workers, peasants, small entrepreneurs—had no possibility for organizing economically and politically, for developing their own ideologies, or for acting collectively (the few exceptions, such as Solidarity in Poland, occurring only when the system was in deep crisis). Still, the dynamics that led to the system's collapse had a class character, and the principal producer of these dynamics was the ruling class. Let me explain this briefly (for a fuller discussion, see Lazić, 1994).

State socialism's command economy systematically produced stagnation and crisis. The ruling class attempted decentralization in order to overcome these problems, transferring some of its authority from the top to lower levels of the ruling hierarchy. But this did not solve the economic problems, while it sharpened conflicts inside the ruling class along both territorial and functional lines. Renewed centralization only aggravated the economic problems, so that in Gorbachev's time a new strategy was tried: to complement decentralization with a controlled and limited liberalization. But liberalization enabled dissident intellectuals to delegitimize the state socialist system. The resulting coincidence of economic, political, and legitimation crises facilitated mass mobilizations, mainly by large segments of intermediate strata and workers, that overthrew the socialist regimes.

The old state socialist system, however, not only prevented class formation among lower social groups who were "rooted" in the system, but it also prevented the bearers of a new system from emerging. More precisely, the command economy did not permit an embryonic entrepreneurial class to emerge. The actors who effected the transformation from state socialism could not, therefore, have constituted a class; they could only be the new and rising elites that took shape under state socialism. There has been another transformational consequence of the specific organizational fusion of economic, political, and cultural subsystems that characterized the state socialist system. Although the elites of the various socialist subsystems were not clearly separable, people who accumulated various kinds of resources have entered different spheres: individuals with accumulated political capital (former "nomenklatura" members) have become entrepreneurs; intellectuals have become leaders of political parties; the nouveau riche have acquired direct political influence, and so on. In other words, the conversion of various forms of economic, political, and social capital during the transformations from state socialism was both fast and massive.

It is quite clear, then, that we cannot analyze these transformations in class terms. The only group that, *stricto sensu,* constituted a class in state socialism—the ruling class, with its organization, defined interests, self-consciousness, ability to act, and so on—has dissolved rapidly. At the same time, new classes have begun to form, so that class relations—the basis of class formation—are just now beginning to appear on the historical stage of postsocialist societies. From this point of view, the contemporary sociological discussion of the nature and role of elites in transformations from state socialism may seem quite appropriate. However, when the discussion centers on whether the elites are "reproducing" or "circulating," it is misleading and conceptually confused.

The most obvious basis for this conclusion is that concentrating on the form of elite change—reproduction or circulation—ignores the crucial aspect of system change, namely, the mechanisms that generate the positions in which classes and elites are located. At conceptual and historical levels it is necessary to distinguish two processes. The first is the collapse of state socialism, which has also meant the collapse of the "nomenklatura" as a ruling class. In this collapse, people who had accumulated (primarily) cultural and social capital played an active role in delegitimizing the system and then in elevating themselves into a part of the new political elite by converting their cultural and social resources into political ones. The second process is the one in which elites have shaped new social relations during the transformation period.

If we consider the theses about elite circulation versus reproduction during postsocialist transformation (for example, Szelényi and Szelényi, 1995), we may reach several conclusions. First, the circulation thesis is more applicable to elites during state socialism than after it. Specifically, when state socialism was inaugurated, the previous ruling class was not only destroyed as a class, but the legitimization of the new socialist system required that members of the old ruling class—especially members of the old elites—be prevented from occupying any command posts. There were very few exceptions to this. Later on, elite circulation continued during state socialism in the sense that, even if the children of nomenklatura members had above-average chances of gaining command positions, the bulk of socialist ruling class members were recruited from lower—in state socialism's final decade, intermediate—social strata. The higher the elite positions, the more this occurred (for data on the former Yugoslavia, see Lazić, 1987, 1994).

The nature of the transformation from state socialism prevents any comparably systematic policy towards elite circulation. The transformation's gradual character has given nomenklatura members time to convert their capital, most often into economic forms. The transformation's liberal character has given them opportunities to remain in politics and even, from time to time, to take high elite posts, according to shifts in voters' attitudes. It is not surprising, therefore, that the available data show a high proportion of former ruling-class members among the new elites (for the Czech Republic, see Mateju and Lim, 1995; for Poland, see Wasilewski and Wnuk-Lipinski, 1995; for Russia, see Hanley, Yershova, and Anderson, 1995; for Hungary, see Sonja Szelényi, 1995; for Yugoslavia, see Lazić, ed., 1995). In short, elite circulation has not been a defining feature of the postsocialist transformation period.

The same data may be used to question the elite reproduction thesis, too. In order to claim that reproduction is the dominant feature of postsocialist transformations, one has not only to ignore the fact that many holders of new elite positions have climbed up from the lower social strata. More important, one must also ignore the key theoretical point that a systemic change has been taking place "outside" individual careers. By employing a terminological parallelism when speaking about political, economic, and other elites in state socialist and in postsocialist societies alike, we overlook the systemic change that has altered fundamentally the social roles of what otherwise look like corresponding elite groups. We ignore, that is, the nature of resources the two sets of elites accumulate and command, the forms their interrelations take, and the bases of conflicts between them. To put this point in aphoristic form: in socialism, elite circulation was part of ruling-class reproduction; in postsocialism, elite reproduction is part of the making of a new ruling class.

Two examples may suffice. First, under state socialism the differentiation of political and economic elites was extremely contingent. Because politics and economics were fused, each political position implied direct economic authority; as a rule, the reverse was also true because managers of big state enterprises were members of the Communist Party's Central Committee or other key Party bodies. The political or economic authority that these interlockings implied was both legal and legitimate. During the postsocialist transformation, however, a divorce between economy and politics has been taking place, so that it is now necessary to *convert* political capital into economic capital, very often by illegal and, as a rule, illegitimate means. Second, under state socialism all intra-elite conflicts were mediated inside the top level of the ruling party hierarchy. During the postsocialist transformation, by contrast, many political conflicts are mediated in parliaments and at elections. At the same time, the state's role in the postsocialist economy is becoming more and more interventionist, but less and less command-like, so that economic competition is moving towards capital, commodity, and labor markets, and so on.

Therefore, instead of speaking about "how much circulation or reproduction is taking place in a post-socialist country," as Ivan Szelényi and Sonja Szelényi (1995: 621) have, it is necessary to distinguish between, on the one hand, the collapse of the nomenklatura as the former ruling class, and, on the other, a new class structuration, in which the elites are playing the formative role. Here social mobility studies may show—as they are already starting to—how these elites (more precisely, their personnel) are being recruited within the new class structure. Stratification surveys may highlight the increasing class differentiation. And surveys of attitudes may turn up elements of emerging class interests. However, in order not to blur "a rather significant change in the institutional structure," as Szelényi and Szelényi (1995: 621) call it, or, more precisely, a structural change in the mode of social reproduction, we must abandon the static and descriptive dualism of elite circulation and reproduction. When speaking about a concrete historical change, at the level of people who have been accumulating economic, political, and cultural capital, or who have been converting previously accumulated capital, it is more appropriate to speak of an *adaptive reconstruction of elites* during postsocialist transformations.

The concept of adaptive reconstruction implies that several processes were unfolding simultaneously in Central and East European countries during the 1990s. First, the command form of social reproduction was dissolving, and in this way the basis upon which the nomenklatura was constituted was removed. Second, a gradual separation of political and economic spheres, together with new mechanisms for acquiring dominant positions in them (market competition and political contestation) imposed on the people who, actually or potentially, control concentrated resources the necessity to adapt in order to keep, or acquire, elite positions. Furthermore, a "sectoral" transfer process took place in the sense that individuals who had belonged to a monolithic ruling class—in which political and economic resources could be distinguished only contingently—were pushed into relatively separate elite "sectors." Depending on the specific path that this process took in each country, former nomenklatura members were more and less successful in converting their accumulated resources into new forms of capital.

THE ADAPTIVE RECONSTRUCTION OF ELITES IN SERBIA

I now want to show how members of the socialist ruling class successfully used a "blocked transformation" in the former Yugoslavia to convert their monopolistic positions into concentrated forms of economic and political capital that are more suited to a postsocialist order. By "blocked transformation" I mean the process in which the old League of Communist societal monopoly was replaced by interlocked positions of economic and political dominance in order to postpone the development of a market economy and political competition (Lazić, 1996).

It is not possible to discuss in detail here the causes of this blocked transformation in Serbia (cf. Lazić and Sekelj, 1997). I can only highlight a few of its aspects. First, it was pure historical coincidence that the old ruling class successfully mobilized the Serb population around an ethnonationalist program precisely at the moment when the state socialist regimes in Central and Eastern Europe abruptly started to collapse. Second, this ruling class—now organized in and around the Socialist Party of Serbia—was able to retain power thanks to the legitimacy of the new postsocialist system. Third, it succeeded, on the basis of general popular support, not only in slowing down the postsocialist transformation—in its own interest—but also in retaining legitimacy despite extremely unfavorable conditions. These conditions included a disintegration of the party's national program, a catastrophic economic crisis, a historically unique form of international isolation, and an overt rebellion by a clear majority of the middle social strata during the winter of 1996–97. The Socialist Party displayed an extraordinary survival capacity in the face of these adverse conditions, any one of which would suffice to destroy most ruling groups. Its survival is understandable only if we take into account the unusual readiness of a large part of the Serb population to support a government that was systematically acting against the population's interests.

This readiness resulted from a complex set of factors that, again, I can only list. First, conditions that might have undermined the ruling group's position were not mutually supportive; on the contrary, they weakened each other. The population accepted an extreme decline in the GDP and living standards—to one third of the pre-1991 level—as a necessary consequence of the civil war that attended the former Yugoslavia's breakup. Most people saw the war as the unavoidable result of a defensive national program. Accordingly, they viewed the sharp economic decline as the result of international sanctions. These were taken as a proof of the great powers' enmity against Serbs, and this enmity was, in turn, seen as the primary cause of the defensive national program's failure.

Second, the economic crisis did not hit all social strata equally. Consequently, members of different strata did not so much compare their living conditions with those of the previous period as they compared their stratum's situation with the situations of other strata. The drop in peasants' living standards, for example, seemed less drastic when they were compared with the deteriorating material circumstances of many urban dwellers (Vujovic, 1995). Not surprisingly, therefore, the Socialist leadership found the peasants to be a bastion of political support. Also, because of the depth of the crisis, in which the economy was almost completely paralyzed, the state's redistributive role became the basic mechanism for the survival of a majority of the population. To many people, therefore, the Socialists and their allies appeared less as the creators of the crisis than as the mainstays of people's livelihoods.

Third, the crisis produced atomization. Because economic enterprises were inactive and paying hardly any regular wages and salaries, the bulk of the population shifted their economic activities into the gray economy

(Mrksic, 1995). Individual survival strategies undermined group solidarities. This is why all attempts at independent union organizing were rather unsuccessful and workers were almost completely absent from the huge protest demonstrations that occurred in Serbian cities during the 1996–97 winter (Babovic, 1997).

Fourth, several sociocultural population traits played an important part in blocking economic and political change. The most significant was a widespread authoritarian orientation that accepted and supported the harsh existing order at face value (Kuzmanovic, 1995). This was associated with traditionalist value orientations, a key element of which is resistance to change.

Finally, the inability of opposition parties to mobilize broad-based support for their program of structural change was a crucial element in the blocked transformation. Their initial failure to gain government power led quickly to internal conflicts and splits. The idea of a "fragmentation of elites" (see chapter 1) is particularly applicable to the Serb opposition parties, and it left them too weak to challenge Socialist Party rule. At the same time, the opposition parties' own undemocratic organizations made their political fortunes hostage to their leaders' vanities and ineptitudes.

PERSONNEL RECONSTRUCTION

The ruling class in socialist Yugoslavia was an open formation throughout its existence. It came to power by revolutionary means and it was recruited initially from the lower social strata. This recruitment pattern was perpetuated, so that the social origins of ruling-class members during the 1980s largely mirrored the adult population's makeup. For example, a survey of political and economic elites in the Yugoslav Republic of Croatia that I conducted during the mid-1980s showed that 32.8, 49.4, 12.2, and 5.6 percent of the elite members' fathers were, respectively, peasants, workers, professionals, and managers/politicians (Lazić, 1987: 85). This meant that the offspring of elite members had only relatively modest chances of "inheriting" an elite position. According to my mid-1980s Croatian data, children of managers/politicians most frequently became professionals, though many of them—close to 40 percent—fell into routine nonmanual and even manual jobs. Because the accumulation of private property was also very limited, even for the top members of the ruling class, elite circulation—as mentioned above—constituted the real intergeneration outlook for ruling-class members. In other words, class reproduction in socialism did not include— indeed, in principle it excluded—personnel reproduction from within the ruling class.

This meant that the process of postsocialist transformation held out two prospects for members of the old ruling class. One was the loss of their monopolistic ruling position. The other was the opportunity to reproduce their privileged social positions intergenerationally if they successfully converted their resources into new forms appropriate to the postsocialist order. I have already observed that their successful retention of political power during the first phase of postsocialist transformation gave members of the old ruling class excellent opportunities to convert resources. A 1993 survey of the occupational origins of seventy-eight owners and top managers of large private companies in Serbia showed how successful persons belonging or connected to the old ruling class were in using such opportunities (see table 7.1).

The data in table 7.1 show that roughly a third of the large entrepreneurs sampled in 1993 had fathers who had held some kind of command position in the socialist system, mainly in its managerial echelon. This suggests the scope of a resource conversion that made an intergeneration reconstruction of the former ruling class possible: the offspring of many members of the old class had become part of the new entrepreneurial elite. This observation is supported by data on the positions the 1993 entrepreneurs held immediately prior to acquiring their elite positions. Almost 45 percent of large entrepreneurs belonged to the command hierarchy (21.6, 18.9, and 4.1 percent, respectively, to the higher managerial, middle managerial, and politician strata) (Lazić, 1995: 158). Finally, the observation is further supported by noting that some 10 percent of 1993 entrepreneurs' spouses themselves held command positions, either managerial or political, at the time the entrepreneurs gained their elite positions. Putting these data together, roughly 60 percent of the members of the new entrepreneurial elite in Serbia in 1993 gained their positions directly or indirectly through paternal or spousal linkages from the old ruling class. It is apparent, in short, that the formation of this elite was rooted in the top level of the Yugoslav socialist hierarchy. A position there (primarily in the state-owned enterprises) was critical for establishing a large private firm in postsocialist Serbia.

However, we should not ignore the fact that many members of the new entrepreneurial elite ascended from lower social strata. The largest group in the sample described in table 7.1 (20.1 percent) started their careers in

Table 7.1 Occupational Origins of the Serb Entrepreneurial Elite, 1993 (Percentage) (N=78)

Occupation of father at 1st position	*Politi-cian*	*Man-ager*	*Lower Mgr.*	*Profess-ional*	*Self-Employed*	*Clerk*	*Manual Worker*	*Peas-ant*	*Other*
Of father	3.18	14.1	5.1	9.0	7.7	9.0	25.6	25.6	1.1
At 1st job	3.9	5.1	17.9	11.5	20.5	3.8	17.9	16.7	2.6

Source: Lazic, ed., 1995, 157.

small private businesses and then climbed to the top of the entrepreneurial tree. Many of the 1993 elite members from quite ordinary occupational backgrounds took advantage of the exceptional circumstances of civil war, international isolation, and the legal system's collapse to enrich themselves rapidly. Putting aside the problem of what kind of entrepreneurial abilities served as the basis for their business success, the fact is that this group of nouveau riches gradually merged with the transformed part of the old ruling class to form the new economic elite.

The same process of elite reconstruction can be seen in the political sphere. The Socialist Party of Serbia won a majority of parliamentary seats in all competitive elections held after 1990. This enabled its leaders to retain control of most state apparatuses and, thereby, keep many members of the old ruling class in political elite positions. However, top leaders of several opposition parties also entered parliament and other representative bodies. Especially after the November 1996 elections, they and their parties took control of municipal governments in most large cities. They accordingly penetrated the political elite, as data in a survey conducted during the spring of 1997 show (see table 7.2).

In the old socialist system, politicians were recruited more or less proportionately from all social strata (cf. Lazić, 1987). The postsocialist pattern is quite different. The data in table 7.2 show that the new political elite in 1997 was overwhelmingly recruited from middle (professional) strata, though it is necessary to stress that the sample studied is extremely small (N=24). However, some additional data corroborate this observation. An almost identical pattern of recruitment from middle strata was found among politicians holding the highest positions in the governments of large cities, 69.6 percent of whom came from professional positions (Lazić and Sekelj, 1997). This observation about the professional backgrounds of political leaders receives further support from the fact that, of the national leaders of the five largest opposition parties in 1997–98 (before the upheaval caused by the struggle over Kosovo in 1999), four had Ph.D. degrees and the fifth was a novelist.

It seems reasonable to conclude that the political elite underwent a process of reconstruction in a way that limited the possibilities for people from lower

Table 7.2   Occupational Origins of the Serb Political Elite, 1997 (Percentage) (N=24)

Occupation of father at 1st position	*Politi-cian*	*Man-ager*	*Lower Mgr.*	*Profess-ional*	*Self-Employed*	*Clerk*	*Manual Worker*	*Peas-ant*	*Other*
Of father	—	10.0	5.0	25.0	10.0	5.0	35.0	10.0	
At 1st job	12.5	—	—	70.8	—	16.6	—	—	

Source: Lazic and Sekelj, 1997, unpublished survey data

social strata with various kinds of expertise to enter its ranks. This is important in view of the fact that the socialist ruling class was very heterogeneous socially. Status inconsistency was characteristic of most of its members and was a reason why class unity—as regards both behavior and consciousness—had often to be imposed from the top instead of being generated from within the class. Moreover, to anyone who has lived in a socialist country, the need for expertise in a political elite is self-evident; the individuals who successively ran state agencies in the fields of culture, manufacturing, defense, and elsewhere, obviously and woefully lacked the necessary expertise.

RECONSTRUCTION OF MATERIAL POSITIONS

All the surveys that probed the material positions of social strata in Yugoslavia during the 1970s and 1980s showed that only the elite part of the socialist ruling class fared much better than the rest of the population. The living standards of the main body of the ruling class did not differ greatly from those of the intermediate class. For example, a survey of social differentiation that I conducted during 1989 found that a "middle" material position was characteristic of most politicians, managers, professionals, clerks, and small entrepreneurs. A "lower middle" position typified most manual workers and peasants. Only 6.2 percent of politicians and 2.6 percent of managers—together with 2.6 percent of professionals—enjoyed a "high" material position (Lazić, 1994: 73). Instead, privileges formed the core of elite lifestyles, and these privileges were only partially convertible into wealth that descendants could inherit. The postsocialist transformation has altered both aspects of the former ruling class: social differentiation on the basis of a "high" material position has become legitimate, and privatization has involved mechanisms for transferring this material position to one's offspring.

I conducted two surveys, one in 1990 and the other in 1997, that focused on the material position of occupational categories in Serbia and their results document the first point. The following indicators were used to construct the composite index of material position in table 7.3: income (personal and family per head), housing (itself a composite of several variables), household fittings and appliances, possession of cars (number and market value), and the ways in which summer and winter holidays are spent. The index scale ranged from 5 (high) to 1 (low). (It should be mentioned that the indicators in the two surveys were almost, but not completely, identical; the same holds for the construction of the indexes, so that the comparison of categories in each survey is the only fully reliable comparison.)

The data in table 7.3 support several observations. First, large entrepreneurs, who hardly existed in 1990, enjoyed the highest material positions in 1997. This is wholly unsurprising. Note, however, that two other categories

Table 7.3   Material Positions of Serb Occupational Categories in 1990 and 1997 (Means of Composite Indexes: 5=High, 1=Low)

Social Category	1990	1997
Large entrepreneurs	—	3.68
Politicians	3.40	3.36
Managers	3.35	3.09
Small entrepreneurs	2.99	3.00
Professionals	3.07	2.15
Clerks	2.69	1.82
Peasants	2.00	1.62
Skilled workers	2.27	1.56
Unskilled workers	2.08	1.42

Sources: for 1990: Lazic, 1994; for 1997: Lazic and Sekelj, unpublished survey data.

involved with private ownership also moved up the material position scale between 1990 and 1997: small entrepreneurs and peasants. It is clear that a new axis of social differentiation was beginning to shape the structure of Serb society during the 1990s. Increased material inequality was another aspect of this emerging axis: between 1990 and 1997 the top strata improved their material positions while those of lower strata deteriorated. Also, the gradation of material inequalities in 1990 was in 1997 replaced by sharper discontinuities. Social polarization was taking place, with the gap between elite and other occupational categories widening. The entrance of small entrepreneurs into the upper group may be explained mostly by the fact that the market has been completely deregulated, internally and externally; this has given small entrepreneurs opportunities to improve their economic position disproportionately, even amidst deep economic crisis.

We should not overlook the fact that politicians fared better in material positions than managers in 1997; moreover, politicians improved their relative material positions during the seven crisis-torn years. In my view, this suggests that a political regulation of social reproduction still prevails in Serbia—a conclusion that partly argues against the increasing importance of private ownership as the basis of growing inequalities. I will say simply that the tension between the political regulation of social reproduction and the emerging mode of capitalist accumulation was factual, not logical; it testified to the tumultuous character of the social change that was occurring.

Finally, the reconstruction of elite material positions appeared to involve two elements: increases in elite wealth (both in absolute terms and in relation to other groups), and, more importantly, a change in the basis of elite wealth. Changing apartment ownership patterns nicely illustrate how these two elements are connected: privatization enabled well-placed people to purchase apartments that are potentially worth hundreds of thousands of U.S. dollars for trifling sums, and these can now be passed to descendants or sold or rented for huge profits. The changed basis of elite wealth has two further components: the conversion of former privileges into private property of all kinds; and the influx of former ruling-class members into the newly emerging entrepreneurial elite (the scope of which was discussed above) to become the society's nouveau riche.

RECONSTRUCTION OF IDEOLOGY

Lastly, I want to show how change in the processes of reproduction effected by the dominant elites has been accompanied by a corresponding change in their ideology. I use "ideology" in its neutral and simple sense of how groups rationalize their interests. However strange it may seem today, a clear majority of the old ruling class members (in Serbia, at least) firmly supported the fundamental principles of socialism well into the 1990s. They condemned both the new multiparty political system and the market economy based on private property (cf. survey data in Lazić, 1994). Although forced by foreign pressures to legalize already existing opposition parties and to hold parliamentary elections at the end of 1990, the Socialist Party froze the legal privatization process until the end of 1997. The spontaneous, de facto rise of the private sector was, naturally, used for the benefit of the ruling party's cadres (Lazić and Sekelj, 1997).

Because a market economy has become more accepted in recent years, research on elite attitudes toward it may seem less important today. Nevertheless, an examination of such attitudes uncovers some interesting patterns. Unfortunately, I did not collect data for such an examination in my spring 1997 survey, so it is necessary to rely on the findings of a survey conducted by the Argument Research Agency during the summer of 1997. In this survey, politicians, all of whom were members of the ruling Socialist Party, and managers of state enterprises were sampled, together with a cross-section of other social categories (see table 7.4). As can be seen in table 7.4, a clear majority in each occupational category thought that expanding the private market was desirable. However, the proportion of each category that did not straightforwardly accept what had become a "common sense" idea was surprisingly large. It was understandable that many workers—in a situation of extreme economic crisis, when the survival of most enterprises depended on continued state subsidies—were suspicious of any break in the direct relation between the state and the economy. And it was unsurprising that politicians and state enterprise managers, whose previous and current positions and power depended on the existing economic order, should see any major privatization as a threat to their status. What needs stressing is that the data indicate the slow pace of postsocialist transformation in Serbia. Specifically, there was obvious resistance among the lower social strata to

Table 7.4   "Should the Size of the Private Economic Sector Be Increased?" 1997 (Percentage) (N=374)

Category	Agree	Undecided	Disagree
Politicians & managers	71.4	14.3	14.3
Entrepreneurs	88.7	8.1	3.2
Professionals	75.4	14.8	9.8
Workers	63.2	24.5	12.3

Source: Argument Research Agency, unpublished survey data, 1997.

faster structural change in the economy, and this resistance aided and abetted the ruling groups that were using the slow pace of transformation to enrich themselves.

Further confirmation of this can be found in the attitudes of elites, but also in the attitudes of other social categories, towards the transformation process in general, as expressed in the same survey (see table 7.5). The attitudes in table 7.5 encapsulated the 1997 status of Serbia's postsocialist transformation quite clearly. Entrepreneurs and professionals supported further change without much hesitation, while politicians, state enterprise managers, and workers were deeply ambivalent about further change. Politically, of course, entrepreneurs and professionals were inferior in both numbers and power. It is quite obvious that the interests of entrepreneurs lie with a market and pluralist transformation, at least in the long run. We must not forget, however, that a majority of entrepreneurs "abandoned" the former ruling class only very recently, and that they, as a rule, used the slowness of marketization to effect successful capital conversions. The politicians and managers in these data were also members of the former ruling class who retained dominant positions. However, they were sharply divided, with roughly half of them accepting (at least verbally) the desirability of further change, while the other half preferred the status quo in which their domination was anchored.

Looking at these attitudinal data from another angle, it is plausible to conclude that those from the old ruling class who entered the entrepre-

Table 7.5   "What Is the Most Acceptable Direction of Social Change?" (Percentage) (N=374)

Category	"Return to Socialism"	"Develop Capitalism and Democracy"	"Maintain Status Quo"
Politicians & managers	14.3	47.6	38.1
Entrepreneurs	8.0	75.9	16.1
Professionals	9.8	77.1	13.1
Workers	14.4	57.2	28.3

Source: Argument Research Agency, unpublished survey data, 1997.

neurial elite, which at the same time absorbed a sizable number of outsiders, held pro-market and pro-liberal orientations that accorded with the emerging social order. The other part of the old class, who still held the dominant political and economic positions, was gradually being forced to change its orientations toward acceptance of political pluralism and step-by-step privatization. But quite consistently, this elite group preferred a slow transformation process on the probably correct assumption that this would help them preserve their positions. All in all, the data indicate that a gradual reconstruction of elite ideology has been taking place in step with the gradual process of postsocialist transformation itself.

CONCLUSION

The data I have examined show that what was happening at the top of Serb society during the postsocialist transformation of the 1990s was not a simple circulation or reproduction of elites. The changes are better viewed as a process of elite reconstruction. With a new reproduction basis and new social roles, elites were being forged from the old socialist cadres at the same time that they were infiltrated by outsiders. These elites were constructing a social order in which they will form the core of a new ruling class.

BIBLIOGRAPHY

Babovic, Marija. 1997. *'Ajmo, 'ajde, svi u setnju* (Let's All Go for a Walk). Belgrade: Medija centar.

Bourdieu, Pierre. 1986. "The Forms of Capital." In *Handbook of Theory and Research for the Sociology of Education,* ed. J. Richardson. New York: Greenwood Press.

Feher, Ferenc. 1984. *Dictatorship over Needs.* Oxford: Blackwell.

Etzioni-Halevy, Eva. 1993. *The Elite Connection.* Cambridge: Polity Press.

Hanley, Eric, Natasha Yershova, and Richard Anderson. 1995. "Russia—Old Wine in a New Bottle? The Circulation and Reproduction of Russian Elites, 1983–1993." Special issue, *Theory and Society* 24 (October): 639–68.

Higley, John, and Richard Gunther, eds. 1992. *Elites and Democratic Consolidation in Latin America and Southern Europe.* Cambridge: Cambridge University Press.

Higley, John, Jan Pakulski, and Wlodzimierz Wesolowski. 1998. "Introduction: Elite Change and Democratic Regimes in Eastern Europe." In *Postcommunist Elites and Democracy in Eastern Europe,* ed. J. Higley, J. Pakulski, and W. Wesolowski. London: Macmillan.

Kuzmanovic, Bogdan. 1995. "Autoritarnost kao socijalnopsholoska karakteristika" (Authoritarianism as a Social–Psychological Characteristic). In *Drustveni karakter i drustvene promene u svetlu nacionalnih sukoba* (Social Character and Social Change in the Light of National Conflicts), ed. Z. Golubovic. Institute of Philosophy, University of Belgrade.

Lazić, Mladen. 1987. *U susret zatvorenom dru{tvu* (Towards a Closed Society). Zagreb: Naprijed.

————. 1994. *Sistem i slom* (System and Breakdown). Belgrade: Filip Vi{nji}.

————. 1996. "Delatni potencijal dru{tvenih grupa" (Action Potential of Social Groups). *Sociologija* 38 (June).

————, ed. 1995. *Society in Crisis.* Belgrade: Filip Vi{nji}.

Lazić, Mladen, and Laslo Sekelj. 1997. "Privatisation in Yugoslavia." *Europe–Asia Studies* 49 (November).

Mateju, Petr, and N. Lim. 1995. "Who Has Gotten Ahead after the Fall of Communism." *Czech Sociological Review* 3 (June).

Mrksic, Danilo. 1995. "The Dual Economy and Social Stratification." In *Society in Crisis,* ed. M. Lazic. Belgrade: Filip Vi{nji}.

Szelényi, Ivan, and Sonja Szelényi. 1995. "Circulation or Reproduction of Elites during the Postcommunist Transformation of Eastern Europe: Introduction." Special issue, *Theory and Society* 24 (October).

Szelényi, Sonja. 1995. "The Making of the Hungarian Postcommunist Elite: Circulation in Politics, Reproduction in the Economy." Special issue, *Theory and Society* 24 (October): 697–722.

Vujovic, Sreten. 1995. "Changes in Living Standards and Way of Life among Social Strata." In *Society in Crisis,* ed. M. Lazic. Belgrade: Filip Vi{nji}.

Wasilewski, Jacek, and Edward Wnuk-Lipinski. 1995. "Poland: Winding Road from the Communist to the Post-Solidarity Elite." Special issue, *Theory and Society* 24 (October): 669–96.

Part II

Economic Elite Change

8

Croatia

Managerial Elite Circulation or Reproduction?

Dusko Sekulic and Zeljka Sporer

What happened to state socialist elites during the transitions from state socialism? Two opposing answers are given. The first answer, based on Pareto's theory of elite circulation, is that new elites, which were submerged during the state socialist period, surfaced and replaced the corrupt and sclerotic old elites. The second, opposing answer is that gradual processes of reform under state socialism enabled rising technocratic elites to gain positions in which they clung to power and survived the transitions. Put more fashionably, the second answer is that the state socialist nomenklatura "converted" their political capital into economic capital by using their connections and control of resources, so that the reproduction of state socialist elites was a main feature of the transitions (Hankiss, 1990; Staniszkis, 1991; Wasilewski, 1998; White and Kryshtanovskaya, 1998).

The negotiated and peaceful character of the transitions lends credence to the reproduction thesis. Except in Romania, they did not involve violent regime overthrows; rather, Communist Party leaders negotiated with their opponents to erect a new regime. This implies two propositions. The first is that elite reproduction was most pronounced in the countries where state socialist reforms had gone farthest—where the command economy was less centralized and bureaucratized and more connected to the world economy, where state socialist elites had more contacts with their Western counterparts, and where, accordingly, the need for technocratic and westernized elites was already substantially met. The other proposition is that the countries with the most reformed state socialist regimes provided more space for counter-elites to develop, even if such regimes were at the same time quite inclusionary and absorptive of counter-elites. In the words of Szelényi and Szelényi, "one can expect a high degree of elite reproduction in countries where the technocracy was co-opted by the nomenklatura, as well as in countries in which there was no counter-elite. By contrast, we expect a high degree of elite circulation in countries where the cooption of the technocracy did not take place, or in countries with a well-formed counter-elite" (1995: 620).

It is plausible to argue that the extent of circulation or reproduction differed across elite sectors. Circulation was probably greatest among political elites, although even there two patterns can be discerned. Where new parties displaced dominant Communist parties in government, political elite circulation was extensive. But where dominant Communist parties managed to repackage themselves as democratic socialist parties and stay in power, there was substantial political elite reproduction. Outside the political sphere, where managerial elites under state socialist regimes felt burdened by the economic system and worked to change it, elite reproduction was extensive. Through buy-outs of state-owned enterprises, or by simply retaining their positions regardless of changes in property ownership, managerial elites largely reproduced themselves.

THE CASE OF CROATIA

What happened to elites in Croatia during and after the transition from self-management socialism? As part of the political and economic system governed by the Yugoslav League of Communists (LCY), Croatia was on the extreme reformist end of the continuum between reform and orthodoxy along which the state socialist countries were arrayed. Yugoslavia was famous for its self-management market economy. Although private property remained quite limited in scope, the market was allowed to function as a prime regulatory mechanism. The economy was open to Western capitalism, and most observers agreed that Western economic forces played a greater role in Yugoslavia than in any other state socialist country. Legally, enterprises were run by worker councils, but the lion's share of economic power was exercised, de facto, by technocratic managers, who amounted to junior partners of the LCY political elite. In alliance with the more modern and reformist parts of the political leadership, the technocrats pushed constantly for more economic reform, greater marketization, and more openness. All in all, reforms and institutional changes were key features of the Yugoslav socialist model, especially after the early 1970s. From this we can conclude that the technocratic part of the Yugoslav economic elite was well developed and that the basis for its reproduction in the postsocialist period was in place (Sekulic, 1985).

In the political sphere, although Yugoslavia was more liberal than other Communist countries, it nevertheless had the same basic power structure, in which the LCY monopolized strategic positions. In spite of relatively wide freedom of the press, significant individual liberties, much openness to foreigners, and much travel by Yugoslavs abroad, the "meta-power" remained in LCY hands. Like all other state socialist countries, moreover, Yugoslavia went through reform cycles. These usually started with a push for political liberalization and marketizing changes in the economy, and they ended when more conservative LCY factions gained the upper hand and slowed or stopped reforms (Baumgartner, Burns, and Sekulic, 1979; Sekulic, 1989).

Yugoslavia had one feature that made it different from other state socialist countries. It was a real federation. Power was concentrated in the hands of the Communist parties of six republics and two autonomous provinces, so that central decision-making involved bargaining among the republic parties. The federal structure was enshrined in the constitution of 1974, which even contained some confederal elements. Especially after Tito's death in 1980, federal power attenuated sharply, so that power shifted decisively to the republics and provinces (Bilandzic, 1985: 358–84). By contrast, in the Soviet Union, which was also a federation, the decisiveness of federal power was not in question until the USSR's last months in 1991.

The "national question" was crucial for understanding the dynamics of change in Yugoslavia (Shoup, 1968; Sekulic, 1997). How to organize and manage relations among Yugoslavia's nationalities was one of the LCY's most important political problems during World War II and once it consolidated power after 1945. Balancing the separate national identities with "Yugoslav patriotism," so that the individual identities were not suppressed while the country remained integrated, was always uppermost in LCY strategies (Moraca, Bilandzic, and Stojanovic, 1977; Jelic, 1981; Sekulic, Hodson, and Massey, 1994). In the end, however, Yugoslavia was destroyed by these national identities and by the ideologies and social movements built upon them (Sekulic, 1992; Cohen, 1993). The path of this destruction was best indicated by the transformation of the Serbian LCY under Slobodan Milosevic from a socialist party into a national–socialist one (Djilas, 1993).

Within the Croatian League of Communists (LCC), tension between a more decentralized (Croatian) and a more centralized (Yugoslav) orientation had long been apparent. During World War II, for example, Croatian Party Secretary Andrija Hebrang, a "nationally" oriented Communist, was replaced by Vladimir Bakaric, who was more sympathetic to the central Party leadership (Irvine, 1993: 201–3). During Yugoslavia's postwar conflict with the Soviet Cominform, Hebrang allegedly committed suicide in jail under circumstances that remain unclear. In 1971, the whole Croatian Party leadership was purged by the center in Belgrade, and many of those purged resurfaced as leaders of new parties and movements during the 1990s (Ramet, 1992: 98–135). Yugoslavia's disintegration during 1991 was propelled by the struggle between the socialist "south," led by Serbia's strongman, Milosevic, and the antisocialist "north," led by new and surging political forces in Slovenia and Croatia.

This interplay between national identities and federal political arrangements is crucial for understanding the extent of elite reproduction and circulation in Croatia. Because of the Ustasha regime's terrorization of the Serb population in Croatia during World War II, Serbs were recruited en masse into the ranks of Communist-led insurgent forces. The direct postwar result was a huge overrepresentation of Serbs in the LCC and, consequently, in all elite positions in Croatia. In Croat popular perceptions, Serb and LCC domination were intertwined. Starting in 1991, the dismantling of the socialist regime in Croatia thus went hand in hand with the displacing of large numbers of Serbs from prominent positions in all public spheres. The subsequent war between Croatia and the rump Yugoslav regime between 1991 and 1995 further eroded the presence of Serbs in Croatian elite positions. This disappearance of the Serb component of the old state socialist regime necessarily resulted in extensive elite circulation.

We can conclude that in Croatia there have been forces that both facilitated and hindered processes of elite circulation and reproduction. On one hand, the reformist orientation of the socialist regime, its openness, and its inclusion of the technocratic intelligentsia favored reproduction, especially in the managerial or business elite. On the other hand, the fact that Croatia fought a war against Serb domination, and that the Yugoslav socialist regime was seen as the main cause of death and destruction during that war, made it extremely difficult for members of the old ruling elite, especially the numerous Serbs among them, to retain or convert their elite statuses.

PRIVATE SECTOR FORMATION

How was Croatia's self-management economy transformed into a capitalist economy based on private ownership? This was not a linear process. In 1990, at the beginning of privatization, the economy contained 10,859 companies, of which 3,637 (35.5 percent) were "socially owned" and 6,785 (62.5 percent) were privately owned; the remainder were mixed companies and agricultural cooperatives (Rohatinski and Vojnic, 1996). It is a mistake, however, to regard the private sector as already dominant in 1990. This is because it was comprised chiefly of very small firms, some of them probably fictitious tax dodges. The relative unimportance of the private sector in 1990 can be seen clearly in the distribution of employment: 97.6 percent of all employees worked in socially owned companies, while the private companies accounted for a mere 1.7 percent of total employment.

At first glance, the 1995 data show a dramatic change in Croatia's ownership structure. By that year, the state-owned sector accounted for only 1.8 percent of companies, and these employed 23.4 percent of the workforce, whereas 94.6 percent of all companies were privately owned, and they employed 40.5 percent of the workforce. Only 3 percent of all companies were in the mixed sector, though they employed 35.3 percent of the workforce. The remaining 0.8 percent of the workforce was located in cooperatively owned enterprises. From these figures we can conclude that a concentration of economic activity in private hands, together with considerable fragmentation of the state-owned and mixed sectors, had occurred. Although the Croatian state continued to play a dominant role in the old state-owned and mixed sectors, together these sectors contained only 4.8 percent of the total number of companies, even though they still employed 58.7 percent of all workers.

In January 1996, the private sector was composed of 127,635 companies (recall that in 1990 the total number of companies of all kinds in Croatia had been 10,859). However, this large number of firms employed much less than half the workforce (40.5 percent). The 1990–95 picture was thus one of an economy in which the state remained a dominant force through direct state ownership and state participation in the mixed sector. By contrast, the private sector still accounted for a relatively small part of total economic activity and it was highly fragmented.

The Croatian economy's development hinges on how this balance between the public and private sectors changes. A new capitalist economy may emerge through the private sector's further expansion, gradually engulfing the state-owned sector. This scenario might be labeled the growth of capitalism "from below." On the other hand, the dominance of the state and mixed sectors, strongly controlled by the managerial elite, may be long lasting. This could be termed the creation of capitalism "from above," and it is the basis for the thesis that a new "managerial capitalism" will develop in Eastern Europe. Let us elaborate these scenarios.

CAPITALISM FROM "BELOW" OR "ABOVE"?

The new capitalist systems in former state socialist societies are being created in the absence of a capitalist class. The transitions from state socialism were not the result of capitalist revolutions; no bourgeoisie propelled them. The small, marginal entrepreneurial category certainly was not strong enough to constitute a significant class forcing economic and regime change. Crucial, instead, was the *idea* of capitalism that penetrated the technocratic intelligentsia, whose members were tired of the centrally planned economy's inefficiencies and, in Yugoslavia, of self-management's failures. Equally crucial was the *idea* of political democracy, which served the humanistic intelligentsia's "class interest" in terms of greater freedom for creative work and aligned it against the state socialist regime.

The goals of technocrats and humanists intersected in the proposition that political democracy is a necessary condition for a market economy. As stated, however, the private sector under state socialism was too small and marginalized to influence the transition in any significant way. Thus, the building of capitalism was left to the transformed state, almost in the same way that the socialist state had earlier sought to build socialism in countries where there was only a weak and undeveloped proletariat. It is important to ask about the identity of these transforming state forces that are building capitalism in ways analogous to those in which the old Communist parties transformed precapitalist societies into state socialist ones.

Eyal, Szelényi, and Townsley (1997) develop a theory that attempts to answer this question. In their view, the capitalism that is being built in postsocialist Eastern Europe is not a simple repetition of the process that occurred much earlier in Western Europe. It is, instead, a process of creating *managerial capitalism,* sui generis. They argue that the theories of managerialism developed earlier in the twentieth century by Berle and Means, Rizzi, and Burnham, were never fully realized in Western capitalism. Although the influence of the managerial class increased, the basic feature of the Western capitalist system—the dominance of private property and ownership—remained unaltered. However, Eyal, Szelényi, and Townsley claim that a full-blown managerial capitalism will characterize the postsocialist countries. In them, capitalism is being built without a capitalist class, so that new managers play the role that a propertied class played in the building of Western capitalism. Of course, building capitalism without a capitalist class is nothing new; other societies that have been "latecomers" to capitalism have used the state as the main force for capitalist accumulation. Examples are post-Meiji Japan and today's China. According to Eyal, Szelényi, and Townsley, in Eastern Europe today the main social category pushing for capitalist formation in the absence of a capitalist class is the intelligentsia, which is transforming these societies in accordance with ideas and models imported from the West, regardless of the fact that local social and economic structures are still quite backward.

The postsocialist intelligentsias are complex and heterogeneous, however. On the one hand, they consist of dissident intellectuals, who are themselves divided into at least two groups. One group is more modern and oriented toward egalitarianism, so that its members criticize the new order for not being sufficiently fair and rational. The second group consists of more traditionalist and nationalist-oriented intellectuals. Because they were to a large extent incorporated into the previous state socialist economic and political order, technocratic managers stand in relations both of cooperation and conflict to these two groups of intellectuals, in the same way that the managers had contradictory relations with the political elite of state socialism. In the Croatian case, we must add the influence of another category, which consists of prominent members of the Croatian diaspora, who returned to Croatia during the early 1990s to take important governmental and economic positions. The returnees' government positions were frequently payoffs for financial support that helped the ruling Croat Democratic Union (HDZ) take and hold political power after 1991. The returnees' economic positions form a seamless web that pervades Croatia.

Postsocialist regimes exhibit large amounts of corruption. The extreme case, of course, is Russia, where the so-called mafia penetrates all economic sectors and stands on nearly equal terms with the state. In other postsocialist regimes, numerous corruption scandals indicate that the state's power and its role in the privatization process have been used to transfer significant assets into private hands, more by political connections and kickbacks than by fair and open tendering processes. The state and political power are, thus, direct instruments for the creation of a new capitalist class. In Bosnia and Herzegovina, which is still in a condition of semi-warfare, this process has reached an extreme point. Discussing Bosnian political parties, Brooke Unger in *The Economist* has observed that "For them the line between politics and business is invisible: [the] Serb Democratic Party (SDS) is a machine for smuggling and extortion, and the other two parties are hardly less venal" (Unger, 1998: 7). Croatia, too, went through a war in which smuggling was critical for provisioning the army and sustaining the newly independent state; thus, the same 1998 issue of *The Economist* judged President Franjo Tudjman's family to be among the wealthiest in Europe.

These considerations cast much doubt on the Eyal–Szelényi–Townsley thesis that we are witnessing the rise of a truly managerial capitalism, at least in Croatia. There is, in fact, little evidence of a new managerial class. Economic activity is more an amalgam of managerial and politocratic power in which the politocracy has the upper hand. The appointment of managers depends directly or indirectly on the state. In order to make really big deals, independent entrepreneurs must obtain the collaboration of state officials, who make sure that their family members acquire as many assets of former "socially owned" companies as possible. By studying the careers of nineteen general managers of large enterprises during the transition period, Vesna Pusic (1992) has shown the importance of political criteria in choosing the new managerial elite in Croatia. Her concluding chapter has the revealing title, "What Have the Rulers Done to the Managers?"

Seen in this light, the managerial capitalism thesis has a different meaning. It is not only that the success of many managers depends on corruption, bribes, and the transfer of assets from the state-owned to the private sector (a process that in Hungary is described by Róna-Tas, 1997); it is also that, often, the only way to ensure managerial survival is by moving into the private sector and opening new firms. The political pressures of the new state on the private sector have made the survival of many state socialist managers impossible because of their ties to the former regime and because of the necessity to find patronage places for people, such as returnees, who are connected with the new regime. Thus, Josip Zupanov (1995: 97–106) lists the options that are open to managers who try to survive the transition: transfer political loyalty to the new rulers, attempt to neutralize the latter's influence by privatizing a state-owned company, or establish a new company by transferring the valuable assets of some state-owned company.

But even if all this is so, does it matter for the development of capitalism? Some economists argue that it does not, in fact, matter how property rights are distributed initially. The most important thing, they claim, is that property rights are distributed and that the market is then allowed to perform its allocative function. The counter argument is that the way in which property rights are distributed initially influences the way in which the market operates later. Specifically, if the initial distribution is made so that one can expect collusion between the state and private owners, then one can also expect that the state will protect "its" economy against foreign or internal competition. State-sponsored property distributions and mafia-like collusions between the newly created entrepreneurs, managers, and state bureaucrats will prevent the market from operating efficiently.

To summarize, the creation of capitalism in Croatia (and other postsocialist countries) involves an imposition "from above," in which the state plays an important role in controlling the economy and creating an entrepreneurial sector that is to a large extent dependent on the state. The managerialism in this process does not reflect some new and independent managerial class but, rather, the state securing the expertise it needs for its continuing control of the economy. Of course, there is some creation of a capitalist class "from below" as obstacles to the private sector's growth are removed and some small companies that are holdovers from state socialism, plus many new companies, expand. This capitalism from below is concentrated in particular sectors, however. As we have seen, the number of Croatian companies increased from 17,000 at the end of 1990 to 133,000 at the end of 1995. But the bulk of this increase occurred in the trade, business, and financial services sectors where the number of companies went from 10,000 to 89,000 (Rohatinski and Vojnic, 1996: 29). Although many of the companies in these sectors have colluded with the state to obtain licenses and other privileges, they at least contain the seeds of a new capitalist class that may survive in an open market.

In probing the composition of this new class, we will address two questions. First, are there important differences between the "pure" managers and the owners who make up the class? Second, does the Croatian case exemplify elite circulation or elite reproduction? In other words, does the new capitalist class consist primarily of newcomers to elite positions or of old state socialist technocrats who have recycled themselves into new positions?

HOW MUCH CIRCULATION? HOW MUCH REPRODUCTION?

To assess the extent of elite circulation and reproduction in Croatia, we examine data collected in collaboration with the Zagreb-based Center for Transitions during 1996. We use elite samples from 1989 and 1996 surveys. The 1989 sample consisted of 147 managers under state socialism, and the 1996 sample contained 130 postsocialist managers. In the 1989 sample were 3 directors of conglomerates, 5 deputy directors, 37 directors and 62 deputy directors of companies, plus 36 directors of the "basic organizations of associated labor" (that is, divisions of large companies). In the 1996 sample were 69 company managers, 26 directors of large companies' divisions, and 25 plant managers.

The positions that members of the 1996 managerial elite held during 1989, the last full year of state socialism, are shown in table 8.1. It can be seen that the main recruitment bases for the new managerial elite were top managerial, political, and professional positions in 1989. Fully 70.8 percent of the 1996 elite held such positions during state socialism's last year, and only one-quarter were then located in clearly non-elite positions. Although the transition involved a shift to capitalism, at least in principle, persons who were private entrepreneurs in 1989 were not present in the 1996 elite to any significant degree; only a few plant managers (8.6 percent) had been private entrepreneurs in 1989.

Table 8.1   1989 Occupational Positions of 1996 Members of Managerial Elite (Percentage) (N = 130)

| | | Position in 1996 | | |
Position in 1989	Total	General Manager	Manager of Sectors	Plant Manager
N	130	69	26	35
Non-elite position*	25.4	21.7	19.2	37.15
Entrepreneur	3.8	2.9	—	8.6
Professional	33.1	34.8	42.3	22.9
Manager or Politician	37.7	40.6	38.5	31.4

Source: Center for Transitions, Zagreb, 1996.
*Worker, lower administrator, other.

Elite reproduction was, at first glance, relatively large: 40.6 percent of the 1996 general managers held elite managerial or political positions in 1989, and this was true of 37.7 percent of the entire managerial category in 1996. Persons with technocratic credentials were more able to survive the transition. But does this confirm the reproduction thesis for Croatia? Szelényi and Szelényi caution that "The distinction between 'circulation' and 'reproduction' is a relative one. Five years are long enough for one to expect some change in the personnel occupying key command positions under any circumstance; a complete turnover of personnel is, however, unimaginable even under the most revolutionary conditions. When we assess 'how much' circulation or reproduction took place in a country, therefore, we always have to think about this question in relative terms" (1995: 621).

Szelényi and Szelényi were addressing elite surveys conducted in Bulgaria, the Czech Republic, Hungary, Poland, and Slovakia during 1993 (see chapter 12). Should their warning about the relativity of circulation and reproduction be applied to our 1996 data for Croatia? How much reproduction is enough to claim that it is the dominant mode of elite change? To establish a yardstick, we can compare the 1989 and 1996 elites. The yardstick consists of the amount of managerial elite turnover that occurred in a comparable period of time during the socialist period. In this way, we can distinguish between the "normal" turnover that could be expected over a period of seven years under self-management socialism and the turnover that occurred during the seven years of postsocialist transition. The difference in turnover between the two periods (if greater during the transition) should be a measure of the elite circulation induced by the transition. Our yardstick can be summarized as follows:

(circulation 1989–96) − (circulation 1982–89) = transition circulation

Table 8.2, which gives the proportions for this comparison, shows a surprising result: transition circulation between 1989 and 1996 amounted to only 7.5 percent of the managerial elite. Put differently, the change in the makeup of the managerial elite was roughly 7.5 percent greater during the transition than during a comparable period of socialist rule. Obviously, the transition involved only a quite limited change in elite composition, and to this extent it is correct to speak of elite reproduction as predominant. However, questions about how newly recruited 1996 elite members differed from those who would have been recruited had state socialism persisted and about the characteristics of those who remained in elite positions throughout the transition are not answered by table 8.2.

The mechanisms producing change in elite composition were different in the two periods. Change during the 1982–89 period was the result of the LCY's "cadre" policy, most specifically, the inclusionary practices of the LCC

Table 8.2   Reproduction and Circulation of Managers in 1989 and 1996 (Percentage)

Managers in 1989 (N= 147)		Managers in 1996 (N= 130)	
Became elite before 1982	53.7	Became elite before 1989	46.2
Became elite 1982–89	46.3	Became elite 1989–96	53.8

Source: Center for Transitions, Zagreb, 1996.

in Croatia. Following an internal struggle for Party leadership, the second half of the 1980s was a period when a more open and reform-minded faction gained the upper hand. This resulted in a deliberate policy of recruiting younger and better-educated individuals into Party ranks, and also into a range of managerial and administrative positions. The high turnover during those years probably reflected the LCC's modernizing efforts. In the 1989–96 period, the character of political control changed because parliamentary democracy was introduced. Nevertheless, political life in Croatia continued to be characterized by the domination of one party, the HDZ, whose hold on government offices was unbroken from the first free election in August 1992 (Druga Tranzicija, 1998). Although it did not have a monopoly of power, the HDZ penetrated all important societal sectors, and it controlled the state apparatus completely. In the economic sector, the state's control of privatization and the fact that it was still the major owner of many large economic entities enabled the HDZ to exert a great deal of political influence over managerial appointments. This approximated the power exercised previously by the LCC. However, the emergence of a truly private sector beyond political control checked HDZ economic dominance in the same way that opposition parties checked the HDZ's political dominance in the parliamentary and electoral sphere.

In any event, the fact that more than half of the managers in 1996 had attained their positions since 1989 mainly reflected the "cadre" policy of the HDZ. In this sense, elite circulation was politically induced in the same way that it was during the last years of state socialism. Still, the turnover within the managerial elite during the first half of the 1990s must also have reflected structural changes in the economy, privatization, and the removal of limits on the private sector's growth. We turn next to some qualitative changes and continuities within the new managerial elite.

POLITICAL PENETRATION

Under Yugoslavia's state and self-management socialism, the LCY penetrated and controlled all important societal sectors. Its main instrument was the nomenklatura system, in which the party screened and selected all aspi-

Table 8.3 LCC Membership among Mass Population and the Managerial Elite in 1989 (Percentage)

Relation to LCC in 1989	Mass Population	Managerial Elite
Never was LCC member	74.7	14.5
Former LCC member	11.9	3.4
LCC member	13.4	82.1
N	2508	145

Source: Center for Transitions, Zagreb, 1996.

rants for important positions. Although the nomenklatura system was less comprehensive and rigid in Yugoslavia than in all other state socialist countries, its basic principles and operation ensured that LCY membership was a prerequisite for any important position. One of the main questions about postsocialist societies is the extent to which the nomenklatura system has been replaced by cronyism and patronage. Let us try to assess this in Croatia during the 1990s.

First, let us use 1989 as a benchmark and start by asking about the extent to which LCC membership was still critical for holding elite positions in that year. We can safely ignore the political elite, in which the LCC's monopoly of political positions meant, perforce, that all position holders were party members. In the self-management economy, however, it was by 1989 less clear that managers were necessarily LCC members. As seen in table 8.3, 119 (82.1 percent) of the 145 managers in our 1989 sample were party members, and this can be compared with the 13.4 percent of the adult population that belonged to the party. In other words, a manager was six times more likely to be a party member than was the average citizen. When we turn to 1996 (table 8.4), the first thing that strikes us is that the greater political freedom stemming from the fall of state socialism did not translate into more intensive political activity as measured by membership in political parties. Only 2.1 percent of the population were members of a political party in 1996, and in this respect it appears that political freedom during the 1990s was in considerable measure the freedom not to be active in party life.

The same held for managers. Whereas in 1989, 82.1 percent of them were LCC members and another 3.4 percent were former members, in 1996 the proportion of managers belonging to *any* party was reduced to 36.9 percent (table 8.4). There was, thus, a tremendous increase in the proportion of politically inactive managers, from less than a fifth in 1989 to nearly two-thirds in 1996. Not surprisingly, a disproportionate number of managers, some 30 percent, belonged to the HDZ in 1996. If we compare this proportion with the 5.5 percent of citizens who were HDZ members, it is apparent that managers were five times more likely to be HDZ members. This ratio was not very different from the 1989 ratio in which managers were 6.6 times

Table 8.4   Party Memberships among Mass Population and Managerial Elite in 1996 (Percentage)

Party Memberships in 1996	Mass Population	Managerial Elite
Not member of any party	92.4	63.1
HDZ member	5.5	30.0
Member of other party	2.1	6.9
N	2202	130

Source: Center for Transitions, Zagreb, 1996.

more likely to be members of the LCC. In 1996, however, a manager was also about 3.3 times more likely to belong to some party other than the LCC than was the average citizen. The fact that managers were twice as likely to belong to the HDZ as to other parties in 1996 reflected the patronage system operated by the HDZ-dominated government, for there is no reason to think that anything in the HDZ's program attracted a disproportionate number of managers to its ranks. On the contrary. Parties like the Croatian Social–Liberal Party (HSLS) and the Croatian National Party (HSN) stood for free markets and other aspects of European liberalism and were much more "business friendly" than the populist and nationalist HDZ. It is reasonable to conclude that the HDZ's influence on economic life resembled the influence exercised by the old LCC. HDZ influence may have been less intensive, but when the generally lower level of political activity during the 1990s is taken into account, HDZ influence was roughly proportionate to that exercised by the LCC under state socialism.

NATIONALITY AS A CAUSE OF ELITE CIRCULATION

National and religious identities played strong roles in Yugoslavia's disintegration. In Croatia, as noted earlier, the overrepresentation of Serbs in strategic positions had long been a source of discontent. In table 8.5, the sizes of the main national groups in Croatia, as recorded in the 1991 census, are compared with the nationalities of the managerial elites studied in the 1989 and 1996 surveys. Although persons designating themselves Serbs and "Yugoslavs" constituted 14.4 percent of the Croatian population in 1991, these two identities were chosen by 27.5 percent of the Croatian managerial elite in 1989, a proportion almost twice as large as that in the population. In the 1996 managerial elite sample, however, there were virtually only Croats (96.2 percent). One reason for this dramatic change was the exodus of Serbs and "Yugoslavs" from Croatia during the war with Serbia between 1991 and 1995. Although no census of the Croatian population has been taken since 1991, three recent mass surveys available to us indicate that

Table 8.5 Nationality Composition of the Croatian Population in 1991 and the Managerial Elite in 1989 and 1996 (Percentage)

Identifying as	Population 1991	Managerial Elite Samples in: 1989	Managerial Elite Samples in: 1996
Croats	78.1	71.7	96.2
Serbs	12.2	17.4	—
Yugoslavs	2.2	10.1	—
Others	7.5	1.8	3.8
N	(census)	145	130

Sources: Croatian Census Office; Center for Transitions, Zagreb, 1996.

the Serb population in Croatia was reduced by two-thirds, to roughly 4 percent of the population, by the war's end.

In addition to the Serb/Yugoslav exodus, there were two reasons why the managerial elite in 1996 consisted almost entirely of Croats. The first and most obvious was the deliberate policy of the HDZ government to promote Croats and replace those Serbs who remained. There were also a significant number of "conversions" by which "Yugoslavs" transformed themselves into Croats. The near total domination of Croats in the 1996 elite thus reflected the policy of the new government, the changed demographic structure, and numerous "conversions." All this amounted to significant elite circulation through which the Serbian part of the former managerial elites was replaced with Croats. This forced circulation was the most important feature that distinguished the new from the old elite.

Nevertheless, the amount of elite circulation was not substantially greater than what could be expected in a normal period of economic development. In this respect, the circulation versus reproduction question should be answered, quantitatively, in favor of reproduction. But what were the qualitative characteristics of the managerial elite after the postsocialist transition? We can say that the old elite largely reproduced itself only if there was no big change in the elite's qualitative aspects. For it is always possible to argue that elite reproduction simply reflected the openness of the old state socialist system to meritocratic recruitment. The argument would be, in other words, that the meritocratically recruited part of the old elite remained in power while persons who satisfied the new political criterion of fidelity to the HDZ replaced those who were in elite positions by virtue of their ties to the LCC.

A MERITOCRATIC SELECTION?

We cannot know with certainty what happened to the state socialist managerial elite in its entirety because we lack longitudinal or "outflow" data tracing where all its members ended up. But by comparing the characteristics of the 1989 elite with those of the holdovers from that elite in 1996, we can form an opinion as to whether the holdovers survived because they had greater meritocratic credentials than those who disappeared. This was the main finding that Jacek Wasilewski reached when he analyzed the outflow of Polish elites from old nomenklatura positions between 1988 and 1993 (Wasilewski, 1995: 112). He discovered that the selection of the old 1988 elite in Poland had been based heavily on educational criteria. Consequently, members of the elite who had little formal education—workers and peasants who had been promoted to elite positions in order to make the holders of top positions seemingly representative of all social categories— became downwardly mobile during the Polish transition.

To see if this happened in Croatia, the educational credentials of the managerial elite in 1989 and 1996 are presented in table 8.6. A distinction is drawn between the survivors from 1989 who were in 1996 elite positions and those who were newly recruited to such positions between 1989 and 1996. It is apparent that the 1989 survivors in the 1996 elite had *lower* education credentials, on average, than did the entire 1989 elite. More than three-quarters of the 1989 elite (76.6 percent) held university degrees, but this was true of little more than half (56.7 percent) of the survivors. Thus, those who survived were not, on average, better qualified for elite positions, at least in formal educational terms, than those who were eliminated. This means that other credentials must in part have accounted for the survivors' success. There was, moreover, no appreciable difference between the credentials of the survivors and those who were newly recruited to managerial elite positions between 1989 and 1996. On average, in other words, the old managerial elite was substantially better educated than the new one—76.6 percent of the old elite as against 52.3 percent of the new elite possessing university degrees.

Much of the explanation for this difference between the old and new managerial elites probably lies in the fact that in the new elite there were sizable numbers of managers who owned or co-owned their companies. These man-

Table 8.6 Educational Credentials of the Managerial Elite, 1989 and 1996 (percentage)

Highest Level of Schooling	*Managerial Elite in:* 1989	1996	*"Old" and "New" Managers Compared* "Old" Managers	"New" Managers
Elementary school	0.7	0.7	—	1.4
Trade school	—	6.9	5.0	8.6
High school	6.9	18.5	16.7	20.0
Two-year college	15.9	21.5	21.7	21.4
University degree	68.3	48.5	50.0	47.1
Graduate degree	8.3	3.8	6.7	1.4
N	145	130	60	70

Source: Center for Transitions, Zagreb, 1996.

ager-owners had lower educational credentials, on average, than did professional managers under state socialism. This is, incidentally, a pattern that Mladen Lazic (1994) has found in Serbia. The difference between the old managerial elite and the new one was thus produced mostly by the entrance of owners who had been barred by ideological, legal, and other obstacles from being members of the managerial elite under state socialism. With these obstacles removed during the postsocialist period, and with the private sector and the companies in it expanding quite rapidly, the owners of the most important companies were picked up by the managerial elite sample in 1996.

The presence of manager-owners in the 1996 elite does not account for all the difference between it and its 1989 precursor. As can be seen in table 8.7, there was a noticeable difference between the average educational credentials of the 1989 elite and that part of the 1996 elite that consisted of managers who were not also owners. Thus, the 76.6 percent of 1989 elite members who had university degrees were an appreciably greater proportion than the 60.8 percent of managers who were not owners and who had university degrees in 1996. In short, even overlooking the entrance of manager-owners and their lower educational credentials, the 1996 elite was still less well educated, again on average, than the 1989 elite.

The data on the educational credentials of the two managerial elites suggest a reinterpretation of the Croatian transition from state socialism. In Central Europe the "class alliance" that undermined state socialism consisted of technocratic–managerial elites and leaders of the humanistic intelligentsia (Eyal, Szélenyi, and Townsley, 1997). In Croatia, however, the situation was different in several respects. First, the relative openness of the LCC and its greater inclusion of technocrats gave the state socialist managerial elite a technocratic flavor, as the 1989 elite's high educational profile indicated. But second, the party-cum-movement that took over in 1990–91 was nationalist and populist in character, and it had relatively limited support among intellectuals and technocrats. Its support was based

Table 8.7 Educations of Manager-Owners and Managers in 1996 (Percentage)

Highest Level of Schooling	Manager-Owners		Managers	
	N	%	N	%
Elementary school	1	2.2	—	—
Trade school	3	6.5	6	7.1
High school	15	32.6	9	10.7
Two-year college	10	21.7	18	21.4
University degree	16	34.8	47	56.0
Graduate degree	1	2.2	4	4.8
N	46		84	

Source: Center for Transitions, Zagreb, 1996.

more on broad nationalist appeals to the less educated and less well-off parts of the population (Sekulic and Sporer, 1997). Groups of political and economic émigrés who returned to become key players in Croatia's postsocialist politics were its other significant source of support.

Although no systematic data on these returnees are available, press reports and other observations suggest that middle-level individuals in the diaspora gave strong support to the HDZ, while most diaspora political and intellectual elites refrained from supporting the HDZ. For example, prominent émigrés like Josip Mestrovic and Vladimir Kusan did not support the HDZ, while more obscure émigrés such as Gojko Susak, who became minister of defense, plus remnants of the Ustasha emigration after World War II, supported the HDZ enthusiastically. Except for a tiny segment of fervent nationalists within the humanistic intelligentsia, the HDZ has lacked broad support among intellectual and technocratic groups inside Croatia. The intelligentsia, instead, mostly supported a coalition of centrist parties in the August 1992 election, although that coalition managed to win only 22 percent of the vote in the election's first round, and after the second round it obtained only six seats in parliament. Articulating the aspirations and orientations of the middle class and the intelligentsia, the centrist parties were not able to penetrate the country's power centers. Only gradually, and then perhaps mostly out of opportunism, were some intellectuals and technocrats induced to ally themselves with the ruling HDZ. It is plausible to suggest that the lower education level of the managerial elite in 1996 reflected these cleavages.

CONCLUSIONS

Different theories about the formation of a new managerial elite in postsocialist countries like Croatia capture parallel, and perhaps converging, processes through which this elite is being formed. Two processes are especially apparent. One is the growth of a genuine private sector consisting of companies that were already privately owned under self-management socialism. These companies are augmented by those recently created by entrepreneurs who have taken advantage of the removal of legal obstacles to private ownership. The second process is the privatization of the formerly state- or socially owned sector. However, much of this newly privatized sector remains under the formal or informal influence of the state and of the managers who operated its enterprises under state socialism.

Ivan Szélenyi and others contend that postsocialist countries are building a new managerial capitalism by jumping over the phase of capitalist development that historically involved the domination of private ownership. What is missing from this prognosis, however, is convincing evidence that it is happening in postsocialist Eastern Europe. It is obvious that the initial conditions of postsocialist economic developments—the large state-owned or state-influenced sectors—differ from the initial conditions of capitalist development in Western Europe. But the fact that there is an emerging capitalist class, centered in the private sector, which is different in some key respects from the managerial elite that dominates the newly privatized sector of former state-owned enterprises, indicates that, in Croatia at least, one can speak seriously about a replication of the historical process of capitalist formation.

As regards the debate over elite circulation versus elite reproduction, the evidence from Croatia is that the quantity of circulation has not been much larger during the postsocialist transition than it was before the transition. This support for the thesis of elite reproduction receives a different spin, however, when qualitative aspects of elite persistence and change are examined. Educational and other qualitative characteristics of the postsocialist managerial elite indicate a significant change that reflects the radical populist and nationalist character of the new postsocialist political order. Contrary to what one might expect, the educational credentials of the postsocialist managerial elite are, on average, significantly lower than those of the elite under state socialism, and this echoes the populist character of the new regime and its bases of mass support. The new elite is less meritocratic than the old one. Likewise, the presence of Serbs and "Yugoslavs" in Croatian elite positions has been entirely eliminated. Finally, political connections and patronage still loom large in selecting persons for elite positions, even if this political screening is less comprehensive and less systematic than it was under state socialism.

BIBLIOGRAPHY

Baumgartner, Tom, Tom R. Burns, and Dusko Sekulic. 1979. "Self-Management, Market and Political Institutions in Conflict: Yugoslav Development Patterns Dialectics." In *Work and Power*, ed. T. Burns, L. E. Karlsson, and V. Rus. London: Sage.

Bilandzic, Dusan. 1985. *Historija Socijalisticke Federativne Republike Jugoslavije* (History of the Socialist Federal Republic of Yugoslavia). Zagreb: Skolska Knjiga.

Cohen, Leonard J. 1993. *Broken Bonds: The Disintegration of Yugoslavia.* Boulder, Colo.: Westview.

Djilas, Alexander. 1993. "A Profile of Slobodan Milosevic." *Foreign Affairs* 72 (3).

Druga Tranzicija. 1998. "Politicki pluralizam u Hrvatskoj 'Od opozicije do vlast' Okrugli stol.1998." (Second Transition: The Political Pluralism in Croatia, from Opposition to Power, Round Table). *Erazmus* 23: 12–38.

Eyal, Gil, Ivan Szelényi, and Eleanor Townsley. 1997. "The Theory of Post-Communist Managerialism." *New Left Review*, no. 222.

Hankiss, Elemer. 1990. *East European Alternatives.* Oxford: Oxford University Press.

Irvine, Jill. A. 1993. *The Croat Question.* Boulder, Colo.: Westview Press.

Jelic, Ivan. 1981. *Komunisticka Partije Hrvatske 1937–45* (The Communist Party of Croatia). Zagreb: Globus.

Lazić, Mladen. 1994. "Preobrazaj ekonomske elite" (Transformation of the Economic Elite). In *Razaranje Drustva: Jugoslovensko drustvo u krizi 90-ti,* ed. M. Lazic, D. Mrksic, S. Vujovic, B. Kuzmanovic, S. Gredelj, S. Cvejic, V. Vuletic. Belgrade: Filip Visnjic.

Moraca, Pero, Dusan Bilandzic, and Stanislav Stojanovic. 1977. *Istorija Saveza Komunista Jugoslavije* (History of the Communist Party of Yugoslavia.). Belgrade: Rad.

Pusic, Vesna. 1992. *Vladaoci I Upravljaci* (Rulers and Managers). Zagreb: Novi Liber.

Ramet, Sabrina P. 1992. *Nationalism and Federalism in Yugoslavia.* Bloomington: Indiana University Press.

Rohatinski, Zeljko, and Dragomir Vojnic. 1996. *Process of Privatization in Croatia.* Zagreb: Central European University, Open Society Institute—Croatia.

Róna-Tas, Ákós. 1997. *The Great Surprise of the Small Transformation: The Demise of Comunism and the Rise of the Private Sector in Hungary.* Ann Arbor: University of Michigan Press.

Sekulic, Dusko. 1985. *Trziste, planiranje i samoupravljanje* (Market, Planning, and Self-Management). Zagreb: Globus.

———. 1989. "Organizations and Society: On Power Relationships." In *The State, Trade Unions, and Self-Management,* ed. G. Szell, P. Blyton, and C. Cornforth. New York: De Gruyter.

———. 1992. "Nationalism versus Democracy: Legacies of Marxism." *International Journal of Politics, Culture, and Society* 6.

———. 1997. "Nations and National Conflict in Successor States of Former Yugoslavia." In *Race, Ethnicity, and Gender: A Global Perspective,* ed. S. P.Oliner and P. T. Gay. London: Kendall & Hunt Publishing Company.

Sekulic, Dusko, Randy Hodson, and Gartth Massey. 1994. "Who Were the Yugoslavs? Failed Sources of a Common Identity in the Former Yugoslavia." *American Sociological Review* 59: 83–97.

Sekulic, Dusko, and Zeljka Sporer. 1997. "Regime Support in Croatia: Determinants of Regime Support in the Past, Present, and Future." In *Australasian Political Studies: Proceedings of the 1997 Annual Conference,* ed. G. Cowder, H. Manning, D. S. Mathieson, A. Parkin, and L. Seabrooke. Adelaide, South Australia: Department of Politics, Flinders University.

Shoup, Paul. 1968. *Communism and the Yugoslav National Question.* New York: Columbia University Press.

Staniszkis, Jadwiga. 1991. *The Dynamics of Breakthrough in Eastern Europe.* Berkeley: University of California Press.

Szelényi, Ivan, and Szonja Szelényi. 1995. "Circulation or Reproduction of Elites during the Postcommunist Transformation of Eastern Europe: Introduction." Special issue, *Theory and Society* 24 (October).

Unger, Brooke. 1998. "A Ghost of a Chance: A Survey of the Balkans." *The Economist.* 24–30 January.

Wasilewski, Jacek. 1995. "The Forming of the New Elite: How Much Nomenklatura is Left?" *Polish Sociological Review* 110.

————. 1998. "Hungary, Poland, and Russia: The Fate of Nomenklatura Elites." In *Elites, Crises, and the Origins of Regimes,* ed. M. Dogan and J. Higley. Lanham, Md.: Rowman & Littlefield Publishers.

White, Stephen, and Olga Kryshtanovskaya. 1998. "Russia: Elite Continuity and Change." In *Elites, Crises, and the Origins of Regimes,* ed. M. Dogan and J. Higley. Lanham, Md.: Rowman & Littlefield Publishers.

Zupanov, Josip. 1995. *Poslije potopa* (After the Deluge). Zagreb: Globus.

9

Hungary

Bankers and Managers after State Socialism

György Lengyel and Attila Bartha

Two theses about the structure and internal workings of economic elites are of continuing interest. One is that managers predominate; the other is that bankers hold a hegemonic position. The intellectual backgrounds of both theses influence the ways in which they are formulated and applied. The thesis of managerial rule goes back to the early 1930s when Berle and Means (1933) examined proprietary forms of modern business enterprises and concluded that the spread of shareholding was dispersing ownership and giving it a corporate form. This meant, in turn, that the power of owners was being replaced by that of managers, who, by monopolizing information and other key aspects of decision-making, were the real controllers of many large companies. More often than not, these managers were able to make their interests prevail over owners' interests.

The thesis of managerial control was further elaborated by James Burnham in his famous book on the "managerial revolution" (Burnham, 1941). Although both the empirical basis and implications of the managerial revolution have been contested, it is one of the most familiar statements in American social science. It prompted J. K. Galbraith's (1967) further thesis about the rise of a "technostructure" that possesses the expertise and information indispensable for running large enterprises. In Galbraith's view, strategic decisions do not pass into the hands of managers, even if the separation of ownership and control is indisputable in modern business enterprise. Rather, the key decisions are taken by committees and other bodies of experts. The networks knitting these collectivities together constitute the

163

technostructure that shapes corporate decisions. The roles of individual managers are less important and are confined mostly to deciding the composition of committees and to rubber-stamping what they recommend.

Somewhat by contrast, Pahl and Winkler (1974) analyzed the composition and functioning of a cross-section of the British economic elite and concluded that managers have a firm sense of autonomy and strive to control resource allocations. Managers stand in relation to traditional owners as professional sports players stand to amateurs. Earlier, Dahrendorf (1959) argued that managers and owners differ not only in social origins, career patterns, and value orientations, but they also have different legitimacy bases. The capitalist owner's legitimacy rests directly on property rights, but the manager relies on delegated property rights for legitimacy. Managerial authority is, accordingly, more like the delegated authority of elected political representatives. In Dahrendorf's view, another source of managerial legitimacy is a consensus, or at least the lack of a dissensus, among the personnel that managers control.

Drawing on these schools of thought, Iván Szelényi (1995) has argued that a postsocialist society is actually a society of managerialism. There are no identifiable ownership groups capable of influencing the most important decisions because it is managers who possess the technical knowledge and other social capital essential for controlling the key factors of production. Consequently, postsocialist struggles do not concentrate on the acquisition of property, but on the control of its distribution. In this respect, postsocialist societies differ from both state socialist and capitalist ones. Though they often seek ownership shares in their companies (especially in prosperous subcontracting firms), postsocialist managers are reluctant to relinquish the advantageous control positions that derive from diffused property structures. The high degree of uncertainty in the postsocialist economic environment makes it a primary goal of managers to oppose those who seek to concentrate property ownership. Szelényi comments that while this situation is typical of economies transiting from socialism to postsocialism, it is probably long lasting. This is because managers possess the most advantageous combinations of economic, cultural, and social capital. They thus have the upper hand over political leaders, who may be more powerfully equipped with cultural and social capital, but who have little or no economic capital. It also makes managers dominant over intellectuals, who possess only cultural capital, and it places them well ahead of the internally differentiated class of small-scale entrepreneurs, who possess little capital of any kind.

ENTER THE BANKERS

It is striking that when analysts of modern market economies discuss alternatives to managerial rule in the economic elite, their attention is drawn to bankers. During the first half of the 1990s in Hungary and other postsocialist countries, bankers became not only a target of populist attacks, but also the focus of broad ideological debate. The antecedents of this debate go back at least to Rudolf Hilferding, whose work followed in the wake of Marxist political economy at the beginning of the twentieth century. Hilferding stressed the crucial importance of centralization and concentration in capitalist economies and the ways in which these trends were spawning cartelization and the ascendancy of finance capital over productive capital—of bank capital over industrial capital. Finance capital's ascendancy was supported strongly by a new middle class of employees in commerce and industry. In Hilferding's view, the main opponents of finance capital had previously been small- and medium-sized factory owners, but because of concentration the latter were increasingly subcontractors to large enterprises and, hence, increasingly supporters of finance capital's ascendancy (Hilferding, 1959).

Hilferding's thesis was resuscitated by several studies during the 1970s and 1980s, which found that bankers and institutional investors more and more control large enterprises. In the United States during the 1960s, New York banks—and, to a lesser extent, insurance companies—gained the dominant positions on many corporate boards of directors. Leaders of financial institutions played decisive roles in making loans and shaping capital flows, even though they did not directly exert managerial control over corporations (Mintz and Schwartz, 1981). Analyzing relations between British industrial enterprises and banks in the same period, Richard Whitley (1989) concluded that the network of overlapping boards was dominated by leaders of financial institutions, and this gave them the largest role in coordinating the policies of industrial enterprises. These and other studies speculated that the ascendancy of financial institutions was forcing corporate managers to pursue short-term profits, making them more receptive to state regulation, and reducing their sensitivity to the social consequences of corporate actions (Useem, 1979; Barton, 1985).

More recently, some sociologists have pointed out that the presence of bankers on corporate boards may simply reflect a strategy of cooptation through which corporations seek to minimize uncertainties in their environments. Fligstein and Brantley (1992) argue that corporate behavior is best understood in terms of the specifics of a corporation and its environment, rather than in terms of struggles for corporate control. Analyzing the French economic elite's internal restructuring after World War II, Pierre Bourdieu (1989) argues that the main change did not involve the ascendancy of managers over owners, or of bankers over managers; rather, the essence of the restructuring was a modification of recruitment channels and a changed operational logic among companies. In place of the specialized schools of science and engineering that had earlier produced "competent" technicians and experts, the channels for economic elite aspirants increasingly became the tertiary educational institutions that improved business and negotiating skills, enabled students to establish contacts, taught them how to perform credibly in public, and gave them financial expertise. Admission into these institutions depended less on previous academic performance than on self-assurance and a cultural heritage acquired from privileged families. Moreover, because the efficiency of enterprise performance was increasingly evaluated in terms of financial indicators, improving applied technologies became an alternative to seeking immediate profits, with the whole operation becoming more subject to marketing strategies. Bourdieu concludes that the result has not been the domination of bankers over managers, but, instead, the strengthening of financial–economic leaders within enterprises and the hiring of a disproportionate number of managing directors who gain their positions through the new recruitment channels.

Exponents of the managerial thesis have also discussed the role of finance capital and the prevalence of bankers on corporate boards. Dahrendorf, for example, approvingly cited Hilferding to observe that the formerly unified role of the capitalist owner has not divided into separate owner and manager roles because a third actor—the finance capitalist or banker controlling monetary funds and having an increasingly independent investment function—has entered the picture. Discussing postsocialist societies, Szelényi makes this view explicit when he claims that the hegemonic economic positions are held by "financial managers"—bankers, managers of investment funds, and advisers to international and national financial organizations. These individuals have a monopoly of the relevant cultural capital and are the purest representatives of a "monetarist ideology." Curiously, Szelényi (1995) subsumes this claim in his discussion of "the manager problem" in postsocialist societies.

In recent Hungarian discussions of these matters, the thesis of banker hegemony has been formulated clearly by Erzsébet Szalai (1994, 1995). Her interviews of managers and her examination of the business press trace a struggle for controlling positions in the banking sphere between an economic-political elite group of "new technocrats," who emerged during the late 1980s, and a "new clientele" of bureaucrats and "yuppies," who surfaced during the 1990s. Szalai concludes that the new technocrats of the late 1980s have won this struggle. They now prevail over the bureaucrats and "yuppies" within the banking elite, and, as such, they constitute the central node in the Hungarian economic elite. Furthermore, Szalai argues, through the exposition of "monetarist values" and through agreements concluded in back rooms, the dualistic socialist tradition of state intervention and informal private bargains lives on.

The main reasons for the survival of this socialist tradition—as Éva Várhegyi (1995) has pointed out—are the establishment of a two-tier banking system during 1987, and the retention of a legal–political framework that has not kept abreast of economic changes. Prior to 1989, monetary policy was governed by fiscal considerations, with enterprises responding to increasingly strict loan terms by simply postponing repayments. After 1989, the banks remained unchanged, but the load of outstanding debts that they inherited from the state socialist era was heavy. To solve this problem, political decisions were needed. It is plausible to assume that the political decisions that were taken reflected a combination of professional considerations, corporate interests, and informal bargaining mechanisms. The indicators of this combination were a segmentation of the banking system and the fact that in 1993 two-thirds of the bank market was dominated by the five large banks whose outstanding debts had been inherited from the former one-tier banking system (Várhegyi, 1995: 24). In 1993, the largest segment of the banking boards, some two-fifths, consisted of managerial personnel within the banks themselves. More than a third of the remaining board members consisted of leaders of other banks and representatives of ministries (Gombás, 1996). However, these high rates of institutional self-representation and mutual cooptation among bank boards must not disguise the fact that, as late as 1994, more than a dozen of the fifteen largest banks were still state-owned (Várhegyi, 1995: 71).

With this discussion of debates and research about the respective places of managers, owners, and bankers in economic elites as background, we want to ask anew which of these groups held the dominant position in the Hungarian economic elite following the transition from state socialism.

THE SOCIAL COMPOSITION OF BANKING AND MANAGERIAL ELITES

When studying the interrelations and structure of the economic elite, or segments of it, distinguishing privileged from dominant positions is a necessary first step. Privileged positions can mainly be described in terms of income, wealth, lifestyles, social distance, and prestige. Indicators of dominant positions include decision-making competence, influence, and the simultaneous holding of other key positions. The privileged and dominant positions of economic elite members are closely interrelated because, clearly, a dominant economic position usually entails considerable privilege. However, the two types of positions do not always coincide: high positions in the economic decision-making hierarchy entail greater competence, but this may or may not be rewarded by greater perquisites.

Data from survey studies of comparable economic elite samples that we conducted in 1990 and 1993 shed light on these distinctions in the Hungarian economic elite.[1] Privileged positions can be identified chiefly by examining aspects of recruitment, such as gender, level of education, age, and social origins. The presence of women in the economic elite was quite limited under state socialism and after the transition; in neither 1990 nor 1993 did women exceed 15 percent of all elite position-holders. However, women were much more conspicuous in the banks, where they held a quarter of all top positions, than in state-owned and private enterprises, where only about one of every ten managers was female. The gender distribution was closely related to gender differences in education. In the first years after the transition, 95 percent of the economic elite held tertiary degrees. But the education leading to these degrees differed by field (economics, engineering, and the law), institutions (universities, colleges), and its full-time or part-time character. Some of these education differences corresponded with gender differences. For example, there were very few female engineers, but more than a quarter of all those with economics degrees were women. The tendency of women to specialize in economics presumably contributed to their more frequent presence in top bank positions.

During the early 1990s, economists became more prevalent in every segment of the economic elite, mainly at the expense of engineers. For those in leadership positions in the banks, a degree in economics came to be indispensable. The proof of this is that all of the bank leaders who were originally trained in engineering apparently felt obligated, with but one exception, to obtain an additional degree in economics. The prevalence of economists also increased among managers, and at the tops of private enterprises economists came to outnumber engineers. Engineers retained their numerical dominance only as leaders of state-owned companies. This change in elite education credentials corresponded to the perceptions of elite members in 1993. Asked to describe the preferred training of "successful company leaders," most respondents deemed training in economics more important than knowledge of engineering, which, in their opinion, was also secondary to legal expertise. This perception probably stemmed mainly from leaders' views of company operations that depended heavily on financial arrangements in postsocialist conditions (Fligstein, 1995).

In terms of education credentials, the economic elite was increasingly homogeneous. While in 1990 more than half the elite had obtained their degrees through part-time evening or correspondence courses, by 1993 nearly three-quarters were graduates of full-time degree programs. In this respect, there was no significant difference between managers and bankers. Although graduates of full-time programs were disproportionately numerous among bankers in 1990, by 1993 such graduates were more or less equally prevalent among managers, with the proportion of managers trained in part-time higher education programs falling below 30 percent.

In terms of average age, the economic elite had been substantially rejuvenated during the second half of the 1980s. In 1984, more than half had been above fifty years of age; in 1990, however, less than two-fifths were fifty

Table 9.1 Occupational Statuses of Parents of Bankers and Managers in 1990 and 1993 (Percentage)

Father's Status	*Bankers 1990*	*Managers 1990*	*Bankers 1993*	*Managers 1993*
Blue-collar	33.3	55.4	23.3	37.6
White-collar	15.0	10.2	10.0	12.2
Manager/professional	45.0	25.4	60.0	45.3
Entrepreneur	6.7	9.0	6.7	5.0
(N)	(60)	(177)	(60)	(181)
Mother's Status				
Blue-collar	57.4	80.0	48.4	67.0
White-collar	21.3	15.8	14.5	13.1
Manager/professional	19.7	2.1	37.1	18.3
Entrepreneur	1.6	2.1	—	1.6
(N)	(61)	(190)	(62)	(191)

Source: Institute of Sociology, Budapest University of Economic Sciences (BUES), 1990 and 1993.

or older. The inroads of more youthful leaders were conspicuous among bankers, where the proportion of leaders above fifty was reduced from 55 to 29 percent. The average age of managers also fell, but the proportion of those above fifty was still 45 percent in 1990. By contrast, the transition from state socialism that began in 1989 did not greatly affect the average age of economic elite members, reducing it merely from 47.6 to 46.3 years.

The major difference between bankers and managers during the early 1990s could be found in their social origins and in the social capital each kind of leader was able to deploy on the basis of his or her family background. Although a decrease in intergeneration mobility—portending a social closure of the economic elite—was the general tendency, its extent varied significantly between bankers and managers (see table 9.1). In 1990, leaders coming from managerial or professional families (measured by father's occupation) amounted to 30.4 percent, with another 6.4 percent having mothers who were managers or professionals. Among the 1990 managers, however, only a quarter had these backgrounds, compared with 45 percent of bank leaders. During the next few years, the proportion of elite members from families of modest or lower social statuses declined considerably. In 1993, nearly half of all elite members came from upper-status families on their father's side, and about a quarter came from such families on their mother's side. Such inherited social capital was clearly more prevalent among banking than managerial members of the elite; 60 percent of the former had fathers who were managers or professionals, while this was true of less than half (45 percent) of enterprise managers.

FINANCIAL STANDING, LIFESTYLES, AND NETWORKS

Indicators of considerable income and wealth, privileged consumption patterns and lifestyles, and exclusive private networks marked the economic elite, and especially its banker component. Respondents in our 1993 survey reported an average monthly net income of 113,000 florins. When the monthly incomes of the several groups making up the elite were compared, however, bankers' incomes were about double those of enterprise managers. The managers' incomes were, in turn, on a rough par with those of cabinet ministers and economic policy committee members in parliament. The high monthly incomes of bank leaders were, thus, conspicuous. Even taking into account significant "veiled incomes" among managers and economic policy-makers, the monthly incomes of bankers (who could also be presumed to have veiled incomes) testified to their much more privileged situations.

Indicators of wealth also revealed bankers' privileged situations. We estimated the average family wealth for the entire economic elite on the basis of its members' homes and apartments, holiday cottages, cars, and art objects. Again, there were obvious differences between the elite segments, though the magnitudes were not as great as for monthly incomes. The average family wealth of bankers was about 40 percent more than that of state-owned enterprise managers and 30 percent more than that of private company managers, senior economic ministry officials, and parliamentary members specializing in economic policies.

How were these income and wealth differences reflected in lifestyle differences? In any society, the lifestyles to be emulated are set by the upper middle class. Ågnes Utasi (1995) has shown that the lifestyles of "status elites" display the preferred values of cosmopolitanism, erudition, and a cultured home. Our surveys produced results consistent with this. As regards enrolling their children in schools abroad, employing domestic servants, and collecting expensive art objects, more than two-fifths of the economic elite followed the lifestyle of Utasi's "status elites." There was, however, considerable polarization in the lifestyles of the economic elite. Among economic ministry leaders, where economic and cultural–scientific strata often intersect, nearly three-fifths followed this lifestyle, while hardly more than one-third of enterprise managers did. Bankers again stood out, with 53.2 percent of them displaying the aforementioned lifestyle.

A final aspect of privilege is the sets of informal relationships—the networks—in which economic elites are enmeshed. As indicated by the occupations of elite members' spouses and of their best friends, the networks were clearly exclusive. Our data show that economic elite members predominantly had intellectual or managerial spouses (65.3 percent) and that their best friends were highly likely to be fellow elite members or other "insiders" (84.1 percent). In this area, however, we found no significant differences between banker, manager, and policy-maker segments of the elite.

To summarize, in terms of income and wealth, bankers were clearly the "elite of the elite." This was also true of their lifestyles, although the top stratum of people in the economic ministries followed similarly exclusive lifestyles. The managers, on average, were a distinct notch or two lower as regards income, wealth, and lifestyle, with a disparity in the monthly incomes of bankers and managers being pronounced. When the occupations of spouses and closest friends were examined, the elite appeared to be quite closed, and neither bankers nor managers stood out in this regard.

CAREER PATTERNS AND MULTIPLE POSITION-HOLDING

The careers of an overwhelming majority of the economic elite were not seriously interrupted by the transition from state socialism. The regime change did not catapult large numbers of formerly junior or subordinate experts and technocrats into elite positions. Those who were already rising arrived in elite positions with substantial managerial experience. This was true of both the manager and banker components of the elite.

Our 1990 survey provided objective measures of economic elite turnover, and our 1993 survey yielded self-reported data that showed uninterrupted careers to be about 20 percent more frequent than our 1990 data indicated. There were two reasons for this 20 percent discrepancy. One was that the actual proportion of leaders with uninterrupted careers did indeed increase between 1990 and 1993; the other was that a large proportion of managers in 1993 assessed their careers as essentially uninterrupted, even though they had experienced minor positional changes that our 1990 survey picked up. Consistent with this, although less than a quarter of the bankers felt that their careers had ebbed and flowed, the corresponding proportion among managers was more than a third (table 9.2). Among bankers there was no difference in the career evaluations of those who made it into the elite before 1990 and those who arrived after 1990, while the proportion of managers who tended to see their careers as uninterrupted was higher among the new elite members in 1993 than among managers in 1990. In short, elite members who reached the top after 1990 more often regarded their careers as uninterrupted than did those who already held such positions in 1990.

A comparison of bankers' and managers' career phases reveals that managers rose to a subelite position more quickly after taking their first job than bankers did. However, managers then had to wait about half again as long as bankers to rise from a subelite to an elite position. At the same time, over their entire careers, bankers experienced far more changes of posts, even as elite members, and they, therefore, spent much shorter periods in each post

Table 9.2   Career Characteristics of the 1993 Economic Elite Segments (Percentage) (N=181)

Elite Segment	Years until Subelite Position	Years from Subelite to 1st Elite Position	Number of Steps in Elite Positions	Total Career Steps	Average Years in One Position	Average Years in one Managerial Position
Bankers	9.4	10.2	3.09	5.18	3.78	3.30
State enterprise managers	6.6	15.9	2.69	4.58	4.91	5.91
Private entrepreneurs	7.7	13.5	2.39	4.42	4.80	5.65
Ministry officials	10.3	9.7	2.36	4.52	4.42	4.09
Parliamentary committee members	9.3	3.6	1.65	3.38	6.78	8.24
Whole economic elite	8.1	3.2	2.59	5.51	4.72	5.10

Source: Institute of Sociology, BUES, 1993.

on average. After a longer initial waiting period, in other words, bankers' careers soared faster and more spectacularly than those of managers. This finding is related to the more elongated hierarchy characteristic of banks (and also of economic ministries, where roughly the same career trajectory and pace could be observed).

In terms of the entire length of careers, there was no significant difference between bankers and managers; their career patterns differed only in the number of career steps. This was related to the creation of the two-tier banking system in 1987, which opened up a large number of subelite posts in banks. What accounts for the contrasting patterns in which bankers rose rapidly only after a long initial waiting period, whereas managers rose rapidly to higher-echelon positions and then had to wait, on average, for fifteen years before moving into an elite position? Apart from the banking sector's expansion after 1987 and the more elongated hierarchies of banks, both of which have already been mentioned, another cause can be identified.

This was a cohort effect. The banking sector's rapid expansion meant that newly appointed bank leaders were likely to be younger than newly appointed enterprise managers. When we disaggregated the career phases of the two segments into age groups, a significant disjunction between the two generations of bankers and managers emerged. There was little age difference between young bankers and young managers when both were at lower and middle echelons. The striking difference was between the older bankers and managers at that stage of their careers, the older bankers having had to wait for elite positions about half again as long as the older company managers. But when bankers and managers moved from a subelite position to their first elite position, both older and younger bankers moved faster than managers.

A corollary of economic elite career patterns—multiple position-holding—was far more characteristic of bankers than of managers (see table 9.3). While half of the bankers belonged to two or more directorial or supervisory boards, the corresponding proportion of managers was barely 20 percent. Nonetheless, the bankers' multiple positions were still far fewer than those found in Western business elites (Whitley, 1989), and they were fewer than those held by the interwar Hungarian economic elite, whose members, on average, held about three times as many positions simultaneously as did the postsocialist economic elite (Lengyel, 1993).

Taking into account all of the managerial, board, and advisory positions charted in our 1993 survey, it emerged that half of the bankers held three or more positions and only 20 percent had just one position, while 40 percent of managers had just one position. Whereas four-fifths of the bankers were members of a directorial board of some company or supervisory agency, this was true of only half the managers. In addition, there was a nontrivial tendency among bankers to hold an influential position in some firm that fell within their bank's sphere of interest. However, the available information was not sufficient to determine whether this kind of interlocking-position holding resulted from mechanisms of cooptation or regulation. Overall, the relatively low rate of multiple position-holding suggested that after the regime transition, cooptation aimed at alleviating environmental uncertainties played more of a role in shaping positional interlocks between banks and enterprises than did regulatory requirements.

Economic elite careers also involve memberships in various professional and political organizations. Managers reported a far greater involvement in professional associations than did bankers. By contrast, over 10 percent of bankers, but only one or two managers, were government advisers. Under state socialism, membership in the Hungarian Workers Party (HSWP) was an indicator of how political factors could influence economic elite careers. Fully

Table 9.3 Multiple Position-Holding among Bankers and Managers in 1993 (Percentage) (N=181)

Elite Segment	1 Position	2 Positions	3 or More Positions
Bankers	19.4	27.4	53.2
Managers	43.7	33.3	23.0
Whole economic elite (N=339)	39.2	33.0	27.8

Source: Institute of Sociology, BUES, 1993.

four-fifths of the economic elite of the planned economy in its last phase were members of the HSWP. In our 1990 survey, three-fourths of the managers and slightly less than two-thirds of the bankers reported former HSWP memberships. Although the rate of former HSWP members dropped to 60 percent in our 1993 survey, former HSWP membership was still a pronounced feature of the elite, especially among enterprise managers. However, age was clearly showing its effects in 1993: four-fifths of the older enterprise managers had been party members, but this was true of only half the younger managers.

To sum up, the career patterns of bankers and managers differed substantially in terms of workplace career and multiple position-holding, as well as HSWP membership under state socialism. The managers reached subelite positions faster, but bankers made it into elite positions faster. The managers' career-related contacts were mainly in professional organizations and in the old HSWP, whereas the bankers were much more frequently involved in outside board and advisory positions.

ATTITUDES TOWARD PRIVATIZATION

The transformation of ownership structures was a crucial aspect of the transition from state socialism (Kornai, 1996). Which privatizing methods were chosen, and at what pace they were implemented, greatly determined who distributed—and under whose control—state-owned property, and who would be its new owners. These privatization choices depended on more than strict economic calculations; they were preeminently political matters. The economic elite, and especially its most dominant segment, heavily influenced the choices that were made and the policies that were implemented. Consequently, the attitudes of bankers, managers, MPs, and ministry officials toward privatization were of great interest to us.

We may construe opinions on the control and speed of privatization as indicators of the economic elite's attitudes. As regards control of privatization, enterprise managers—quite understandably—held opinions that differed substantially from those of the rest of the economic elite. Barely half of them approved of the government's arbiter role; the other half preferred privatization under the direction of the enterprise managers themselves. By contrast, some 70 percent of respondents in the economic ministries and parliamentary committees and nearly two thirds of the bankers advocated a centrally controlled privatization process. As for the pace of privatization, two-thirds of the elite in late 1993 urged that it be accelerated. There were, however, marked differences among the elite segments: 84 percent of MPs and some 70 percent of large enterprise managers wanted to speed up privatization, while nearly two-fifths of top ministry officials and 42 percent of the bankers did not.

How can these attitudinal differences be explained? Our analysis revealed that a respondent's location in the elite was a principal factor shaping his or her attitude. Compared with bankers, the probability of favoring accelerated privatization was, *ceteris paribus,* 4.5 times greater among MPs and 2.4 times greater among company managers. Like the elite of the economic ministries, the bankers seemed to want a slower and better-regulated privatization. On the other hand, opinions on the control of privatization did not relate unambiguously to respondents' locations within the elite. Level of income and extent of multiple position-holding appeared to shape attitudes on this question just as strongly as location. Elite members with higher incomes and greater numbers of positions preferred government-controlled privatization disproportionately. Thus, the most privileged elite groups—bankers and other high-income and multiple-position respondents—wanted a slower and more controlled privatization. Obviously, they found the status quo, or only gradual changes in it, congenial. As things turned out, privatization generally had both a controlled character and a rapid pace during the mid-1990s. Consequently, neither bankers nor managers can be viewed as winners in privatization.

CONCLUSIONS

This chapter has examined the Hungarian economic elite after the transition from state socialism in light of competing theses about managerial rule and bank hegemony in capitalist economies. Contrary to much writing about economic elites in postsocialist conditions, our survey data from 1990 and 1993 do not lend much support to the idea that large enterprise managers played the decisive roles. First, our data show the clearly privileged position that the banking segment of the elite enjoyed. Largely made up of younger people, who were born in Budapest families headed by professionals and managers, bank leaders had the greatest incomes and personal wealth, and they followed high-status lifestyles. Nearly all of them began their careers as economists who had been able to study full-time at the Budapest University of Economic Sciences. Although they took longer to reach subelite positions than did managers in large enterprises, they ultimately moved faster than managers into elite positions. As measured by the occupations of their spouses and closest friends, as well as by the extent of their multiple position-holding and influential advisory roles, the bankers' networks were broader than those of managers. The managers, by contrast, were significantly less privileged in terms of income, wealth, lifestyle, and family-based social capital. Although they probably had greater decision-making autonomy within their enterprises, managers could not be regarded as the dominant group within the elite, if only because their economic–political networks were more limited than bankers' networks were.

Should we conclude, then, that bankers hold a hegemonic position in the postsocialist Hungarian economic elite? The evidence is not all on one side. While it is true that bankers held a greater range of positions during the early 1990s, this concentration of influence and power was still relatively puny by the standards of the interwar Hungarian and more recent Western economic elites. On the one hand, the general character of privatization in Hungary has accorded rather closely with the preferences of the leading bankers; on the other hand, its pace has been closer to what the managers have wanted.

On balance, neither managerial rule or banker hegemony was the main feature of the economic elite during the years immediately following the transition. It is more accurate to say that different and to some extent conflicting and competing segments of the elite kept a watchful eye on each other. There was a ragged but mutual control of economic and political change, rather than the victory of one group in a battle for control. It remains to be seen whether bankers or managers eventually triumph, or if they together institutionalize patterns of control and cooperation that induce the elite as a whole to play the economic game with positive-sum outcomes.

NOTES

1. The 1990 survey preceded the June elections of that year. The sample of 371 economic leaders consisted of three segments: main department heads and higher-ranking officials of the economic ministries; presidents, managing directors, and their deputies in the principal banks; managing directors and other key executives in a 16 percent sample of all large manufacturing companies. The 1993 survey utilized a sample consisting of 341 key leaders in five sectors: large state-owned enterprises; large private enterprises; major banks; economic ministries and government agencies; and the economic committees of parliament.

BIBLIOGRAPHY

Barton, Allen H. 1985. "Determinants of Economic Attitudes in the American Business Elite." *American Journal of Sociology* 91 (February): 54–86.

Berle, Adolph A., and Gardiner Means. *The Modern Corporation and Private Property.* New York: Macmillan.

Bourdieu, Pierre. 1989. *La noblesse d'État.* Paris: Ed. de Minuit.

Burnham, James. 1941. *The Managerial Revolution.* New York: G. P. Putnam.

Dahrendorf, Ralf. 1959. *Class and Class Conflict in an Industrial Society.* London: Routledge.

Fligstein, Neil. 1995. "Networks of Power or the Finance Conception of Control?" *American Sociological Review* 60: 500–503.

Fligstein, Neil, and Peter Brantley. 1992. "Bank Control, Owner Control, or Organizational Dynamics: Who Controls the Large Modern Corporation?" *American Journal of Sociology* 98 (April): 280–307.

Galbraith, John Kenneth. 1967. *The New Industrial State*. Boston: Houghton-Mifflin.

Gombás, Éva. 1996. "The Banking System in Hungary." Budapest, unpublished manuscript.

Hilferding, Rudolf. 1959. *A finánctőke* (Finance Capital). Budapest: K.J.K.

Kanter, Rosabeth Moss. 1993. *Men and Women of the Corporation*. New York: Basic Books, 2nd ed.

Koontz, Harold, Cyril O'Donnel, and Heinz Weihrich. 1984. *Management*. New York: McGraw-Hill.

Kornai, János. 1996. "Négy jellegzetesség: A magyar gazdasági fejlôdés politikai gazdaságtani megközelítésben. Második rész" (Four Characteristics: The Hungarian Economic Development in Political Economic Approach. Second Part). *Közgazdasági Szemle* 1: 1–29.

Lengyel, György. 1993. *A multipozicionális gazdasági elit a két világháború között*. (The Multipositional Economic Elite in the Interwar Period). Budapest: E.L.T.E.

Lengyel, György, and Attila Bartha. 1995. "Az iskolapadból a csúcsra: A gazdasági elit képzettsége és karriermintái a kilencvenes évek elsô felében" (From the School-Bench to the Top: Education and Career Patterns of the Economic Elite in the First Half of the Nineties). *Educatio* 4: 598–613.

Lengyel, György, and Dobrinka Kostova. 1996. "The New Economic Elites: Similarities and Differences." In *The Transformation of East-European Economic Elites: Hungary, Yugoslavia and Bulgaria,* ed. G. Lengyel. Budapest: Budapest University of Economic Sciences.

Mintz, Beth, and Michael Schwartz. 1981. "Interlocking Directorates and Interest Group Formation." *American Sociological Review* 46: 851–69.

Pahl, Ray, and John Winkler. 1974. "The Economic Elite: Theory and Practice." In *Elites and Power in British Society,* ed. P. Stanworth and A. Giddens, 102–22. Cambridge: Cambridge University Press.

Szalai, Erzsébet. 1994. *Utelágazás: Hatalom és értelmiség az államszocializmus után* (Crossroad: Power and Intellectuals after State Socialism). Budapest: Pesti Szalon, Savaria U. P., Szombathely.

———. 1995. "Kastély" (The Castle). *Kritika* 9: 8–13.

Szelényi, Iván. 1995. *The Rise of Managerialism: The New Class after the Fall of Communism*. Budapest: Collegium for Advanced Studies.

Useem, Michael. 1979. "Studying the Corporation and the Corporate Elite." *The American Sociologist* 14 (May): 97–107.

Utasi, Ágnes. 1995. "Középosztály és életstílusok" (Middle Class and Lifestyles). *Társadalmi Szemle* 3: 3–13.

Várhegyi, Éva. 1995. *Bankok versenyben: A magyar bankpiac állapota, fejlôdése és jövôje* (Banks in Competition: Conditions, Development, and Future of the Hungarian Bank Market). Budapest: Pénzügykutató Rt.

Whitley, Richard. 1989. "A City és az ipar" (The City and Industry). In *A menedzser* (The Manager), ed. G. Lengyel. Budapest: E.L.T.E.

10

Russia

The Oil Elite's Evolution, Divisions, and Outlooks

David Lane

The rise of oil companies in the capitalist world was associated with the entrepreneurship of leading capitalists, the dominance of corporate capital, and the quest by national governments to exert influence over natural resources for both strategic and financial purposes (Yergin, 1991). The situation of Russia's vital oil industry is, by comparison, unique. The government, led by state employees, developed the country's vast resources in oil and gas. During the transition from state socialism, Russia has had no indigenous capitalist class with sufficient means to purchase its petroleum and other natural resources. Moreover, the Russian state has been intentionally weakened in the process of dismantling state socialism. In this chapter, I consider the ways in which the Russian oil industry has been privatized and its leadership has been formed. I show that previous management positions in the oil sector have been converted into economic capital. I examine divisions within the sector between managerial and financial interests, elite conflicts over the extent and type of state regulation and control, the main forms of interest articulation and, finally, I offer some generalizations about Russian capitalism today.

Although the Russian oil industry has made a relatively successful transition to a market economy, it is characterized by significant differences of interest between managerial, financial, and political interests, between local and central political authorities, and between different sectors of government and their constituent interests. The elites lack cohesion and the industry faces a particularly hostile parliamentary elite. The tendency of free market capitalism toward "disintegration" is amplified in Russia by what might be called a "chaotic economic formation." After analyzing this situation, I argue that an alternative form of coordination and cohesion might be achieved through a more corporatist capitalism.

THE TRANSITION: THE FORMATION OF COMPANIES AND AN OIL ELITE

Mikhail Gorbachev's reforms opened a window of opportunity for the management and administrators of the oil industry, who became benefactors of his reform policy. The end of the 1980s gave the leaders of enterprises unprecedented prerogatives as their rights over production were extended to finance and marketing. In the terminal Gorbachev period, enterprises sought to maximize short-term profit, and investment was neglected. The price on the domestic market of oil and oil derivatives in 1990–92 was approximately 5 percent of world prices. Many production units, refineries, and commercial intermediaries bought products at the home price and received export quotas and licenses to sell on the foreign market. The difference between the fixed domestic price and international market prices led to enormous fortunes being made, legally and illegally.

With the dissolution of the Soviet ministries in 1990–91 and the shift of control from the USSR to the republics and regions, a spontaneous process of privatization began. Enterprises and organs of local administration began to form independent companies. The management of local companies, as well as leaders of local administration, took over assets in the oil industry. The new state political structures, however, were weak, and management, being in control of productive assets, was strongly positioned to act in its own interest in matters of production, refining, and sales. In 1991, the All-Union ministries of the USSR were liquidated and a single Ministry of Fuel and Power of the Russian Federation was formed (Mintop, *Ministerstvo topliva i energetiki RF*). But its activity was confined to the legal and general regulation of the fuel and power complex and it had no direct control over production activities. It became a channel between government and industry. Perhaps even more important was the fact that institutional reforms were not imposed from the top, but developed with participation by the executives of the oil industry, including those in the enterprises themselves.

The entropy and disorganization that followed the command-administrative system's disintegration was accompanied by a shift to the market, begun in 1992 by Ygor Gaidar's government. To maintain state control, the government of the Russian Federation formulated plans to create several holding companies. The intention was to reorganize the oil companies on a vertically integrated basis according to the model of the leading Western oil companies, with which the Russian oil directors were well acquainted. In 1990–91, for example, before he started to establish Lukoil, Vagit Alekperov visited the headquarters of some large Western oil corporations, and he was well aware of their structure and organization. By the middle of 1992, it was proposed to organize the industry into ten or twelve large, vertically integrated companies able to compete, it was expected, on Russian and world markets. Unlike Middle Eastern governments that, in the years after World War II, sought control through nationalization (or at least the threat of nationalization), for reasons of political legitimacy and state weakness the Russian government had to privatize the companies and adopt a market strategy. The economic rents paid by the fuel industries, however, were crucial to the well-being of the economy, and it was recognized that some form of government control was essential.

The central government asserted its right to the tax income from this major export industry. As with the claims of Iraq over Kuwait, the assertion of this right was questioned by many of the regional republics, and it was a fundamental cause of the (largely successful) movements for greater autonomy, bordering on de facto independence, in Tatarstan and Chechnya. (Chechnya's material interest lay in obtaining the royalties from a pipeline running through its territory, plus the profits from a small amount of production and refining.)

"Official" privatization of the oil industry occurred from 1993 to 1997. This involved redistributing the assets of production enterprises that were the subjects of the "spontaneous" privatization noted above, and, concurrently, organizing vertically integrated holding companies. Some of the holding companies have had strong financial and managerial controls over their subsidiary companies; in other holding companies, however, the "subsidiaries" maintain effective control over their physical assets. Divisions within and between holding and subsidiary companies reflect differences in the ownership and control of assets. The principal actors are the government of the Russian Republic, the governments of regions and localities, financial institutions (such as the banks), and management executives in the industry. The forms that the political struggle for control take are not unlike those of the struggle during the post–World War II period between the governments of what later became the OPEC states, Western governments, and the oil companies. The difference is that the Western oil companies were major established powers, whereas the Russian ones are still forming. In the Russian case, moreover, the government is faced with an entrenched management that in the past controlled production.

The structuring of the oil industry resulted from discussions between the industry's management and the first head of Mintop, Vladimír Lopukhin, and the State Committee for the Management of State Property

(*Goskomimushchestvo*—GKI), led by Anatoly Chubais. There were divisions within the political elite about the course of privatization. The radical reformers, especially those around Chubais and the GKI, wanted to ensure greater competition. They believed that privatization in the fuel and power industries should be done quickly and according to the rules common to all industries. But managers of the producing and distributing oil units were sufficiently well organized politically to resist the reformers' plans for privatization. Consequently, oil and gas, as strategic industries, were not subject to the open privatization procedures of other industries, and oil and gas prices continued to be regulated after the price liberalization of 1 January 1992.

The top oil managers supported Mintop's scheme for restructuring the industry. These envisaged restricting privatization and creating controlling stock packages in the newly established companies to keep these companies as state property for three years. However, the government's ownership right was also a contested terrain within the political apparatuses. The industrial ministries (and committees) shared Mintop's view that state ownership should be an important instrument of control over the oil companies, as well as a source of profits that could be redistributed to other government projects.

The general laws for privatization of the oil complex were laid down by presidential decree in November 1992. Crucially, the government would have majority ownership rights in the holding companies, which, in turn, would have a majority interest in the subsidiaries (those that had been formed earlier during "spontaneous" privatization). The government's intention was to privatize assets and form competing companies while giving the state a significant level of control over the privatized companies. The problem here, for the market reformers, was that if the subsidiaries, which operated in local markets, were controlled by the holding companies, then the latter would act as local monopolies over the supply of fuel.

The strictest governmental control was maintained in the transportation of oil and oil products. Fifty-one percent of share capital in the companies Transneft and Transnefteprodukt remained under federal government ownership. The objective was to keep the transport of fuel under government control. This control, it was contended, would ensure that the fuel companies continued to function without interruption during the transition to a free market, and it would also give the government effective regulation of oil exports. Another argument in favor of this slow privatization was financial. The market value of the Russian oil industry's assets was at least two hundred billion dollars. Neither Russian citizens or private financial institutions could raise such sums, nor could potential Western investors find such amounts easily. It was argued that rapid privatization in this context could only lead to undervaluing the state's assets.

THE RISE OF FINANCE CAPITAL

The intention of the early Yeltsin administration to maintain significant state ownership in the oil industry was not realized, and during the mid-1990s the government began to sell its share of the industry's assets. An unmistakable shift in policy towards greater company autonomy occurred through a "loans-for-shares" scheme, devised by Vladimir Potanin, the president of Uneksimbank. This involved investors (banks or financial institutions) lending the government money in return for the state's share packages in partially privatized companies. If the loans were not repaid the ownership and rights of control (including the right to sell assets) would lie with the lenders. In 1995, Mintop actively opposed loans-for-shares auctions because they would sever the link that ensured direct government control. But Potanin's scheme prevailed.

The fight over the Potanin scheme illustrated the divisions between ruling elite factions. Liberal reformers in the Ministries of Economics and Finance and in the GKI opposed "home industry" factions within the government and the presidential apparatus. The reformers advocated a minimal role for the state, and their views coincided, for the most part, with those of the IMF and its demands for a more rigorous privatization policy. Anatoly Chubais and the GKI supported the extension of privatization and

Table 10.1   Government Ownership Shares in Russian Oil Companies, 1994–97

Company	Percentage of Government Holding			
	1994	1995	1996	1997
Sidanko	100	85*	51*	—
Vostsibneftegaz	100	85	38	—
Sibneft	N/A	100*	51*	0
Yukos	86	53*	0.1	0.1
Surgutneftegaz	40.1	40.1*	40.1*	—
Komitek	100	100	92	0–22
Lukoil	42.1	26*	16.6*	6.6
NorsiOil	N/A	100	85.4	45
Tatneft	46.6	46.6	35.1	20–25
Transneft	100	100	75	51
Rosneft	N/A	100	100	51
Tiumen Oil	N/A	100	100	51
Sibur	100	85	85	51
Vostochnaya Oil	100	85	85	51
Slavneft	93.5	92	90.1	56–68
Onako	100	85	85	85

Source: Eugene M. Khartukov, *Oil and Gas Journal,* 18 August 1997, 38.
*Wholly or partly in the hands of the "pledge holder."

favored the loans-for-shares deals. What tipped the scales in favor of the liberal reformers around Chubais was the Russian government's precarious financial position. This allowed Yeltsin to authorize that shares be "swapped" for loans, which the government could then use as subsidies for its other programs.

The significant shift of ownership to the private sector, in which the banks and financial companies, often working through nominees, secured control of most oil industry assets, is shown in table 10.1. In 1997, the government relinquished ownership rights in a large number of companies. The pipeline operators, Transneft and Rosneft, were partly privatized through a 25 percent offer of their stock to existing and former employees, and another 25 percent was to be offered to the investment market. Despite political pressure from the Duma and from regional authorities, President Yeltsin—confronting serious budget deficits—lifted restrictions on the sale of oil assets in 1997, and an unprecedented rate of de-statization ensued.

The major players in the privatization sweepstakes were Russian banks, particularly Alfa Bank (40 percent of Tiumen Oil), Uneximbank (85 percent of Sidanko), Menatep (85 percent of Yukos), and SBS/Berezovsky (99 percent of Sibneft) acting through intermediaries such as Laguna, Interros Oil, Sins, Rifainoil, Monblan, and Finansovaia Neftianaia Korporatsiia (FNK); Imperial Bank (owned by Lukoil and Gazprom) purchased 5 percent of Lukoil shares.

Due to the uncertain legal status of capital, the difficulty of repatriating profits, the extent of crime and corruption, and the hostility toward foreign capitalists in parts of the government, the oil industry and the Russian parliament, foreign direct investment in the oil industry has been small. In 1996, Russian and foreign joint ventures accounted for 7 percent of oil production and 12.5 percent of exports, though the exports grew by about 15 percent in 1997. Laws have limited foreign share holdings in oil companies, and foreign shareholders have effectively been excluded from the boards of companies because they had fewer shares than was necessary to qualify for election. In 1997, however, President Yeltsin lifted the legal ceiling of 15 percent of shares that could be owned by foreigners, although companies themselves could still fix a ceiling. A law on production sharing, which gives foreign investors rights to export income, was signed in June 1997, but it only applied to a small number of production sites. Despite these problems, external actors may become more important as the entrenched oil management seeks alliances and capital to strengthen its position. Joint ventures—as between Shell and Gazprom, Sidanko and British Petroleum, Lukoil and ARCO, Yukos and AMOCO—may become more significant. In 1998–99, however, Western companies were still somewhat hesitant to form strategic alliances with Russian oil companies.

MANAGERIAL CONTROL?

Ownership is one important aspect of the organization of companies, but it cannot be assumed to effect their control. This is because owners are confronted with managerial and technocratic personnel, who may be owners in their own right. Possessing knowledge about the organization of a company and also being masters over its productive activities, managerial and technocratic personnel exert influence on a company's strategic plans. Because decision-making processes are secret and restricted to the inner circle of company directors, it is usually very difficult to discover who controls companies and to determine to what extent ownership rights are translated into control.

Initially, the executives and managers who controlled production enterprises in the old Soviet oil industry benefited from the Soviet ministerial system's dissolution. During the period of reforms since 1991, the oil and gas managerial strata (in contrast to the leaders of most other industries) have seldom directly criticized the main direction of President Yeltsin's policies. And, unlike other industries, there have been virtually no large-scale strikes or mass antigovernment demonstrations in the oil and gas industry. As the chief of Lukoil, Vagit Alekperov, has put it: "The direction of economic reforms, carried out by the President, generally suits us" (*Finansovye izvestiia*, 27 March 1997).

The process of consolidating into vertically integrated companies has weakened the managements of subsidiary enterprises. The managements of holding companies have had to break the resistance of those who manage production units and refineries. There has also been competition between the holding companies for the most promising enterprises, together with a growing struggle between them for markets, access to new fields, and quotas for transporting oil through export pipelines.

The communication environment has also been changing, with many oil executives moving their headquarters from Siberia to Moscow, where they interact with Western businessmen and Russian bankers. The former corporate unity of the oil elite has been weakened somewhat by the incursions of outsiders into top administrative echelons. These outsiders are men who possess skills and knowledge in financial management and marketing. As recently as 1995, the boards of directors of vertically integrated oil companies still consisted wholly of leading oil managers and ministry officials. Since 1996, however, bankers and financiers have been recruited to a number of boards, notably those of Yukos, Sidanko, and Sibneft. Representatives of other business companies have also started to appear as vice-presidents of oil companies (for example, Zia Bazhaev in Sidanko, and Mukharbek Aushev in Lukoil). In 1998, two financiers with major interests in Yukos and Sibneft—Mikhail Khodorkovsky (Menatep Bank and Yukos chairman) and

Boris Berezovsky (a major shareholder in Sibneft, with significant stakes in LogoVaz and other companies)—engineered a proposal for a merger between Yukos and Sibneft.

The outcome of all this is that there are significant political divisions between different interests within the oil industry and between the industry's leaders and people outside it. However, the ascendant group is now located in the banking and financial services sector. I want to examine how the backgrounds of the ascendant banking and finance leaders differ from those of the oil managers and how these background differences are related to differing orientations toward the oil industry. Using interview survey data, I also want to examine the different outlooks of wider political and economic elites within the energy sector.

RECRUITMENT OF THE OIL AND BANKING ELITES

Current interpretations of Russia's economic and political transition from state socialism stress the nomenklatura's "reproduction" with the implication that the elites lack commitment to a market system and that Russia's pluralist institutions are merely a new shell for the old dominant class. There are three problems with this approach. First, "nomenklatura" was a very general category that subsumed many different occupational groups and executive and administrative roles in diverse sectors of the Soviet polity and economy. Often people with political capital (in the Komsomol and Party apparatus) are not distinguished from those with economic capital (in the economic administration and management) and from those with general cultural capital (a position in higher education, a capability in research, or a command of symbols as in the media). A second problem lies in the nature of the new economic elite itself. Researchers do not distinguish between the leaders of different sectors of the economy—banking and financial services, manufacturing and construction, retail, entertainment and show business, the media, the energy industries, and so on. This oversight is particularly important in a large, continental economy like Russia. Third, existing research does not take account of the values and beliefs of the elites. It is merely assumed that old wine in new bottles will taste like old wine; in other words, there is no allowance for the elites' conversion to a new belief system or their adaptations to the new circumstances of a marketized economy. To avoid these problems, I analyze the social origins of the oil elite, compare them with those of the banking and financial service elite, and consider the values and outlook of the oil leadership; finally, I draw some comparisons with the political elite.

I defined the oil elite initially as members of the boards of directors of holding companies during 1995–96. Recall that this was before bankers and directors in the financial sector had secured a presence on oil company boards. To establish the backgrounds and careers of the oil elite, biographical encyclopedias and databases were searched for details of their life histories. After excluding entries with very little information, fifty-five biographies were analyzed to give a composite picture of the contemporary leaders of the oil industry. By way of comparison, I will also discuss the backgrounds of 118 leading people in banking and financial services. These individuals were selected from published studies of the one hundred "most influential" Russian entrepreneurs and bankers, and from handbooks of leading businesspeople published in Moscow during 1996 and 1997.

While it is often contended that younger people rise rapidly to elite positions during regime transitions, a study of the Russian oil elite severely modifies this view. On 1 January 1997, 49 percent of my elite sample were aged over fifty, and 89 percent were over forty. In the banking elite the figures were lower: 34 percent were over fifty, and 73 percent were over forty. The first observation to make is that the power and benefits of economic leadership in contemporary Russia accrue to middle-aged men; very few in both elite groups were women: only 7 of 118 in the sample of bankers and financiers and none among the fifty-five oil leaders. Unlike other members of the new banking and financial service elite, of whom 37 percent were born in Moscow or Leningrad, all the oil leaders were born in the provinces of the former USSR. By higher education, 79 percent of the oil elite had graduated in faculties of applied science and engineering (compared to only 34 percent of the banking and financial service elite), while only 11 percent of oil leaders held economics degrees (compared with 53 percent of banker and financiers). Just 3 percent of the banking and financial elite members had been to higher Party school and no member of the oil elite had been there.

Membership in the former Communist Party of the Soviet Union (CPSU) could be construed as one form of identification with the old regime. However, data on CPSU membership from biographies may be misleading for two reasons. First, former Party membership may be denied or minimized by the subjects, and second, Party membership may have been a formality with little, if any, political significance. Bearing these caveats in mind, approximately a third of the oil and banking elites in my samples had been Party members. It is important to distinguish those who had some position in the Party or Komsomol apparatuses and to assess whether that position was a consequential one. To ascertain this, positions in the Party and Komsomol apparatuses were weighted by rank in the hierarchy (that is, a weight of 10 was given for the post of secretary of the Central Committee of the CPSU, and prorated down to 1 for a local Party secretary) then this figure was multiplied by the years in post. This gave an average Party/Komsomol index of 8 per person for the bankers and 4 for the oil executives—showing a much greater salience of previous political capital for the banking elite than for the oil elite. The positions occupied in the Party were on the average middling ones, only one banker having been a member of the CPSU Central Committee. However, it is worth emphasizing that, especially in the oil elite, a large majority had had no position in the Party apparat.

The other important elite sector in the Soviet political system was the government apparatus. Therefore, all positions held by members of the banking and oil elites in the Soviet government apparatus before 1 July 1990 were studied. Those occupying positions in the economic administration (for example, in Gosplan and the State Bank) came to sixteen (29 percent) of the oil elite, whereas the figure was sixty-six (56 percent) for the banking elite.

It is not a simple matter to determine the occupational backgrounds of Russian elites. Not only did people transit, usually upward, between positions, but also, during the latter period of perestroika, there were important internal shifts as individuals sensed which way the ship bearing Communism was going (or sinking). To overcome this problem, I calculated the proportion of time that individuals spent in different positions in the seven years prior to the beginning of the USSR's collapse, that is, from August 1981 to December 1988. It was from these positions that Russian elites emerged after state socialism.

This research reveals interesting differences between the banking and oil elites. For the oil elite, by far the most common position during the 1980s was that of an oil industry executive; posts in production enterprises accounted for 54 percent of the elite's total career time in that period. A professional position was the second most common. Members of the oil elite spent relatively little time in Party and government executive posts. By contrast, the largest group in the banking and financial services elite came from administrative positions in Soviet economic agencies such as Gosbank (24 percent of the elite's total career time during the 1980s), other government entities (10 percent), and professional positions (14 percent). Reflecting the banking elite's somewhat younger age, more bankers and financiers had been students, and this contributes to the generally held, but also rather misleading, impression that the new Russian business elite as a whole is young.

These findings suggest making a distinction between two career types. On the one hand are the government, Party, and administrative elites of the Soviet system—consisting of people whom we might define as members of the "administrative" class. These people had careers in the administrative organs and during the transition from state socialism they "reproduced" such forms of capital as they had already acquired. By contrast, previous Soviet elite members did not figure prominently among the new oil and banking elites, where what might be called a "substitution" reproduction occurred. During the transition from state socialism, that is, the people who formed these postsocialist elites simply moved further up the ladders they were already climbing. Their continued upward mobility was not materially different from what they could have expected if state socialism had remained in place. The only significant change for them was that they now had individual rights to economic assets. The data also show that a considerable number of people in the oil elite, and especially in the banking elite, came from outside these two sectors, and thus they might be considered part of an elite circulation.

My conclusion confirms the research of Eyal, Szelényi, and Townsley (1997), who claim (with respect to Eastern Europe generally) that the transfer of executive capital was the most important asset of the new economic elites. While it is true that many oil and banking executives previously had positions in the Party and state apparatuses, their Party positions do not appear to have been particularly important. However, among the banking elite, administrative capital and general cultural capital appear to have been important assets. This was also evident in educational profiles showing the oil elite's members to have come predominantly from applied science and engineering. Overall, it also needs to be remembered that the Russian economic elite is embedded in a comprehensive economy that makes for far greater elite diversification than in the other East European countries.

VALUES AND OUTLOOKS:
OIL EXECUTIVES AND POLITICIANS COMPARED

Another aspect of Russian elite change has to do with the values and beliefs of the new elites. Do they act in a market environment in traditional "apparatchik" ways or are they profit-seeking, accumulation-making entrepreneurs? What is their attitude to government control and the market system? To answer these questions one would ideally interview strategic members of the oil and other economic elite groups. Practically, however, this proved impossible because many of the major oil companies refused to allow their executives to be approached, while in other cases oil executives had insufficient time or interest to make themselves available for interviews. Despite these obstacles, interviews were conducted with fifty oil executives who held jobs as director, deputy director, president, or vice-president in large oil companies. Forty of these men worked in Moscow, five in Bashkiriia, and five in Tatarstan. Fifteen supplementary interviews using a more limited range of questions were carried out with other oil executives in Moscow. In total, sixty-five leaders of the oil sector were interviewed. For purposes of comparison, thirty interviews were conducted with holders of key political positions in relevant state administrative agencies and Duma members who had a special interest in the energy sector administration and members of the Duma of the Russian Republic having an interest in the energy sector.

For simplicity's sake, I will label these thirty individuals "politicians." All of the interviews with oil executives and politicians were conducted between June and October 1997.

The sample of oil executives interviewed was similar in many ways to the oil elite that I earlier identified through biographical research. They were male and middle-aged. The largest group among them had been educated in engineering, though a fair number of both the oil executives and the politicians had studied economics and management. A much higher proportion of the interviewees, in comparison with the oil elite identified through biographies, had been born and educated in Moscow, which indicated that they had worked in the commercial rather than the production and management areas of the oil industry. While all were directors or presidents or vice-presidents, there was probably some inflation of titles and many of the oil executives interviewed did not sit on their company's board of directors. A large majority of the interviewees had not participated in the apparatuses of the Komsomol or CPSU. Their identification with new post-Soviet political parties was weak: only a minority of the oil executives and about half of the politicians identified with a specific party, and only half of the oil executives thought it important to be active in politics.

It is widely agreed that stable pluralistic political systems are characterized by elites that share fundamental outlooks and norms; for example, that existing economic structures, such as forms of ownership, management, and the mode of state intervention are acceptable, and that change should occur within the existing structure of political interest articulations. To illustrate this, a study of top bureaucrats in half a dozen stable West European democracies during the early 1970s found that 60 percent thought their political system was "fundamentally sound, with little need for change" and another 37 percent thought it "fundamentally sound though some reforms are necessary" (Aberbach, Putnam, and Rockman, 1981: 195). I have elsewhere shown that, unlike elites in Western democracies, Soviet and Russian political elites, under Gorbachev and Yeltsin respectively, were fundamentally divided on such issues. Interviewed in 1994, none of the Gorbachev elite and only 1 percent of the Yeltsin elite agreed with the first of the above responses (that is, little need for change), though 51 percent and 40 percent, respectively, agreed with the second (that is, some reforms were necessary). At the other end of the scale, not one member of the West European bureaucratic elites during the early 1970s saw his or her political system as "basically unsound and should be completely replaced," whereas the proportions of the Gorbachev and Yeltsin political elites that held this view of the Soviet and post-Soviet systems were 18 percent and 40 percent, respectively (Lane, 1997: 871).

Very little is known about the attitudes of Russian economic elites toward the legitimacy and effectiveness of the new economic order. Therefore, I altered the questions used in my 1994 political elite study to make them relevant to the executives of the oil industry and politicians interviewed in 1997. I first asked for their perceptions of the Soviet oil industry before perestroika, that is, before Gorbachev came to power (see table 10.2). The extent of disagreement among the oil elite was substantial, and this has implications for the feasibility of further post-Soviet reforms. Just one half of the oil executives (50.8 percent) believed that the Soviet oil industry was sound, even if it needed reforming. The politicians interviewed were even more positive about the old system, with over 63 percent holding this view. On the other hand, significant minorities of the oil executives and politicians thought that the Soviet oil industry had been completely ineffective and was not capable of being salvaged.

Further light is shed on the oil executives' dispositions when we consider their attitudes to the reforms that took place in the political system after 1992 (table 10.2). They were again divided, with a majority advocating considerable change—though note that half of the politicians called for a complete change in the existing system. Obviously, these key elite groups harbored much doubt about the new political system's adequacy. I also asked specifically about the existing economic system's effectiveness, and the responses are also shown in table 10.2. Here there was a striking difference between the oil executives and the politicians. Among the former, less than one in ten thought a complete change necessary, while fully half of the politicians held this view. Among the oil executives, more than half thought that the present economic system is not effective, but that reforms can be carried out. It seems clear from all of the responses shown in table 10.2 that a critical mass of oil executives had little confidence in the current system and wanted more reform. Politicians, the majority of whom advocated fundamental political and economic change, voiced disillusionment with the current system even more frequently.

Large numbers of the 1997 respondents believed that corruption and criminalization were widespread. Over three-quarters of the oil executives and politicians agreed that corruption was prevalent, while two-fifths of the oil executives and four-fifths of the politicians thought that Russian economic life in general had a criminal character, though more than half the oil elite (57.6 percent) thought that, although crime was widespread, the economy in general was healthy. In a similar vein, the tax system's inadequacies led over 70 percent of the oil executives and more than half the politicians to agree that "the prime task of government is to establish order in the taxation system."

The substantially asymmetrical attitudes of oil executives and politicians toward the postsocialist system were also evident in their views about the types of property that "should predominate in the near future." Only two members of the oil elite plumped for state ownership, 61.5 percent favored

192   *David Lane*

Table 10.2   Elite Perceptions of the Soviet Oil Industry's Effectiveness and the Effectiveness of the Political and Economic Systems in 1997 (Percentage) (N=95)

Elite Perceptions	Soviet Oil Industry Before Perestroika		Political Reforms since 1992		Current Economic System	
	A	B	A	B	A	B
Effective; almost no need for change	7.7	13.3	4.5	—	1.5	—
Effective; some need for change	43.1	50.0	27.7	10.0	32.3	10.0
Not effective, but reforms could have been/should be made	18.5	26.7	52.3	40.0	53.8	36.7
Completely in-effective and beyond reforms	23.1	10.0	13.8	50.0	7.7	50.0
No response	7.7	—	1.5	—	4.6	3.3
N	65	30	65	30	65	30

Source: David Lane and VTzIOM, Moscow, 1997 Survey.

A = Oil executives

B = Politicians

Questions:

1. Consider the oil industry in the period before perestroika (before Gorbachev came to power); do you think the industry at that time was [alternatives listed in table]?

2. As a result of the political and economic reforms that have taken place since 1992, is the present political system [alternatives listed in table]?

3. The present economic system in the Russian Federation is [alternatives listed in table].

joint stock company property, while 6 percent wanted more individual forms of property ownership. The politicians displayed the reverse set of preferences, with 70 percent favoring state ownership and only 23 percent wanting joint stock-companies. There was, however, considerable agreement that the economy should ultimately be a mixed one. This emerged from responses to a question asking respondents to choose between a liberal, a social democratic, and a paternalist system. The overwhelming preference (81.5 percent of oil executives and two-thirds of politicians) was for a social democratic system, though just over a fifth of the politicians opted for a more paternalistic system.

I asked a number of questions to gauge how the oil executives assessed their companies' development and position in the economy. Attitudes about profit maximization and the role of the government were probed. The oil executives generally favored a market-type system in which companies enjoy free pricing and little government control (78.4 percent). There were significant exceptions, however, and 10 percent of the oil executives, along with a quarter of the politicians, strongly disagreed with this. There was little agreement in either group about the roles being played by regional authorities (see table 10.3). Not surprisingly, moreover, the executives, unlike the politicians, were resolutely opposed to increased government price controls on oil products in the economy (table 10.3). Likewise, more than three-quarters of the oil executives opposed increased control by politicians over economic affairs, while more than 60 percent of the politicians saw a need for increased control, and they—the politicians— were also more skeptical about market relations, with over 70 percent of them supporting government price controls on oil products in the domestic market (table 10.3). In sum, with regard to views about the situation of the oil industry and policies toward it, there was significant agreement among oil executives, but overall there was a wide gap between their preferences and those of politicians. This indicates that it is clearly premature to discuss the emergence of Russian elite unity over vital questions of oil policy and politics.

Table 10.3   Elite Agreement and Disagreement about Regional Authorities, Oil Price Controls, and Increased Political Control of Economic Affairs (Percentage) (N=95)

Elites Agree/Disagree	Regional Authorities Hamper Oil Industry		Should Control Oil Prices		Do Not Increase Politicians' Control	
	A	B	A	B	A	B
Agree completely	24.6	6.7	15.4	36.7	39.3	—
Agree with reservations	41.5	34.5	20.0	36.7	42.6	36.7
Disagree with reservations	26.2	37.9	29.2	13.3	11.5	43.3
Disagree completely	7.7	20.7	32.3	13.3	6.6	20.0
N	65	30	65	30	65	30

Source: David Lane and VTzIOM, Moscow, 1997.

A = Oil executives

B = Politicians

Questions:

1. Do you agree that regional authorities present one of the greatest problems facing the management of the Russian oil sector?

2. Do you agree that the freeing of prices in the oil sector was a mistake and the government should introduce control over prices of oil products in the internal market?

3. Do you agree that at present, under existing conditions, it does not make sense to talk about an increase in the control of politicians over economic affairs?

WIDER ELITE DIVISIONS

The politicians' views, summarized above, appear to be representative of the attitudes of most deputies in the Duma, who regularly call for strengthening state control of the oil and gas sector and for massively redistributing resources from this sector to others that are unable to compete on the world market (for example, the processing industries and agriculture) and to support social welfare. These deputies would restore the state monopoly over the export of oil, gas, and oil derivatives, while maintaining state revenues through government ownership of shares in the energy complex.

The left-wing opposition earlier opposed privatization and insisted on annulling the loan-for-shares auctions. But by the end of the 1990s there was no (official) campaign for the renationalization of the oil companies and Gazprom, even by the Communists. The nationalist–Communist–agrarian faction now advocates the regulation of energy prices for and their maintenance at levels much lower than world prices. It supports transferring much of the public tax burden to the energy complex and using rents and profits in the oil and gas industries to support other domestic industries. It seeks to limit the access of foreign investors to the strategic sectors of the economy, particularly the energy sector. For example, the left opposition blocked the introduction of a production-sharing law in a form that would have been acceptable both to foreign investors and to the Russian oil companies. This opposition helps to explain why the oil and gas elite has unequivocally supported Yeltsin and his administration.

In the upper house of the Russian parliament, the Council of the Federation, in which representatives of the regions sit, a minority represents the interests of the energy sector. Most of the regions lack energy resources, and their enterprises and communal services are as a rule unable to pay the rising prices of fuel and power that are a consequence of Russian producers' reducing the differential between domestic and export prices. Most of the regions and their representatives support regulating fuel prices.

One can point, however, to the formation, in 1994, of one lobbying group that has supported the oil and gas industry. This is the bloc of representatives from the oil and gas territories, the so-called Association of Economic Inter-Relationships. Among its members have been spokesmen for the Tiumen, Tomsk, Orenburg, and Sakhalin regions, the Khanty-Mansiisk and Yamalo-Nenetsk autonomous territories, plus the Bashkiria, Tartarstan, and Komi Republics. In its first few years of existence, however, the association was not very active in support of the companies as such; it was more concerned to support regional interests against those of the center generally.

The oil and gas companies do not, therefore, enjoy much support in parliament. The hostility of many members of the Duma is potentially a significant problem for the oil elite because the Duma may block or significantly influence legislation affecting their well-being. Accordingly, the industry may find it necessary to intensify pressure on deputies. On the eve of the 1995 parliamentary elections, for instance, some leaders of the oil industry tried to organize their own pre-election campaign, in which a leading role was to be played by an interest group known as SISTEK (Union of Information and Collaboration in the Fuel and Power Complex). The intention was to finance ninety-four regional newspapers through which electioneering (propaganda in support of candidates) would be carried out. It was proposed that once the new parliament was formed, SISTEK supporters would try to persuade nonaligned deputies to back the lobby (*Kommersant,* 16 August 1995). The Union of Oil and Gas Industrialists, led by Vladimir Medvedev, endorsed the plan. However, the oil and gas elites did not formally support it and, in the election, they promoted the Our Home is Russia movement, of which Viktor Chernomyrdin was a prominent member.

The oil elite's practice of pursuing its interests behind the scenes may have limits, and one may expect the companies to take a more prominent public role in the future. Oil and gas companies have already bought into the media industry, for example. Gazprom has a large share in the NTV channel and in regional newspapers; Lukoil bought Izvestiia only to lose control of it to Uneksimbank. Moreover, as banks and other financial institutions increase their control of the oil companies, they may use their own control of the media to influence public opinion in favor of the oil companies (for example, Most Bank controls NTV and the *Segodniia* and *Moskovski Komsomolets* newspapers). Also, the Yeltsin administration's policies, as well as the advisory role of external agencies such as the IMF and the World Bank, may not coincide with the oil companies' interests. This has already been apparent with respect to the collection of taxes from the energy sector, and it has led to the president of Gazprom, Rem Viakhirev, to call for deputies in the Duma to defend the industry against government revenue demands.

FROM "CHAOTIC" ECONOMIC FORMATION TO A CORPORATIST CAPITALISM?

My analysis of the oil industry prompts some concluding observations about the type of capitalism that is developing in Russia. I hypothesize that we are witnessing an extreme type of disorganized capitalism there, which might be called a "chaotic" economic formation. I avoid using the term "chaotic capitalism" because of the extensive bartering, as well as the absence of a class pursuing accumulation through the valorization of surplus value, that characterize the Russian scene at present.

Advocates of markets insist that they not only secure the coordination of economic activities, but they also enhance the efficiency and effectiveness of modern enterprises. The market promotes coordination and coherence because the forces of demand and supply embedded in a competitive price system lead to a rational and more or less optimal allocation of resources. In social and political life, moreover, there is a market analogue in the guise of a democratic competition between groups and a pluralistic, multifaceted conception of society. This market model was recommended by influential Western economic advisers as the basis for postsocialist economies, and it has formed the intellectual backdrop for the radical reforms that have taken place in Russia and in Central and Eastern Europe during the 1990s.

But the operation of "free markets" has been increasingly criticized in market economies on the grounds that competition leads to "disorganized" capitalism (Lash and Urry, 1989). Its attendant characteristics are recurrent recessions, high inflation and unemployment rates, and a fragmented political structure and civil society. The relations between economy, state, and society, it is contended, are asymmetric. This has certainly been evident in Russia during the transition from state socialism, to such an extreme that the label of a "chaotic" economic formation may be more appropriate there. A chaotic economic formation is defined by the following features: a lack of coordination between social and economic systems and inadequate cohesion of goals, laws, governing institutions, and economic life; deep elite disunity; the absence of a mediating class system; a weak state characterized by criminalization and corruption; inadequate political interest articulation; and an economy lacking systemic accumulation and distinguished by decline, inflation, and unemployment. As the market ceases to function, economic exchange increasingly takes place through networks pervaded by corruption.

In contemporary Russia, industries vary greatly in their capacity to adapt to market conditions, particularly when their exposure to global competition is taken into account. As a consequence of marketization, the energy and minerals industries have, on the whole, adapted to the world market, whereas manufacturing and agriculture have not. The adoption of a free-market policy by the oil and gas industries, for instance, would entail raising domestic prices to world levels and this would be highly detrimental (at least in the short run) to the industries that have not adapted to the market. It would severely depress the production that serves the home market and domestic consumers. Russia is not Kuwait; it is an important world power, it has a comprehensive industrial economy, a major military capacity, and a highly educated and urban population. The Russian economy's weakness impacts on the politics of Russian oil, which, should it internally adopt a market policy, would have unacceptable political and social costs.

The initial postsocialist arrangements for the oil and gas industries led in the direction of the state providing a shell for coordination. The intention of the early Yeltsin government, in support of the Fuel and Energy Ministry, was to retain a large part of oil and gas assets in state ownership, so as to provide the basis for an evolving system of state capitalism. This system was to consist of competing, partly privatized and partly state-owned companies in a market setting. Gazprom is the model example of what was intended.

By 1998, however, state assets in the oil industry had been sold and the industry was largely in private hands. There were numerous reasons for this change. The radical reformers in the government and presidential apparatus were ideologically committed to it; outside interests such as Western governments, financial services, and the IMF strongly supported it. The oil companies themselves profited from it and, in attempting to strengthen their market position, they sought further capital investments not only from Russian banks and financial institutions but also from foreigners. Oil executives as a whole appeared to accept the movement to a company-owned oil industry operating on market principles. The yawning government budget deficits, themselves a consequence of state attempts to counter the disorganization of the economy, were a further factor leading to the sale of government assets.

Ironically perhaps, the feudal sheikdoms of Kuwait, the Muslim traditionalists of Iran, and the military dictatorship of Iraq provide a stronger political framework for the preservation of their respective national oil industries than does the fragmented and weak government of Yeltsin's Russia. In Russia, the ruling elites are badly divided. The Ministry of Finance, The Ministry of the Economy, GKI, and GKAP hold to a free-market ideology and orientation. However, other ministries, particularly Industry, Agriculture, Science, Defense, and possibly Foreign Affairs, as well as regional political authorities, may well adopt a more corporatist and interventionist approach in order to support their various home and nationalist constituencies. Moreover, the two chambers of parliament do not in general support a free-market policy. Politicians are more sympathetic to the support of other Russian industries through low oil prices, and they want greater state involvement and control. There is, in short, a major cleavage over control of the oil industry. In this context, the policies of external international agencies, such as the IMF, play an important role in restructuring the economy. However, this can only lead to strengthening the market and weakening the government still further.

The clash of interests between the oil and gas industry, the dominant factions in parliament, the market-oriented coordinating apparatuses, and the fragmented governmental ministries and departments all point to the state's inability to coordinate capitalism in Russia. These factors have contributed to a chaotic situation. There is no clear elite compact concerning the extent of state regulation and market competition.

I believe that the political and economic forces loose in Russia today may yet bring about a revival and strengthening of the state. Even a deregulated, privatized oil industry is subject to political intervention—as the modern history of the Middle East shows. It seems unlikely that the federal government will reclaim the assets of the major oil companies. Not only is the Russian state divided between federal and regional bodies, but also Western governments and international agencies are likely to demand a privatized and open economy. Moreover, there is a potential constellation of political interests between dominant circles in the Duma and industries and ministries operating principally in the domestic market. Opposing these groups are the relatively successful export industries, such as oil, backed by the radical market reformers and external forces. There is an elective affinity here between the doctrine of free markets and economic interests in Russia. But the free-market policy, which has so far predominated, has led neither to stability nor yet to breakdown; it has simply led to chaos. In this context, the political becomes a major determinant of the economic. A key factor is the presidency. Further internal dislocation and a new nationalist or Communist president, or even a politically "reconverted" Yeltsin, could well turn the country in the direction of corporate, state-led capitalism.

NOTES

The research reported in this chapter was supported by a grant from the British Social and Economic Research Council. I acknowledge the research assistance of Iskander Seifulmulukov on the oil industry and also the staff of VTzIOM, who supervised the surveys.

BIBLIOGRAPHY

Aberbach, Joel D., Robert D. Putnam, and Bert A. Rockman. 1981. *Bureaucrats and Politicians in Western Democracies.* Cambridge, Mass.: Harvard University Press.
Eyal, G., I. Szelényi, and E. Townsley. 1997. "The Theory of Post-Communist Managerialism." *New Left Review,* no. 222.
Lane, David S. 1997. "Transition Under 'Eltsin: The Nomenklatura and Political Elite Circulation." *Political Studies* 45 (December).
Lash, Scott, and John Urry. 1989. *The End of Organized Capitalism.* London: Polity Press.
Yergin, Daniel. 1991. *The Prize.* New York: Simon and Schuster.

11

Bulgaria

Economic Elite Change during the 1990s

Dobrinka Kostova

Bulgaria's peaceful transition from state socialism began in November 1989 when the leader of the Communist Party, Todor Zhivkov, was forced from power through an internal party coup. Four relatively free and fair parliamentary elections (1990, 1991, 1994, and 1997) have since taken place. Two elite camps—one associated with the Bulgarian Socialist Party (BSP, the successor to the old Communist Party), the other with the Union of Democratic Forces (ODS, a handful of opposition parties after 1989 that coalesced in 1994)—have struggled for political dominance throughout the 1990s. Following an economically disastrous period of rule by the BSP between 1994 and 1996, the ODS gained government power in early 1997 after massive street protests against the BSP government forced an early election. National economic insolvency required the creation of an internationally supervised currency board arrangement on 1 July 1997.

In transiting from a centralized command economy to a market-oriented one, Bulgaria has traveled a rocky road, the end of which is not yet in sight. On the one hand, a number of successful privately owned companies have been established, and this has mainly occurred through individual initiatives "from below" (Lengyel and Kostova, 1996). On the other hand, the growing number of private firms is a somewhat misleading indicator of marketization because the amounts of production, employment, exports, and taxes that they account for are still not large. Additionally, many of these private firms have a parasitic relation to the state-owned or state-controlled sector, some existing only on paper to serve as tax havens or as vehicles for obtaining favorable bank loans and other financial credits (Kostova, 1996). Their titular owners often retain jobs in the bloated but relatively safe state sector so that the private firms serve mainly as secondary sources of income. The emergence of private owners, entrepreneurs, and businessmen has nevertheless led to significant changes in individual behavior and social statuses. These changes are manifested in purchasing luxury automobiles, building homes with swimming pools, frequenting exclusive restaurants and clubs, holding charity balls, and engaging in other activities associated historically with the nouveau riche (Sampson, 1994).

More generally, the Bulgarian transition has involved differentiation between and within political, economic, media, military, and cultural–scientific elites. The economic elite, for example, consists of new economic actors in the private sector, people prominent in the large black market, owners of restituted property that was confiscated by the socialist state, as well as people who were key players in the old command economy. This economic elite differentiation creates many contradictions and conflicts as groups pursue their particular interests and try to force political decisions that serve those interests. The important questions today are who has the economic initiative and who is ready to risk adaptations to the new economic situation—in short, who controls the economy? An even more basic question is whether it in fact matters who does this. The "who controls?" question pertains to changes in economic elites that are occurring throughout Eastern Europe. The "does it matter?" question pertains to outcomes in Bulgaria's rather chaotic economic circumstances.

Data for the analysis of the Bulgarian economic elite in this chapter are derived from surveys I conducted in the fall of 1990, the winter of 1994, and the spring of 1998. In all three surveys, the elite was identified positionally in two steps, first by locating the largest and otherwise most important economic enterprises and government agencies regulating them, and second by listing and then interviewing the top position-holders in these enterprises and agencies. Specifically, the economic elite studied here includes (1) directors and deputy directors of the largest private companies and state-owned enterprises; (2) presidents and vice-presidents of the largest banks; (3) ministers, deputy ministers, and department heads in the economic ministries and specialized government economic regulatory agencies; (4) key politicians in the parliamentary committees charged with formulating and overseeing the implementation of economic policies, together with key politicians in the various political parties. The surveys covered 303 leaders in 1990, 338 in 1994, and 256 in 1998, and the survey instruments asked for a wide range of information about life history, current social status, family background, personal values, economic interests, and perceptions of the economic and political landscape. Administered at intervals of four years, the three surveys make it possible to assess the extent of change and continuity in the makeup and outlooks of the economic elite. They provide rich data that bear on hypotheses about elite adaptation and change during a tumultuous period in Bulgaria.

ELITE RECRUITMENT

To what extent have factors that shape the holding of top economic positions changed during the transition period? Have social origins become more or less important? Has personal diligence and ingenuity played a larger role in elite careers? To shed light on these and similar questions, I will concentrate on economic elite members' educations, professional experiences, and political activities. Variables in this analysis include age, gender, family settings, educational levels and specializations, and the occupational statuses and durations of previous positions. I use these variables to illuminate larger analytical points about elite recruitment patterns and the factors and circumstances shaping them.

Age and Gender

A nearly universal feature of elites is the predominance of older persons in them. At the beginning of the Bulgarian transition, there was a strong difference between the average ages of elite and non-elite persons, but my surveys show a steady shift toward a more youthful elite as the 1990s progressed. In 1990 and 1994, three-fifths or more of the elite had already passed their fiftieth birthdays. By 1998, however, three-quarters of all elite members were less than fifty and nearly half were less than forty. Clearly, a major generation change in the economic elite's makeup had occurred. Presumably, younger persons were more able to adapt to the rapid economic, political, and social changes that followed the demise of state socialism.

The gender composition of the economic elite changed much less: males continued to outnumber females by roughly four to one. My 1994 and 1998 surveys recorded slight increases in the proportion of women holding elite positions, but this was probably due mainly to the increased willingness of women to participate in the surveys, as suggested by the fact that nearly all refusals to participate in those surveys came from men. Women are still conspicuous by their absence from top elite positions. They held less than 6 percent of the uppermost positions in 1994, and only about 10 percent of such positions in 1998. Predominantly, women were located in second-echelon "deputy" positions in all sectors of the elite. The most significant determinant of a woman's entry into the elite was her holding of a prior professional or managerial position, but this was a narrower recruitment platform than males enjoyed. It is also noteworthy that the age differential among women in elite positions was less than that of men, with the women being, on average, five years younger than the men. However, this almost certainly reflects the younger retirement age for employed women in Bulgaria.

Women's chances of reaching elite positions appeared to be somewhat more strongly affected by their father's occupational status than was the case for men. Most fathers of elite women were managers or professionals (70 percent). A somewhat smaller proportion of elite men had fathers in such high-status positions (64 percent). Overall, women entered elite positions from less diverse jobs than men, and the strongest predictor of their elite positions was a previous job as a higher state official or a middle-level manager in some economic enterprise. University degrees were vital for women's chances of gaining elite positions, but this is also true of men. In sum, a comparison of the gender makeup of the elite in 1990 and 1998 showed that no large increase in women's chances of reaching elite positions occurred during the decade after the end of state socialism.

Family Settings

Elite careers involve social dislocations because people climbing toward elite positions often distance themselves from their earlier social circles and, at least sometimes, from a first marriage. In 1990, very few members of the economic elite (1.3 percent) had been divorced, but in 1994 3.9 percent had been divorced, and by 1998 the proportion of divorced persons had doubled again, to 8.3 percent. Where first marriages do not break down, a spouse's occupational status may change and more or less parallel the rising status of the aspiring elite member. In 1990, 55.1 percent of elite members' spouses worked as professionals, and this proportion rose to 64.5 percent in 1994 before falling back to 58.6 percent in 1998, in which year about a tenth of spouses had stopped working, perhaps because labor market opportunities for them to do so had decreased severely in the economic crisis of 1996–97. There was, nevertheless, substantial equivalence between the educational and professional credentials of elite members and their spouses. In this respect, elite families remained more or less homogeneous despite the upheavals of the transition period.

When the family settings from which elite members came are considered more broadly, to include characteristics of parents, homogeneity remained a central characteristic. While parents of economic elite members under state socialism (as measured when the transition began in 1990) were predominantly peasants and workers (62.3 percent), and only rarely professionals (13.8 percent), by 1998 economic elite members were much more frequently the offspring of fathers (and often mothers) who performed nonmanual work (65 percent), and they were much less frequently the children of peasants or workers (35 percent). This marked shift in the occupational profiles of elite members' parents was to some extent a consequence of the elite's increasing youthfulness and of concomitant changes in the makeup of the economy and workforce, but it also reflected the fact that elite members began to come from more privileged family backgrounds in the postsocialist years.

Education

A distinctive feature of the economic elite during the 1990s was its high level of education. My surveys turned up not a single person with less than a secondary education, although there was a slight increase in the proportion of persons who had only a secondary education between 1990 (6.6 percent) and 1994 (9.6 percent). In 1998, however, all elite respondents had completed a university education. In 1990, the dominant educational specializations were economics and engineering (91 percent). The proportion of economists and engineers decreased to 71 percent in 1994, but it then moved back up to 85 percent in 1998. Meanwhile, a significant increase in the proportion of lawyers in top economic positions occurred. Lawyers were nearly absent in 1990 (2 percent), but in both 1994 and 1998 roughly one of every six elite members was a lawyer or held a university degree in a field other than economics and engineering.

The high educational credentials of elite persons in Bulgaria are not a new phenomenon. Under state socialism, most persons in elite positions were university-educated, a pattern that accorded with the generally well-educated population fostered by the state socialist regime. In terms of elite education profiles, then, continuity outweighed change, even though the regime and society changed profoundly. Moreover, there was no dramatic change in the distribution of specialized university education among the elite; as mentioned above, economics and engineering continued to predominate. However, the shift to a market economy created opportunities that enabled some people with entrepreneurial skills but with limited formal education to reach elite positions. In addition, because a market economy places a premium on legal knowledge, lawyers became more conspicuous in the elite.

When I asked them about the importance of education for the holding of top economic positions, members of the elite gave it much emphasis, and they most often singled out an education in economics. Nine of every ten respondents mentioned training in economics as critical for top positions, eight of every ten also mentioned the law, and seven added engineering to their list of the most salient types of education. A more detailed factor analysis of these and other elite opinions indicated that education was perceived as more important to success than having the right party and political connections or even having the ability to manage employees.

Party Affiliations and Political Networks

Competitions for economic power and privilege involve exclusionary practices among individuals and social groups, as well as conflicts between principles and ideologies. Under state socialism, political loyalty and Communist Party ties were given priority over wealth and other economic and social attributes in selecting elites. During the 1990s, party affiliation, as measured by party membership, has decreased greatly in importance. In 1990, members of the formerly communist Bulgarian Socialist Party (BSP) constituted 58.1 percent of the economic elite, and an additional 19.8 percent reported that they had terminated their BSP membership just a few months earlier. In 1994, by contrast, only 9.2 percent were still BSP members, while 46.2 percent reported having left the party. Perhaps reflecting the BSP's failed economic policies between 1994 and 1996, just 1.6 percent of the elite were BSP members in 1998. One of the most dramatic changes during the 1990s was the steadily increasing proportion of elite members who belonged to no party: from 19.1 percent in 1990, to 34 percent in 1994, to 72 percent in 1998.

The virtual disappearance of BSP members from the economic elite resulted from two developments. The first was the party's declining influence and overall social control. The second was a spreading recognition among elite persons that membership in the BSP or some other party did not provide much protection for economic activities. In the face of the several governmental alternations among parties and coalitions that occurred after 1989, people in top economic positions increasingly avoided close affiliation with a party.

This decrease in party membership suggested that a shift in mechanisms of political influence occurred, from a dependence on party connections to a dependence on more diffuse political and economic power networks. It is difficult in interviews to gather empirical material about such networks. However, a comparison of the times at which various elite members obtained their positions with successive political events provides an indicator of the networks' importance. For example, following the parliamentary elections in April 1997 and the creation of the new ODS coalition government, 65 percent of the top state economic administrators interviewed in 1998 had gained their positions within the preceding twelve months. Indeed, half of the entire 1998 sample had obtained their positions during the preceding year. In 1998, more generally, 85 percent of the elite sample had held no high-level position under the old state socialist regime. In sum, a fairly sweeping circulation of the economic elite occurred between 1989 and 1998, and this accelerated greatly as networks connected to the forces making up the ODS government after early 1997 came to the fore.

Careers

Elite education profiles and elite opinions about education's importance, discussed above, were linked closely to the careers that elite members followed. During the 1990s, the managerial ladder became the most important route to top economic positions. Under state socialism, elite recruitment typically required a university education, but it also gave preference to a working-class occupational background. By contrast, most members of the postsocialist economic elite began their careers in nonmanual jobs.

There were some interesting differences between the career patterns associated with the various components of the economic elite. Most of those who hold state administrative positions had pursued careers within the intelligentsia; 60 percent of the company managers had careers that began in lower-level managerial positions, and the other 40 percent of managers began as manual workers. The careers of bankers and politicians were more diverse. Nevertheless, if the position held by elite members immediately before they assumed their elite position is examined, it becomes clear that most entered the intelligentsia before being recruited to the elite itself. Put differently, experience as manager or a professional was the most important and proximate platform for moving into an elite position.

The data also reveal some differences between careers in the public and private sectors. In the public sector, a previous managerial position tended to be critical for gaining elite status. Nonmanual jobs in the public sector were correlated with eventual elite positions in that sector. In the private sector, by contrast, previous private sector jobs were not correlated with eventual private sector elite positions. This implies that the recruitment process in private firms and banks included requirements that differed from those in the public sector. The private sector elite consisted of individuals for whom private business employment was not their first job. Most frequently, they were first self-employed in the shadow economy or were exposed to private business practices via their fathers' activities in the presocialist period. The data also indicate that being employed in the public sector under state socialism while at the same time pursuing some private business activity was a frequent path to business elite positions in the 1990s. However, the most conspicuous difference between careers leading to elite positions in the private or public sectors was the lesser importance of educational credentials for top private entrepreneurial positions.

The analysis of private business careers confirms the importance of at least some experience in market-related activities for eventual elite positions in the private sector. Such experience provided individuals with opportunities to gain the knowledge and contacts that are crucial to successful market activities. In this respect, there was no difference between men and women in the elite, though education appeared to be of greater importance for women in top private sector positions than it was for men in the same kinds of positions. In sum, careers leading to top positions in the public and private sectors differed quite markedly, with previous exposure to the market being the most distinguishing feature of the elite's private sector component.

CONCLUSIONS

Changes in politics and political institutions were rapid and fundamental in Bulgaria during the 1990s. However, the economic system changed more slowly. Although the proclaimed goal was to dismantle the old socialist economy, the extent of actual dismantling remained quite limited. In this respect, the makeup and role of the economic elite was of vital importance because economic reforms depend on leaders who are able to propose and implement them. During the decade after state socialism, a somewhat mixed economy emerged. It involved an important redistribution of property between survivors of the old elite and members of the new and still emerging economic elite. Bulgaria is still far from being a robust pluralist society, but during the 1990s a significant differentiation of economic and political elites occurred, with other elite groups, such as military and police commanders, being relegated to more secondary power positions. Political and economic elites became more clearly separated from each other, and they displayed a rough parity in power and influence. Cutting across this more differentiated elite structure was the growing importance of the rule of law—of clearer distinctions between what are and what are not legal activities—and in this respect conflicts between the old and emerging elites were especially deep. The aim of the transition from state socialism was to undermine the old elites and their institutions. But during the 1990s, although formal institutions were altered greatly, the old and new elites merged, and in doing so they truncated the transition from state socialism.

My longitudinal data on changes in the economic elite permit some conclusions about how this happened. First, the data show that the elite became more heterogeneous in its composition. Between 1990 and 1994 it was relatively open to new members. After 1994, however, the elite became increasingly closed to outsiders, especially as people associated with the BSP government between 1994 and 1996 regained some of the prominence that they or their colleagues had lost during the early 1990s. In this respect, patterns of elite recruitment displayed continuity and also some discontinuity with the elite configuration under state socialism. Second, the earlier importance of working-class origins for attaining an economic elite position was replaced by an emphasis on experience as professional managers and experts. Third, the elite's age profile became more youthful than that of the old socialist elite, and this suggested that there was a premium on elite members' adaptability to new and changing conditions. Fourth, high education credentials continued to be vital for elite positions in the public sector, but they were somewhat less important in the new private sector. Fifth, party membership and other official party involvement declined greatly in their importance, and they were replaced by participation in more diffuse political networks. In sum, the 1990s were a period of significant change in the Bulgarian economic elite, and this was a precondition for transforming Bulgaria's economy. However, the lion's share of this economic transformation still lies ahead.

BIBLIOGRAPHY

Kostova, Dobrinka. 1996. "Strategies and Legacies of the Economic Elite in Bulgaria." In *The Transformation of East European Economic Elites,* ed. G. Lengyel. Budapest: Budapest University of Economic Sciences.

Lengyel, György. 1996. "The Hungarian Economic Elite in the First Half of the 1990s." In *The Transformation of East European Economic Elites,* ed. G. Lengyel. Budapest: Budapest University of Economic Sciences.

Lengyel, György, and Dobrinka Kostova. 1996. "The New Economic Elites: Similarities and Differences." In *The Transformation of East European Economic Elites,* ed. G. Lengyel. Budapest: Budapest University of Economic Sciences.

Sampson, Steven. 1994. "Money without Culture, Culture without Money: Eastern Europe's Nouveaux Riches." *Anthropological Journal for European Cultures,* 3 (April): 7–30.

12

Bulgaria, the Czech Republic, Hungary, and Poland

Presocialist and Socialist Legacies among Business Elites

Ákos Róna-Tas and József Böröcz

> Men make their own history, but they do not make it just as they please; they do not make it under circumstances chosen by themselves, but under circumstances directly encountered, given and transmitted from the past. The tradition of all the dead generations weighs like a nightmare on the brain of the living.
> —Karl Marx, *The 18th Brumaire of Louis Bonaparte*

Continuity and change have been at the center of the debate about the postsocialist transitions in Central and Eastern Europe. In the heady days of the fall of the state socialist political orders there, many believed that a sudden rupture with the past was possible. Revolutionary designs were hatched to change the failed socialist systems into vigorous capitalist ones. Today, a decade after the landslide electoral victory of Solidarity in Poland installed the first noncommunist government in the then still existing Soviet bloc, few would share the widespread optimism of those early days. Continuities with the state socialist past are all too apparent. From lingering foreign indebtedness and lopsided industrial structures to the return of Communist successor parties to power, the stamp of state socialism has been hard to erase (Crawford and Lijphart, 1995).

Yet, for anyone familiar with Central and East European history, it is difficult to miss another set of continuities. In many respects, the postsocialist countries seem to have returned to the trajectory that was interrupted by the state socialist takeover in 1948 (Janos, 1994; Good, 1994). To anyone who takes a look at the geography of economic success and failure since state socialism fell, this pattern is quite apparent. The more successful countries at the end of the 1990s were the ones that were more developed before 1948 and that had been part of the Hapsburg Empire forty years before that. During the interwar period, these countries tied their economic fortunes to Germany, and since 1989 they have again built strong economic and cultural ties to their powerful German neighbor and to the European Community. By contrast, countries in the eastern and southern flanks of the region, which suffered from backwardness before state socialist rule, are again finding themselves left behind.

Both pre- and post-1948 continuities have featured prominently in political debates in all these countries. A return to the pre-1948 past was a major theme in the revolutions of 1989. Memories of figures during the interwar period such as Masaryk, Pilsudski, Horthy, and Stamboliiski loomed large in their respective countries. Pre-1948 political parties reappeared and many political institutions of the past were resurrected. State socialism's legacies were also hotly debated. From demands to punish those responsible for the worst excesses of state socialist rule to alarm over resilient Communist Party officials reinventing themselves as private entrepreneurs, the legacies of state socialism have been fought over and debated endlessly.

The very fact that we can distinguish between pre-1948 and post-1948 legacies suggests that the changes can be very real. No one would seriously suggest that the countries of Central and Eastern Europe are the same as they were ten, let alone fifty, years ago. We do not wish to argue that quick and profound changes never happen. Our contention is that change during the postsocialist transformations has not been a single process; it has, instead, involved a multiplicity of processes marching to different drummers (Dahrendorf, 1990).

Time has been internal to these processes. That is, some aspects of social life have changed rapidly; others have advanced at a more leisurely pace. Laws, regulations, governments—formal institutions, in short—changed overnight. Habits, friendship networks, residential patterns, human capital have changed much more slowly. Thus, what looks like a single process has harbored different time scales. For instance, the privatization of shops, bars, and restaurants happened rapidly, but the privatization of larger enterprises has proceeded at a slower pace. Events have also unfolded on different time scales. This hardly comes as a surprise to historians, who know well that there are processes of the *longue durée* while others make up what is sometimes called "eventful history" (Braudel, 1980; Isaac and Griffin, 1989). What makes different time scales interesting is that processes unfolding at different tempos are often linked. The speed and direction of change in one process can depend on change in others.

Neoclassical institutionalism—the paradigm within which much of the postsocialist transformation has been designed—is uninterested in history and continuities. From its perspective, the transformation from state socialism is a movement between two equilibrium points, two economic structures, or two systems. Key institutions can be engineered and others will fall into line as society as a whole follows the functional imperatives of modern capitalism.[1] Individuals act on future expectations, not on past experiences (Krugman, 1991). Once the proper institutions and incentives are in place, individuals choose their pursuits in the proper direction. According to this approach, people's characteristics are instrumental assets, "capital" (human, social, or financial), tools they can use, acquire, shed, and trade in order to promote their chosen ends, and people act in response to changing opportunities.

What is neglected in this approach is that mentalities, skills, and social networks are not so pliable. Most people do not easily change the deep values they have internalized through early socialization. They rarely learn new skills and unlearn old ones quickly, especially skills that are intangible and personal. Nor are people likely to switch friends and acquaintances en masse. Much of the continuity one finds between socialist and postsocialist societies can be traced to these rigidities in individual lives.

It is worth recalling that the first state socialist leaders in 1948 and thereafter were very much aware of these rigidities. Driven by a revolutionary zeal similar to that which guides today's social engineers, they made an attempt to demolish such rigidities and continuities. The isolation and neutralization of people with the "wrong" class mentality, programs of re-education and indoctrination, geographical relocations, the elimination or strict control of formal organizations of all kinds—from trade unions to circles of stamp collectors—were all attempts by the early state socialist rulers to break the grip of the past. As we will argue, even their ruthless efforts did not succeed completely.

Should one conclude, therefore, that the legacies of state socialism are so deep and tied so strongly to several hundred years of history that any postsocialist change is only a ripple on the surface of an immense historical ocean? That any attempt at sudden change is futile? Cultural historicists argue exactly this (for example, Jowitt, 1992; McDaniel, 1996). They are fond of pointing to culture, which changes only glacially, if at all. They believe that shared meanings lock people into a collective destiny. If neoclassical institutionalism assumes that people are rational decision makers facing the future without much or any regard to the past, cultural historicists believe that people face the past without much thought about the future. They are prisoners of their culture and do whatever tradition dictates. Yet, the cultural historicist argument, though often delivered with great erudition, is rarely convincing. Cultural historicists are often guilty of picking selectively from past traditions, weaving a seamless interpretation leading up to the present. Their explanations tend to be holistic, whereby history and culture act as an undivided force through mechanisms that remain unspecified. The fact that traditions are always contested by countervailing currents remains either unacknowledged or, if noticed, it never leads to an explanation of the existence of contending traditions. Because cultural-historicism claims tend to be interpretative, it is far from clear how they can be proven wrong.

Evolutionary theorists try to strike a balance between the two positions (for example, Poznanski, 1996; Murrell, 1993). They agree with neoliberal institutionalists that individuals are the proper unit of analysis and they oppose the holism of cultural historicists. But evolutionary theorists are skeptical about the hyper-rationality of neoliberal institutionalism. They believe that the future is inherently unpredictable, so that strategic action cannot be based on the probability calculus that the rational person imagined by neoclassical economics is assumed to follow (Schumpeter, 1934; Hayek, 1978; O'Driscoll and Rizzo, 1985). Instead, people proceed by trial and error, imitation and adaptation, discovery and innovation, slowly perfecting their behavior through learning (Alchian, 1950; Nelson and Winter, 1982; Nelson, 1995). They act on past experiences, not on future expectations, and to this extent the past is of prime importance. Their knowledge is often unspoken, implicit, personal (Polanyi, 1962), and they tend to fall back on routines, "soft institutions," and even cultural "frames" (Poznanski, 1992; Pelikan, 1992; North, 1992; Denzau and North, 1994). Evolutionists emphasize decentralized spontaneous processes, and they take a conservative policy stance.

Evolutionists point correctly to the deficiencies of the neoliberal model, and they provide a more realistic description of social change. They also rightly stress the dynamic aspect of economic life, as opposed to its equilibrating tendencies. Our own approach borrows many ideas from the evolutionary school, but we are skeptical about its faith in spontaneous processes. We also think that evolutionists are overly optimistic about learning. Learning from experience does not always lead in the direction of optimal solutions (see, for example, Dawes, 1988; March, 1991). Moreover, evolutionists rarely deliver on their promise of methodological individualism. They often investigate organizations or entire economies, but rarely individuals. This is why we turn now to individual life histories.

LIFE HISTORIES OF ELITE MEMBERS

When talking about life histories we are not concerned with the overall coherence, meaning, or even the narrative of individual lives (Bourdieu.

1987). What we want to do is identify and speculate about a few mechanisms that play important roles in the selection of business elites.

Individual life histories of elite members are especially important. Elites possess power that makes their presence in society commanding. That life histories are important is clearly demonstrated by the scrutiny that the backgrounds and careers of political elite members receive during election campaigns. Life histories of economic elite members, by contrast, are more elusive, even though the power they wield is no less than that of politicians. To understand what kinds of life histories lead to elite positions in the economy can give us insight into historical continuities in two ways. First, finding out the recruitment mechanism for top economic positions can reveal how scarce goods are allocated in the economy. In the context of Central and Eastern Europe, this addresses some of the bitterest political debates over the distributive aspects of the postsocialist transformation. Second, because economic elites play a crucial role in the emerging postsocialist economies, their composition sheds light on what they will do and how they will run their companies and, thus, on the ways they will influence the further development of economic institutions.

Using data collected in four postsocialist countries—Bulgaria, the Czech Republic, Hungary, and Poland—we argue that, despite apparent dissimilarities, the process of economic elite recruitment in all four countries has been surprisingly similar. In them, strong and nearly uniform recruitment mechanisms link an individual's past to his or her present, and they tie the collective presocialist and state socialist pasts to a collective postsocialist present.

In reducing recent Central and East European history to the life histories of economic elite members we ignore a number of factors that do not attach to individuals. A country's geographical location, its size, and its industrial structure exemplify elements that cannot be addressed readily within our framework. Our claims must, therefore, be modest because we do not know the extent to which continuities that are discernible through individual life histories matter compared to such impersonal factors.

THE FOUR COUNTRIES

Without attempting to give a full historical account of the diversity of the four countries on which we focus, we provide a short sketch highlighting some of their differences in order to bring the uniformity of the elite recruitment mechanisms we uncover into sharper relief. The four countries' presocialist period was marked by vastly different degrees of economic "backwardness." Before World War II, the Czech part of Czechoslovakia was almost on a par with its West European neighbors in terms of industrialization, urbanization, and the emergence of the various class segments characteristic of industrial capitalism. Bulgaria, by contrast, was clearly on the periphery of the capitalist world economy, while Hungary and Poland were located somewhere in between.

After about 1948, the initial Soviet-imposed system of Stalinist rule created a high degree of standardization among these countries. However, the period after 1956 loosened Stalinism's standardizing effects and put the four societies on radically different routes, despite strong economic growth in all of them. The post-1956 "normalization" in Hungary involved at first severe and later gradually decreasing political oppression, together with large-scale, centralized investment in industrial modernization. "Normalization" in Hungary also led to the effective collectivization of agriculture, albeit with a series of compromises that included the acceptance of private household plots. In Poland, on the other hand, agricultural land and production remained highly fragmented in the hands of millions of small, usually grossly undercapitalized farmers. The post-1956 period saw in Czechoslovakia a period of economic growth and the emergence of a formal doctrine about the desirability of gradual political reforms, a process that was, however, crushed in the 1968 Prague Spring repression. As a result, the post-1968 situations of the four societies became even more disparate.

After 1968 it was Czechoslovakia's turn to experience a freezing of social, political, and economic experimentation under state socialist "normalization," offset by a relatively comfortable economic environment. Hungary, meanwhile, embarked on a path of ambitious economic reforms involving the radical decentralization of the control functions of state ownership, the creation of previously unknown levels of strategic decision making, and the placing of quasi-proprietorial power in the hands of managers under the general umbrella of a reformed planning system. These Hungarian changes were soon imitated in Poland and, later and in a weaker fashion, in Bulgaria. In all three countries, however, the reforms took extremely erratic paths, following closely the dynamics of power struggles within the political leaderships.

The global oil crisis of the early 1970s hit the two most reformist, industrializing economies—Hungary and Poland—the hardest. But instead of adjusting to the technological and organizational imperatives of a suddenly high-cost energy environment, they went on a foreign borrowing spree to sustain the investment and consumption levels that had become important components of the political status quo. This was accompanied by the emergence of the first relatively open manifestations of political dissent and the rapidly increasing political toleration of hidden, unregulated, untaxed, and unrecorded, informal economic transactions that soon became an integral part of state socialist economic practices all across Central and Eastern Europe.

The early 1980s witnessed the dramatic moral, political, cultural, and economic disintegration of state socialist arrangements. This manifested itself most visibly in the Polish political and economic crisis of 1980, which culminated in the declaration of martial law at the end of 1981. Poland's ensuing but sluggish "normalization," exacerbated by a collapse of the country's foreign debt structures, sent living standards into a tailspin. In Hungary, the crisis of state socialism was marked by the express legalization of various complex, hybrid organizational constructs along with a host of new, explicitly "capitalist" property forms, while political apathy and social "peace" were financed from a second, even more ruinous wave of external borrowing by the state.[2]

The final collapse of state socialism took different forms in the four countries. While in Poland and Hungary the Communists negotiated themselves out of power, in Bulgaria a mixture of negotiations and popular demonstrations led to the end of the one-party state. In Czechoslovakia popular pressure brought down state socialist rule. Each country then followed its own path to a market economy (Stark, 1992). Poland took the big bang approach; the Czechs took a centrally navigated evolutionary route, while in Hungary gradualism resulted from political mistakes and compromises. Bulgaria made little progress and at the end of the 1990s it still lags far behind in reforming its economy.

THEORY AND HYPOTHESES

Our central theoretical claim is that the mentalities, skills, and networks that are rooted in both the presocialist and the state socialist eras shape the recruitment of economic elites. These social attributes of elites are resources of a peculiarly *sticky* kind. Mentalities, skills, and networks are sticky because they are difficult to discard or hand over to others. It is even more difficult to take them from people forcibly. They are assets that are stuck to people and cannot be altered independently. They pose the problem of the indivisibility of individuals, so to speak. But just as such assets are stuck to people, people are also stuck with their own assets. That is, everyone has his or her own mentality, skills, and networks, and it is very difficult to abandon or change these because their accumulation is path-dependent. By this we mean that personal assets develop in such a way that they are subject to increasing returns to scale—a self-reinforcing process—so that they are at least as reflective of the initial conditions in which they began to accumulate as they are of current incentives (David, 1985; Arthur, 1994). The strength of individual assets and attributes is a function of the long time they take to form, and this is a key reason why they are difficult to alter. It follows that institutional change must accommodate the sticky properties of individuals. To understand their role in social change it is not enough to build an argument about how different personal assets become valorized; we also have to develop an explanation about how they emerge.

Developing a mentality depends on the interaction between the self and the social environment in a self-reinforcing cycle. The more one acquires a set of values, a repertoire of behavior, a habitus (Bourdieu, 1977), a set of taken-for-granted assumptions about the world, the more others recognize one by these traits. Others' expectations are guided by these traits, and the expectations of others, in turn, make one behave in more predictable ways. Since initial conditions are crucial, one's early family experiences are decisive. In Central and Eastern Europe, these family experiences are the main conduit of values from the presocialist past.

Personal networks are equally subject to a self-reinforcing process.[3] There is an increasing return to scale, both extensively and intensively. Because each tie with a partner gives one access to other potential partners, the breadth of one's network grows relatively slowly in the beginning, but its growth accelerates greatly once one has acquired many ties. The potential number of people one can approach increases with the number of people one has already approached. Moreover, trust and confidence in a particular relationship are difficult to establish, but over time as neither partner violates the other's trust nor confidence, their maintenance becomes easy. Furthermore, building trust and confidence with one person makes it easier to build trust and confidence with a friend of that person, assuming that the friend trusts the person with whom one has the initial relationship of trust and confidence. Entering a network of people through the wrong ties can brand a person for life in that network. Similarly, violating trust and confidence in the early stages of a relationship makes the violator an enemy rather than a friend.

Skills and knowledge acquired during state socialism were also subject to a self-reinforcing process (Arthur, 1994) because in learning new skills one also learned how to evaluate success and failure in that system. Perceptions of success and failure were not completely exogenous. For example, company managers who learned how to produce the most in quantity or the best in quality focused on achieving those ends and considered themselves successful if they fulfilled them. If the goods they produced could not be sold, they faulted the state socialist system while remaining convinced that the ultimate value was in production and that their market failure was only temporary. By the same token, those who learned under state socialism that growth in size was the best indicator of success tried continually to expand and were extremely reluctant to downsize. Even if they did whatever it took to muddle through, they did it with the expectation that their time would come. People could also be locked into virtuous circles, as successful companies often are, when they discovered a market where they did very well. Yet it often happened that they kept to their routines even when the circumstances in which these routines worked had changed.

Neither stickiness nor path-dependence is absolute. The usual way to unstick assets is through formal institutionalization. Institutionalization makes assets travel better. Mentalities can be formalized as legal or religious prescriptions. Skills can be formalized and transferred in the educational system as credentials. Networks can be formalized as organizations and transformed into organizational memberships. The self-reinforcing dynamics of these assets are not absolute either. Mentalities can encounter crises when people have to reevaluate who they are. Networks can reach their limit when getting to know yet another person or making still another friend becomes almost impossible. There can come a point when new experiences add little to the knowledge that one already possesses. People can reinvent themselves, build new networks, and learn new skills. People *do* change in response to changed opportunity structures, but not to the degree that neoclassical institutionalists believe they do.

From these theoretical considerations we derive several hypotheses.

Presocialist Continuity Hypotheses

The role of presocialist bourgeois values. People who were exposed before state socialist rule through their families to bourgeois values pertaining to business developed a mentality that puts them at an advantage in entering the postsocialist business elite. Thus, people whose family owned a business before the socialist takeovers are overrepresented in the economic elite. The content of these bourgeois values varies somewhat from country to country, and even within any given country there is variation among them according to the nature and size of the business in question. What all share is the importance of personal autonomy—a value little appreciated under state socialism where most people were employees of the state. Many of the presocialist values passed down through families are the ones neoliberal institutionalism assumes in its *Homo oeconomicus*—rational calculation, instrumental thinking, and individualism.

Ivan Szelényi advanced a similar analysis in studying Hungarian agriculture. He found that people who held land before state socialism were more likely to engage in private commercial farming under socialism (Szelényi, 1988). We will separate business and land ownership before state socialism and investigate the effect of each separately.

Some postsocialist observers argue that the reason why business ownership before 1948 gives an advantage to people today has little to do with the transmission of values and mentality and can simply be explained by restitution of properties that were confiscated. It is claimed that getting back one's grandparents' or parents' property has been a ticket into the new business elite, especially where the property returned is substantial. While it would not explain the prevalence of pre-1948 business families among top postsocialist managers who are not owners of their firms, restitution might account for this pattern among owner-managers.

Though restitution of property has been a hot political issue in all four countries (Gelpern, 1993), only the Czech Republic required the restitution of all property confiscated by the state socialist regime after 1948. But this threshold date meant that large businesses have rarely been returned to their earlier owners because by 1948 most such enterprises had already been nationalized either during the war by the German occupiers or by the Benes government of 1945–47 in its attempts to stabilize the postwar economy and punish ethnic Germans. In postsocialist Bulgaria, land was returned to its previous owners, but little else was restituted. Though postsocialist Hungary enacted no restitution laws, its center–right government did enact a scheme by which people whose property had been confiscated received compensation vouchers at a steep discount on the property's original value, with a cap of five million florins (ca. U.S.$50,000). However, these vouchers had only limited circulation and their market value dropped quickly to a small fraction of their already low nominal value. The only exception was land, where the government, using some legal ingenuity, allowed for a process of voucher auctions that often resulted in the return of land confiscated under state socialism (Comisso, 1995). Finally, Poland enacted no restitution or compensation laws, even though such laws were repeatedly proposed in the Sejm. In sum, if restitution or compensation played any role in the four countries, its role pertained almost solely to land. We can hypothesize that those from families that owned land before 1948 would be overrepresented in the owner segment of the business elite (Frydman et al., 1993).

The role of presocialist cultural capital. People who belonged to families that spurred them to acquire high levels of education in the presocialist era retained their cultural capital—mostly as basic cultural skills—throughout the state socialist era, despite attempts by the socialist regimes to eradicate such cultural advantages.[4] If the effects of cultural capital and business-related values are separated, each should have had a positive effect on individuals' chances of entering the postsocialist economic elite.

State Socialist Continuity Hypotheses

The role of networks. In all state socialist countries the Communist Party was the most powerful organization. On its demise it left an intricate, nation-wide web of social relations that survived mostly as informal ties.[5] These old Party ties were important during the postsocialist transformation because they had a wide geographic span and because many former Party members remained in the state bureaucracy. Thus, the ties pervaded much of the state even when the successor parties to the Communists—the socialist and social democratic parties—were initially without government power, as was the case in Hungary, Poland, and the Czech Republic. We expected that people who were members of the Communist Party during the 1980s would be more likely to show up in the new business elites (Hankiss, 1990; Staniszkis, 1991; Róna-Tas, 1994).

There are various other networks that are essential for anyone running a business (Stark, 1996). Personal ties to suppliers, contractors, and distributors were essential under state socialism for the day-to-day operation of any company. Moreover, a company itself can be seen as a network of social relations. These networks survived and gave a clear advantage to people who were already in management positions during the socialist period. One could start a new business and take these networks along. Therefore, state socialist managers enjoyed a clear postsocialist advantage in the business world.

Because the private sector was kept small, traditional, and local under state socialism, people in the private sector had little access to networks of managers. In Hungary and Poland the private sector was given access to the state sector, where small private partnerships or cooperatives often acted as subcontractors (Róna-Tas, 1999; Stark, 1989; Johnson and Loveman, 1995). Many of these people kept their jobs in the state sector, however, and they worked only part-time as private entrepreneurs, using their state jobs to secure important channels to customers and suppliers for their entrepreneurial efforts.

The role of knowledge and skills. Networks and knowledge are often intimately intertwined. Knowing people and knowing things are not easy to disentangle. For example, by familiarizing themselves with the people who supply them with materials, managers also find out the location of needed inputs and the means of obtaining them. Such knowledge develops with experience and it is very difficult to pass on in a standardized form.

Educational credentials indicate knowledge but they also indicate that the person holding the credentials attended a certain school and became acquainted with many people in his or her own profession. An overrepresentation of people with high education credentials could be expected in the new business elites, not just because these people had scarce expertise, but also because they were members of professional networks that formed during their university years.

Age and gender. Because mentalities, networks, and skills take time to develop, we might expect that the new business elites would not be very young. Indeed, they should be older than the general population because, all else being equal, older persons have more experience and wider and more robust networks. Moreover, older persons were closer to the presocialist era and could thus be expected to display pre-1948 bourgeois values more clearly.

Like age inequalities, gender inequalities can be also seen as the results of a self-reinforcing process. It is easy to understand why: the distribution of domestic labor and work careers starts with the initial child-rearing responsibilities that are assigned to women. From this start, several mechanisms lock women into domesticity and lock them out of careers outside the home. Here, however, we cannot explore the gender dimension in any detail and must leave it for future analysis. We can only employ gender as a control variable. Since gender is related to so many of the variables in which we are interested, we include it in our models to filter out gender composition effects.

BUSINESS ELITE CONTOURS IN 1993

Our data were gathered during 1993 in Bulgaria, the Czech Republic, Hungary, and Poland.[6] In each country we conducted a representative survey of the general population and a separate elite survey using a similar questionnaire. The new business elite was selected in each country by randomly sampling the largest companies (as measured by total sales). The chief executive officers of these companies were then interviewed. In the interview questionnaire we asked each chief executive officer about his or her business property. Those who partly or fully owned their companies were classified as owner-managers; the others were classified as managers (see table 12.1). Thus, each of the four business elites consisted of two groups: the owner-managers and the managers of large companies. Our elite samples did not include owners who played no role in managing their companies. In 1993, the number of individuals who were solely owners was relatively small. Private companies not managed by their owners were mostly either companies in foreign ownership or companies with large numbers of shareholders. Our elite samples did not include economic policy makers either. Ministry or privatization agency officials could be powerful players in the economy, but they were political appointees and were part of the political elite.

WHO WERE THE MEMBERS OF THE NEW BUSINESS ELITES?

There were very few women in the new business elites in 1993. Except for Bulgaria, the ratio of women was one in ten or less (see chapter 11). Among owner-managers the proportion of women was smaller still. In all four countries the mean age of the business elite was over forty, and in Hungary it was close to fifty years. Comparing these age profiles of the elites to the age profiles of their respective general populations, significant differences emerged only in Poland and Hungary. In both countries the general population was on average about five years younger than the business elite. This was not surprising. Given that Poland and Hungary had histories of experimenting with market reforms, in both of them market experience accumulated during state socialism should have counted for more. Average ages can be mis-

Table 12.1   Number of Respondents in Each Country Subsample in 1993

Subsample	Bulgaria	Czech Republic	Hungary	Poland
General population	4919	4737	4221	3520
Managers	320	679	373	480
Owner-managers	74	121	205	54

leading, however. While age is one reasonable proxy for experience, it also reflects other life cycle attributes that promote or inhibit economic success. Nevertheless, one would expect that both the very young and the very old had fewer chances of ending up among the new business elites. The young had less experience; the old had weaker health and less willingness to start new ventures.[7]

Did a person's pre-1948 family history matter? Yes, but with some unexpected twists. The new business elite in each country was much more likely to have descended from grandparents who owned a business in 1948 than to have risen from the general population. This pattern stood out. It was least apparent in Poland, where we found the lowest proportion of elite persons who descended from business-owning grandparents. The difference between Poland and the other countries was most probably due to the World War II elimination of Jews and the postwar expulsion of Germans, two ethnic groups that were highly overrepresented among business owners in the presocialist era.

We found a weaker but similar relation in all four countries between parents' business ownership in 1948 and a postsocialist business elite position. Why, we might ask, were grandparents more important precursors of business elite positions in the early 1990s than parents, when most people were, of course, raised by their parents? The answer, we believe, is that many in the new business elites were too young to have had a parent who was old enough to have owned a business in 1948. The average member of the new business elites was born after 1948; thus, his or her parents were only in their late teens or early twenties when the average future business elite member was born. This explanation is supported by the only exception to the pattern: Bulgaria's owner-managers, who were marginally less likely to have come from families where parents owned a business, were the youngest of all groups in our business elite samples.

If the legacy of grandparents' pre-1948 business ownership was clear and uniform and followed our expectations, the legacy of pre-1948 land ownership was more ambiguous and largely contradicted our expectations. With the exception of the Czech Republic, the new business elite was not more likely to have come from families with pre-1948 land ownership. While there was no significant difference in this respect between the elite and the general population in Hungary, the relation was negative in Bulgaria and

Poland. In those two countries, the families of top business leaders were *less* likely to have owned land in the presocialist era than the general population.

The reason why pre-1948 land ownership had negative or no effects on elite membership in three of the four countries has to do with the nature of the land market and the postsocialist recession in agriculture. Land restitution, like restitution of any kind, proved to be a lengthy process, in which establishing the claims of often-contending heirs dragged on in the courts. Moreover, the policy of land restitution had to resolve thorny issues about the fates of agricultural cooperatives, which had to be forced or induced to give up their lands to new or old owners. Thus, at the time of our survey, land restitution and compensation was still in progress in Bulgaria, the Czech Republic, and Hungary. Moreover, most of the lands returned were small and had strings attached in order to prevent speculation. At the same time, in all four countries agriculture plunged into a deep recession (Agocs and Agocs, 1994).[8] As a result of all this, it was next to impossible to enter the owner–manager segment of the business elites through farming.

The reason why the Czech Republic was an exception can be explained not so much by its strong embrace of restitution, but by considering the nature of Czech agriculture before state socialism. Historically the Czech lands had been highly industrialized. The reason why Czechs reported the lowest proportion of land ownership in 1948 was because Czech agriculture had been relatively small-scale compared to agriculture in the other three countries. The residential pattern of many small towns that developed in the Czech lands integrated the smaller peasantry with city- or town-dwelling artisans, entrepreneurs, and business people much better than in Bulgaria, Hungary, or Poland, where the peasantry lived its own, separate life in small villages, far from the large industrial and commercial centers. Consequently, cultural differences between the landowning peasantry and small business owners were considerably less in the Czech Republic than elsewhere.

The new business elites in all four countries came disproportionately from families with very high education profiles in 1948. This pattern was striking and it raised the possibility that our previous explanation of the importance of presocialist business property was simply registering a correlate of high education profiles: business owners were better educated and so they sent more of their offspring into successful careers. However, multivariate analysis that we performed but do not present here showed this not to have been the case.

Turning to the legacies of the state socialist era, we looked first at education. As we expected, members of the new business elites were much better educated than the general populations in 1993. There were very few among either their manager or owner–manager segments who did not have some kind of tertiary degree.

We also found that very large proportions of the persons making up the four elites were already managers before the fall of state socialism. The percentage of socialist managers was somewhat higher among managers than owner-managers, but even in the latter category over three-fourths held some managerial position before 1989. In Bulgaria, this percentage was lower, which is again partly explained by the lower average age of the Bulgarian business elite in 1993. But it was clear that the overwhelming majority of the new business elites had managerial experience under state socialism.

The role of former Communist Party cadres in the postsocialist transformations has generated heated political debate. Our data showed that over half of the new business elites were Party members in 1988, compared to between one-tenth and one-eighth of the general populations. Former Party members were, thus, strongly overrepresented among the business leaders. Those who held Party offices were also much more likely to end up in the new business elites. It cannot be disputed that former Communists did very well in the transition from state socialism, and this was evident even in 1993, when the successor parties to the Communists had not yet gained political power in Poland, Hungary, and the Czech Republic and had to share power in Bulgaria. However, multivariate analysis showed that former Party functionaries did not have an advantage, once their education, managerial experiences, and simple Party memberships were taken into account.

Finally, those with experience in the private sector under state socialism (the so-called second economy) were overrepresented in the new business elites, especially those who kept their state sector jobs. Not surprisingly, this finding was stronger for owner-managers. Poland diverged somewhat from the general pattern because it had the largest proportion of self-employed people in the general population under state socialism and because its agriculture was not collectivized. Even in Poland, however, most self-employed people were peasants with little chance of making it into the business elite.

CONCLUSIONS

Despite important differences among the four countries, the recruitment of the new business elites followed a surprisingly uniform pattern. Continuities with the presocialist past were evident everywhere. People carry mentalities over generations. They also seem to retain their skills and networks through turbulent times. The business elites that emerged in postsocialist Central and Eastern Europe are today shaping their countries' economies by wielding power over the distribution of property. They also have an important role in setting the informal ground rules of business, and those who follow them will have to adapt to these rules. Moreover, the elites have begun to emerge as a political force, converting their money into political influence. The window of opportunity for major redistributive changes that opened to a small crack with the collapse of state socialism has now closed. Property rights, mores, and political power have locked the new economic elites into their positions for years to come.

NOTES

We would like to thank Éva Fodor for her generous help in preparing the data and Alya Guseva for helping us with the data analysis.

1. In the sociological literature, the most articulate representative of this position is Victor Nee (1989, 1991).

2. For more detail on Bulgaria, see Crampton (1987), Lampe (1986), and Creed (1991); for Czechoslovakia, see Wolchik (1991) and Teichova (1988); for Hungary, see Róna-Tas (1999) and Berend (1990); for Poland, see Poznanski (1996) and Mizsei (1990). For the region as a whole, see Rothschild (1989) and Adam (1989, 1993).

3. On the role of networks in Eastern Europe, see Böröcz (1993), Böröcz and Stanworth (1995), Czak and Sik (1987), and Sik (1994).

4. Kelley and Klein (1981) found similar re-stratification in postrevolutionary Bolivia.

5. Many of these informal networks were very soon reorganized as business clubs.

6. The research was aided by a grant from the Joint Committee on Eastern Europe of the American Council of Learned Societies and the Social Science Research Council.

7. In a multivariate model, not presented here, we analyzed the nonlinear effect of age.

8. This recession was partially due to uncertainties about ownership rights.

BIBLIOGRAPHY

Adam, Jan. 1989. *Economic Reforms in the Soviet Union and Eastern Europe since the 1960s.* London: Macmillan.

———. 1993. *Planning and Market in Soviet and East European Thought. 1960–1992.* London: Macmillan.

Agocs, Peter, and Sandor Agocs. 1994. "'The Change Was But an Unfulfilled Promise': Agriculture and the Rural Population in Post-Communist Hungary." *East European Politics and Societies* 8: 32–58.

Alchian, Armen A. 1950. "Uncertainty, Evolution, and Economic Theory." *Journal of Political Economy* 58: 211–22.

Arthur, W. Brian. 1994. *Increasing Returns and Path Dependence in the Economy.* Ann Arbor: University of Michigan Press.

Berend, Ivan T. 1990. *The Hungarian Economic Reforms.* 1953–1988. Cambridge: Cambridge University Press.

Böröcz, József. 1993. "Simulating the Great Transformation: Property Change under Prolonged Informality in Hungary." *Archives Européennes de Sociologie* 34: 81–106.

Böröcz, József, and Ákos Róna-Tas. 1995. "Formation of New Economic Elites: Hungary, Poland, and Russia." *Theory and Society* 24/5: 751–81.

Böröcz, József, and Caleb Southworth. 1995. "Kapcsolatok és jövedelem: Magyarország, 1986–87" (Social Networks and Income: Hungary, 1986–87). *Szociológiai Szemle* 2.

Bourdieu, Pierre. 1977. *Outline of a Theory of Practice.* Cambridge: Cambridge University Press.

———. 1987. "The Biographical Illusion." Working Papers and Proceedings of the Center for Psychosocial Studies, no. 14, University of Chicago.

Braudel, Fernand. 1980. *On History.* Chicago: University of Chicago Press.

Comisso, Ellen. 1995. "Legacies of the Past or New Institutions? The Struggle over Restitution in Hungary." *Comparative Political Studies* 28, no. 2: 200–238.

Crampton, R. J. 1987. *A Short History of Modern Bulgaria.* Cambridge: Cambridge University Press.

Crawford, Beverly, and Arendt Lijphart. 1995. "Explaining Political and Economic Change in Post-Communist Eastern Europe: Old Legacies, New Institutions, Hegemonic Norms, and International Pressures." *Comparative Political Studies* 28, no. 2: 171–99.

Creed, Gerald W. 1991. "Between Economy and Ideology: Local Perspectives on Political and Economic Reform in Bulgaria." *Socialism and Democracy* 12: 45–65.

Czak, Ágnes, and Endre Sik. 1987. "Managers' Reciprocal Transactions." In *Education, Mobility, and Network of Leaders in a Planned Economy,* ed. György Lengyel, 141–71. Budapest: Karl Marx University of Economic Sciences, Department of Sociology.

Dahrendorf, Ralf. 1990. *Reflections on the Revolution in Europe.* New York: Random House.

David, Paul. 1985. "Understanding the Economics of QWERTY: The Necessity of History." In *Economics, History and the Modern Historian,* ed. W. Parker. London: Macmillan.

Dawes, Robyn M. 1988. *Rational Choice in an Uncertain World.* San Diego: Harcourt Brace Jovanovich.

Denzau, Arthur T., and Douglass C. North. 1994. "Shared Mental Models: Ideologies and Institutions." *Kyklos* 47, no. 1: 3–31.

Frydman, Roman, Andrzej Rapaczynski, John Earle, et al. 1993. *The Privatization Process in Central Europe.* New York: Central European University Press.

Gelpern, Anna. 1993. "The Laws and Politics of Reprivatization in East–Central Europe: A Comparison." *University of Pennsylvania Journal of International Business Law* 14, no. 3: 315–72.

Good, David F. 1994. "The Economic Transformation of Central and Eastern Europe in Historical Perspective." In *Economic Transformations in East and Central Europe: Legacies from the Past and Policies for the Future,* ed. D. F. Good. London: Routledge.

Hankiss, Elemer. 1990. *East European Alternatives.* Oxford: Clarendon Press.

Hayek, Friedrich August von. 1978. "The Pretence of Knowledge." In *New Studies in Philosophy, Politics, Economics, and the History of Ideas.* London: Routledge.

Isaac, Larry W., and Larry J. Griffin. 1989. "Ahistoricism in Time-Series Analyses of Historical Process." *American Sociological Review* 54, no. 6: 873–91.

Janos, Andrew. 1994. "Continuity and Change in Eastern Europe: Strategies of Post-Communist Politics." *East European Politics and Societies* 2: 1–32.

Johnson, Simon, and Gary Loveman. 1995. *Starting Over in Eastern Europe: Entrepreneurship and Economic Renewal.* Boston: Harvard Business School Press.

Jowitt, Kenneth. 1992. *New World Disorder.* Berkeley: University of California Press.

Kelley, Jonathan, and Herbert S. Klein. 1981. *Revolution and the Rebirth of Inequality: A Theory Applied to the National Revolution in Bolivia.* Berkeley: University of California Press.

Krugman, Paul. 1991. "History vs. Expectations." *Quarterly Journal of Economics* 4: 651–77.

Lampe, John R. 1986. *The Bulgarian Economy in the Twentieth Century.* London: Croom Helm.

March, James. 1991. "Exploration and Exploitation in Organizational Learning." *Organization Science* 2, no. 1: 71–87.

McDaniel, Timothy. 1996. *The Agony of the Russian Idea.* Princeton , N.J.: Princeton University Press.

Mizsei, Kálmán. 1990. *Lengyelország. Válságok, reformpótlékok, és reformok* (Poland. Crises, Reform Substitutes, and Reforms). Budapest: Közgazdasági és Jogi Könyvkiadó.

Murrell, Peter. 1993. "What is Shock Therapy? What Did It Sow in Poland and Russia?" *Post-Soviet Affairs* 9, no. 2: 111–40.

Nee, Victor. 1989. "A Theory of Market Transition: From Redistribution to Markets in State Socialism." *American Sociological Review* 54: 663–81.

———. 1991. "Social Inequalities in Reforming State Socialism: Between Redistribution and Markets in China." *American Sociological Review* 56: 267–82.

Nelson, Richard R. 1995. "Evolutionary Economics." *Journal of Economic Literature* (March).

Nelson, Richard R., and Sidney G. Winter. 1982. *An Evolutionary Theory of Economic Change.* Cambridge: Harvard University Press.

North, Douglass C. 1992. "Institutions, Ideology, and Economic Performance." *Cato Journal* 11, no. 3 : 477–96.

O'Driscoll, Gerald P., Jr,. and Mario J. Rizzo. 1985. *The Economics of Time and Ignorance: With a Contribution by Roger W. Garrison.* New York: Blackwell.

Pelikan, P. 1992. "The Dynamics of Economic Systems, or How to Transform a Failed Socialist Economy." *Journal of Evolutionary Economics* 2: 39–63.

Polanyi, Michael. 1962. *Personal Knowledge: Towards a Post-Critical Philosophy.* Chicago: University of Chicago Press.

Poznanski, Kazimierz Z. 1992. "Property Rights Perspective on Evolution of Communist-Type Economies." In *Constructing Capitalism: The Reemergence of Civil Society and Liberal Economy in the Post-Communist World,* ed. Kazimierz Z. Poznanski. Boulder, Colo.: Westview.

———. 1996. *Poland's Protracted Transition.* Cambridge: Cambridge University Press.

Róna-Tas, Ákos. 1994. "The First Shall Be Last? Entrepreneurship and Communist Cadres in the Transition." *American Journal of Sociology* 100, no. 1: 40–69.

————. 1999. *The Great Surprise of the Small Transformation: The Demise of Communism and the Rise of the Private Sector in Hungary.* Ann Arbor: University of Michigan Press.

Rothschild, Joseph. 1989. *Return to Diversity: A Political History of East Central Europe since World War II.* Oxford: Oxford University Press.

Schumpeter, Joseph. 1934. *Theory of Economic Development.* Cambridge: Harvard University Press.

Sik, Endre. 1994. "From the Multicoloured to the Black and White Economy: The Hungarian Second Economy and the Transformation." *International Journal of Urban and Regional Research,* 18, no. 1: 46–70.

Staniszkis, Jadwiga. 1991. *The Dynamics of the Breakthrough in Eastern Europe: The Polish Experience.* Berkeley: University of California Press.

Stark, David. 1989. "Coexisting Organizational Forms in Hungary's Emerging Mixed Economy." In *Remaking of the Economic Institutions of Socialism: China and Eastern Europe,* ed. V. Nee and D. Stark. Stanford, Calif.: Stanford University Press.

————. 1992. "Path Dependence and Privatization Strategies in East Central Europe." *East European Politics and Societies* 6, no. 1: 17–54.

————. 1996. "Recombinant Property in East European Capitalism." *American Journal of Sociology* 101, no. 4: 993–1027.

Szelényi, Ivan. 1988. *Socialist Entrepreneurs: Embourgeoisement in Rural Hungary.* Madison: University of Wisconsin Press.

Teichova, Alice. 1988. *The Czechoslovak Economy. 1918–1980.* London: Routledge.

Wolchik, Sharon L. 1991. *Czechoslovakia in Transition: Politics, Economics, and Society.* London: Pinter.

Epilogue

Elite Theory versus Marxism

The Twentieth Century's Verdict

John Higley and Jan Pakulski

The Marxist and elite paradigms have always pointed toward starkly different—one may say mutually incompatible and fundamentally opposed—theories of political and social change. This polarity reflects the paradigms' divergent philosophical roots, sociohistorical origins, and political functions. Marxism had strong Hegelian roots and it was deeply embedded in the radical tradition of utopian socialism; the elite paradigm was rooted in the neo-Kantian fact–value distinction and it was firmly anchored in the positivist tradition. The Marxist paradigm was shaped by the new political order that gestated in the Vienna Peace of 1815 and then froze; the elite paradigm was the product of that order's eventual collapse in the revolutionary upheavals sparked by socialist, communist, and fascist movements during the years surrounding World War I. Most important, Marxism claimed to be both the theoretical tool for unlocking history's secrets and the ideological and political tool of a rising social force, the industrial proletariat; the elite paradigm had more modest explanatory aims and a much more somber tone, and it sought to ride no political horse. Its formulators—Gaetano Mosca, Vilfredo Pareto, Robert Michels, and Max Weber—pursued a rigorous science of politics, and they dismissed and ridiculed the Marxist claim of revealing, not to mention shaping, history's logic.

In the Marxist paradigm, class membership influences all aspects of social and political life. Class divisions articulate themselves in social disparities and in conflicting norms, solidarities, identities, and political allegiances. Arising from fundamental economic relationships, classes are the principal actors on history's stage, with all major social and political changes propelled by their struggles. This explanatory focus is supplemented by an eschatology that sees class conflicts as moving history toward a classless end when all people will enjoy a free, equal, and prosperous condition. In the elite paradigm, by contrast, tiny but powerful minorities are made up of autonomous social and political actors who are interested primarily in maintaining and enhancing their power, so that their power struggles are not reducible to classes or other collectivities. By holding that it is elite choices and power competitions, rather than economics and class-like collectivities, that shape political and to some extent wider social orders, format political and many social divisions, and enflame or contain major conflicts, the elite paradigm reverses Marxism's causal arrow. As for eschatology, the Marxist vision of a classless society is replaced by a sobering projection of continuous—one is tempted to say "eternal"—elite circulations and struggles.

These paradigmatic polarities have pervaded the assumptive and normative underpinnings of Marxist and elite theories of political and social change. Regarding politics as the outgrowth of economics, Marxist theory has depicted industrialization as diffusing power in a propertied ruling class and as heralding that class's showdown with an ever larger and more self-conscious proletarian class. Elite theory, by contrast, stresses the autonomy of politics and the vital link between political power and bureaucratic organization, rather than property. It denies that unorganized masses have the capacity to form a solidary class that could undertake politically and socially transforming actions. According to elite theory, all that can realistically be hoped for in an age of bureaucratic organization is effective rule by powerful, organizationally-based, self-interested, but nonetheless responsive and responsible elites.

During the twentieth century, the confrontation between the Marxist and elite theories was only partly weakened or blurred by a third paradigm and set of theories. This third paradigm consisted of the more participatory and citizen-oriented democratic precepts that derived principally from the liberal thought of Alexis de Tocqueville and John Stuart Mill. But the democratic theories that emanated from these precepts have always had a more limited reach than the Marxist and elite theories. They have been concerned primarily with the foundations and workings of mainly Western (especially Anglo-American) political systems during the twentieth century. Attempts to apply democratic theories to other parts of the world and other historical periods have focused on many phenomena: economic growth and market economies, middle classes, political cultures, civil societies, religious beliefs, political institutions, state autonomy, and foreign pressures. However, these applications have been vitiated by disagreements about the causal importance and interrelations of such diverse phenomena. Moreover, claims that democratic theories have a global reach depend to an uncomfortable degree on assuming that the democratic politics of a score of Western countries, during some or all of the twentieth century, approximate the destination toward which the politics of all other countries are moving. Yet, the huge demographic, environmental, natural resource, and ethnonational barriers to such a worldwide democratizing trend, as well as the malfunctioning of Western democracies themselves, make this assumption dubious at best. Consequently, democratic theories have not achieved the explanatory force and scope of the Marxist and elite theories; they have served more as a normative vision than as an explanation of political and social change.

Two points need stressing. First, the Marxist and elite paradigms gave birth to competing theories about how social and political change occurs and what is, therefore, possible. Second, the differential development of the Marxist and elite theories has depended less on evidence for and against them than on their ideological attractiveness, that is, their capacity to give normative and programmatic backbone to organized political forces. Let us briefly examine the twentieth-century fortunes of Marxist and elite theories in light of these points.

MARXISM'S HARD TWENTIETH-CENTURY ROAD

The plausibility of Marxist theory, with its strong emphasis on class formations and interests, was closely linked, as we have said, to conditions in nineteenth-century Western Europe at a relatively early stage of industrialization: the spread of large factories in growing cities; the movement of impoverished peasants into urban ghettos and the disorders that resulted; the repressive Vienna Peace orchestrated by aristocratic and autocratic states that neither the budding socialist movements accompanying the industrial revolution nor the abortive "Springtime of the Peoples" in 1848 managed to undermine. The plausibility of elite theories was linked to conditions in early twentieth-century Western Europe at a more advanced stage of industrialization: the rapid growth of strong interventionist states; the rise of corporate bureaucracies, both public and private; the proliferation of charismatically led political mobilizations, especially of communist and fascist varieties; the emergence of powerful and manipulative mass communications media.

Given the different conditions to which the Marxist and elite theories were linked, one would expect to observe a decline in the fortunes of Marxist theory during the twentieth-century age of étatism, national mobilizations, and totalizing wars. In fact, Marxism's attractiveness began to fade as the nineteenth century neared its end. In the years immediately before and after World War I, however, it was embraced and reformulated as a theoretical and ideological tool of radical and reformist leaders of the European left—Communists, socialists, and social democrats alike.

The elite theory adumbrated by Mosca, Pareto, Michels, and Weber also enjoyed a brief period of popularity in those stormy early decades of the twentieth century. But the decisive factor shaping elite theory's subsequent fortunes was less a decline in its plausibility than a lack of ties to organized political forces. Unlike Marxist theories, elite theory did not find a powerful "theory carrier" and it consequently went into a long eclipse. This happened, paradoxically enough, at a time when elite theory's plausibility was probably greater than that of the reformulated Marxist theory. The "carrying" political factor was, thus, decisive. Later, the defeat of fascism in World War II, in which the Soviet Union played a major part, gave a powerful boost to Marxist theory in continental Europe (though much less in the Anglo-American countries, whose liberal leaders and intellectuals claimed the primary credit for fascism's defeat), and it enabled the European left to gain the high moral ground, especially in the universities. In addition, after World War II, Marxism became the ruling political formula in the Soviet-controlled state socialist countries of Central and Eastern Europe; and it became a fashionable blueprint for economic, social, and political development in emerging Third World countries.

Twentieth-century political developments thus turned Marxism into a major worldwide intellectual and political movement. But the same developments had a devastating impact on Marxist theory's explanatory power. Arraying the twentieth-century evidence for and against fifteen key hypotheses of Marxist theory, the American sociologist Richard F. Hamilton (1995) has found none of them confirmed, seven flatly disproved, and the other eight hypotheses receiving contingent, situation-specific support, but with their causal implications either problematic or rejected. Thus, the predicted showdown between a dominant bourgeois class and a de-skilled, impoverished but ever-growing proletariat did not eventuate, and proletarian revolution did not occur in any of the advanced capitalist countries where it was expected. In those countries, the petite bourgeoisie did not collapse into the proletariat but instead formed part of a growing and prosperous middle class, the dangerous lumpenproletariat disappeared, and intellectuals, who were supposed to join and help lead the proletarian revolution, dispersed in all directions, not a few of them playing important roles in fascist movements and regimes aimed at arresting the spread of socialism. Concentration of private property, while great, stopped short of the predicted "monopoly" configuration. Likewise, the state's autonomy and scope remained much greater than would be characteristic of a state that functioned as an executive committee for managing the bourgeoisie's common affairs. Mid-century corporatist deals paved the way for the incorporation of working-class parties into governments and for egalitarian reforms. Although economic crises punctuated the century, they did not display the cumulating intensity expected by Marxist theories, nor did nationalism wither in the face of international capitalism; rather, nationalism remained a dominant force that strongly shaped even the proletariat's actions, most conspicuously during the century's two world wars.

At the twentieth century's end, Marxist theory consisted of several dissipating streams (Pakulski and Waters, 1996). Its more orthodox streams had degenerated into empirically confounded, vague, or highly dubious concepts and contentions. Its adjusted "critical" streams had fragmented and lost their distinctiveness. They appealed primarily to intellectuals who regarded capitalism's market mechanisms with special distaste, and who, in spite of everything, continued to believe that a truly egalitarian society is somehow possible. To a considerable extent, Marxist theory's adherents were confined to those who simply could not stomach an explanation of political change based on what was always the principal twentieth-century alternative: elite theory.

THE ECLIPSE OF ELITE THEORY

Political and social developments during the twentieth century left the tenets of elite theory comparatively unscathed, though they contributed to a precipitous decline in its popularity among political activists and intellectuals, and thus sent it into prolonged eclipse. During the 1920s, fascism's demagogic appeals to nationalist and racist sentiments, which were used to justify the crushing of socialist forces, displaced the rationalistic rebuttal of Marxist theory that Mosca, Pareto, Michels, and Weber had offered. Seizures of power and its undisguised concentration in small cliques of fanatical leaders led to elite circulations in Italy, Germany, Austria, several countries of Eastern Europe, and, to a lesser extent, Spain, Japan, and some countries of Latin America. While it is doubtful that the early elite theorists accurately predicted the rise of fascist elites, there was nothing about this rise that was inconsistent with the theorists' emphasis on the inescapability of elite domination, the forms this can take, and the inexorable circulation of elites.

The ugliness of fascism and its threat to Western civilization sobered many persons who had blithely regarded the gradual progression of Western countries toward a vague socialist condition as unproblematic. To a limited degree, the rise of fascist elites rekindled interest in elite theory (for example, Mannheim, 1940; Burnham, 1943; Lasswell and Lerner, 1965). Overwhelmingly, however, the revulsion against fascism translated into a strong reaffirmation of democratic beliefs, so that the explanation for fascism was mainly sought in other directions: as lower-middle-class extremism reinforced by authoritarian tendencies among working classes (Lipset, 1960); as the product of an "authoritarian personality" syndrome (Fromm, 1941;

Adorno et al., 1950); as the result of an antidemocratic stream in European philosophy (Arendt, 1951); or as the consequence of mass society (Kornhauser, 1959). Indeed, without convincing reasons being given, some came to view elite theory itself as leading to fascism (for example, Beetham, 1977).

In the euphoria that attended the fascist powers' defeat in 1945 and during the two halcyon decades of sustained economic growth that began a few years later in the most advanced Western countries, elite theory went into deeper eclipse. Pareto, Mosca, and Michels fell into a disciplinary no-man's-land between political science and sociology, being relegated by each field to the status of minor figures (Etzioni-Halevy, 1993). Weber's legacy was reinterpreted in the sociological tradition as a corrective to, rather than a confrontation with, Marxist theory, and the elite-centered theses in his work remained underdeveloped, subsumed under the headings of "charisma" and "bureaucracy." More important, influential parts of the academic and intellectual establishments—especially the liberal left in America and democratic socialists in Western Europe—condemned elite theory as inherently conservative, simplistic, and antidemocratic (see, for example, Bachrach, 1967; Beetham, 1977).

It was not that scholars and intellectuals were unaware of elites and their role in social and political change. Rather, a combination of socioeconomic and sociocultural conditions hindered the development and restricted the popularity of elite theory. It was Marxist theory's diluted and diverse streams that provided the idioms for intellectuals who were critical of liberal democracy's shortcomings. This was partly a matter of preemption because, as noted, Marxist theorizing emerged from the horrors of World War II wearing an anti-fascist mantle, and it had powerful carriers in the form of large Communist, socialist, and social democratic parties. The popularity of Marxist theory was also partly the result of terminological adjustments made to it by the New Left during the 1950s and 1960s. And, finally, its popularity was in part a consequence of elite theory's perceived guilt-by-association with fascism.

On both sides of the Atlantic, moreover, the postwar period was marked by exceptionally promising conditions. Economic growth and the consolidation of welfare states enabled governing elites to avoid hard choices and to placate discontented groups with subventions and other seemingly cost-free redistributive measures (Field and Higley, 1980, 1986). A belief that the welfare state was perhaps the final solution to major social conflicts and problems became widespread (see, for example, Tingsten, 1955; Myrdal, 1960; Briggs, 1961; Beer, 1965). Many commented on how domestic issues were being reduced to discussions between bureaucrats and experts, and how the function of political leaders was more and more that of shaping and selling to mass electorates the justifications for specific policies that bureaucrats and experts produced (for example, Meynaud, 1965; Thoenes, 1966).

Steady economic growth and welfare state expansions increased social mobility from a variety of non-elite statuses to elite positions. Many newly arrived elite persons consequently tended to see themselves as identified with the social categories from which they hailed and in which they continued to have close personal ties.

All this made elites seem less socially and politically distinct, less threatening to and more empathetic with mass populations. As a result, the global and historical reach of elite theory was largely ignored, the elite concept was seldom employed in public and scholarly discourse in other than a pejorative way, and a view of elites (often dubbed "policymakers," "decision makers," or just "opinion leaders") as a relatively prosaic aspect of the democratic landscape prevailed. Within social science circles, this view was reinforced by the ascendancy of survey and other quantitative research methods better suited to investigating mass attitudes and behaviors than to studying the dissembling political opinions, secretive behaviors, and situationally contingent actions of elites.

What passed for elite theory during the twentieth century's third quarter was, therefore, a protracted discussion, which exhibited little urgency, about the roles of elites in Western democratic political systems. This discussion centered on the modifications of classical democratic theory made principally by Joseph Schumpeter (1941), Raymond Aron (1950), Giovanni Sartori (1965), and Robert Dahl (1971). The discussion is familiar and well reviewed elsewhere (Parry, 1969; Putnam, 1976; Sartori, 1987), so it is enough to say here that thinking about elites was sidetracked onto a set of essentially empirical questions about their existence, social composition, and policy attitudes at community and national levels in democracies. Were there elites at all? If so, as C. Wright Mills (1956), Robert Dahl (1960), Arnold Rose (1967), and many other (mainly American) scholars asked, were they of a "power" or a "plural" kind? To what extent was elite social composition unrepresentative of the wider citizenry? How did research methods used to study elites shape the answers to these questions? These were a-theoretical matters because they seldom linked elites to basic patterns of political change or continuity, they were explored in an historical and comparative void, and they were mainly concerned with measuring trivial correlates of elite status (Zuckerman, 1977).

Nor did elite theory fare any better when discussion turned to the politics of non-Western developing countries. Many political adventurers in those countries were strongly attracted to Marxist theory because they could use it to justify their revolutionary seizure and wielding of government power. Elite theory's denial of the Marxist program and its emphasis on the inevitability of elite domination were hardly useful to such adventurers. Although it was clear to Westerners who looked at them that all developing countries were dominated by elites, most of which were internally divided, thoroughly corrupt, prone to violent struggles, and, hence, incapable of operating democratic regimes, this tended to be seen as a temporary problem that Western example and aid would in time overcome. Even when, in the 1970s, the failure of most developing countries to move in democratic directions became so apparent as to require explanation, the strong tendency was to seek answers in Marxist notions of dependency and the workings of a capitalist world-system (for example, Wallerstein, 1974).

THE END OF ELITE THEORY'S ECLIPSE

Three major trends during the twentieth century's final two decades forced more serious consideration of elites. The first trend was the economic advances of Japan and the "Asian Tiger" countries. These advances occurred against the predictions of dependency theorists and, until the late 1990s, without the recurring economic depressions that Marxist theory prophesied for capitalist countries. The Asian successes involved tutelage and reforms from above carried out by strong state elites (Johnson, 1982; Evans, Rueschemeyer, and Skocpol, 1985; Kataoka, 1998). The economic performances of Japan and the Tigers thus helped to revive interest in elites and their role in fostering economic development. The political liberalizations that were eventually initiated by elites in Korea and Taiwan, and the ways in which elites managed the two countries' transitions from authoritarian to democratic regimes, heightened this interest (Higley, Huang, and Lin, 1998).

The second elite-centered trend unfolded among the state socialist countries of Eastern Europe. As the early elite theorists had anticipated, state socialist regimes testified strongly to the centrality of elites. Once such regimes were consolidated in Yugoslavia, Albania, Central and Eastern Europe, China, North Korea, Cuba, and Vietnam, it became less easy to view the dominance of ruthless party elites, such as the Soviet Union had experienced under Stalin, as merely a transitional or aberrant condition. Rather, it was obvious that revolution and military conquest in these countries had led only to a circulation of elites, with the new state socialist elites being more thoroughly entrenched than those they displaced. The extreme longevity of elite tenures under state socialism, the repression of all competing elites, and the fiasco of Mao's ostensible effort to combat elite entrenchment through "cultural revolution" were strikingly consistent with elite theory.

This did not escape the attention of some scholars in the state socialist countries. But in seeking to use elite theory to illuminate power relations in their countries, these scholars confronted difficult political–ideological and censorship restrictions. They accordingly embraced elite theory by stealth, under the label of "developed class analysis," studies of "political-ideological leadership," the "new class," and, in one case, a survey of national "opinion leaders" in state socialist Yugoslavia (Barton, Denitch, and Kadushin, 1973). One of the authors of chapter 5 in this volume, Polish sociologist Wlodzimierz Wesolowski (1977), drew a clear theoretical distinction between Marxian economic class divisions and elite–mass relations. He argued that the political elite in state socialist countries like Poland should be viewed as autonomous from the dominant class in its articulations, actions, and general social functions. Among Western students of the state socialist countries, elite-centered analyses formed the scholarly mainstream, even if they were conducted with little reference to classical elite theory. In this enterprise, typologies of elites more complex than those offered by the early elite theorists were constructed, the organization and dynamics of elite–mass relations were studied, and close attention was given to the political effects of elite successions in the state socialist countries (for example, Beck 1973; Welsh, 1979; Bunce, 1981; Lane, 1988; Brown, 1989).

One may view these scholarly developments as an ultimate historical irony. The triumph of Marxist-inspired politics in the state socialist countries contributed to the waning of Marxist theory by generating social and political configurations clearly at odds with its tenets and very much in line with the predictions of its most ardent critics, the original elite theorists. The Soviet Union's demise between 1989 and 1991 further attested to the relevance of elite theory. It was driven by elite conflicts and elite-imposed reforms that, in turn, opened a window of opportunity for reformist elites in the Soviet satellite countries, backed in a few instances by sudden mass mobilizations (Higley and Pakulski, 1993, 1995; Tökés, 1996; Lane, 1996; Linz and Stepan, 1996; Hough, 1997; Kotz and Weir, 1997). As earlier and elsewhere during the twentieth century, the rise and fall of state socialism was in largest measure a story of elite struggles, circulations, and failures.

The elite-driven demise of the Soviet Union and its satellite regimes constituted an especially dramatic category in the "third wave" of transitions from authoritarian to putatively democratic regimes that coincided with the twentieth century's final quarter (Huntington, 1991). This was the third major trend that helped end elite theory's long eclipse. In the extensive literature studying the third wave transitions, the calculations and actions of elites figure on nearly every page. Summarizing more than two dozen such studies carried out under their direction, Larry Diamond, Juan J. Linz, and Seymour Martin Lipset (1995: 19) observed that "Time and again across our cases we find the values, goals, skills, and styles of political leaders and elites making a difference in the fate of democracy." Samuel P. Huntington's (1991) comprehensive analysis of thirty-five third wave countries highlighted the interplay among political elites in the courses and outcomes of democratic transitions. Juan J. Linz and Alfred Stepan's (1996) rigorous analyses of the democratic transition paths taken by thirteen Southern European, South American, and East European countries between 1974 and 1991 showed the decisive importance of relatively unconstrained choices made by elites during those transitions.

In sum, a mixture of political and theoretical developments revived interest in elite theory during the twentieth century's last decades. The main political developments were the obvious centrality of elite choices and actions in guiding the spectacular economic and political changes in Asian societies, in fostering but also managing the collapse of state socialism, and in shaping many of the other regime transitions in democratization's third wave. Principal theoretical developments were the exhaustion of Marxist theory's credibility and the reformulation of democratic theory in a more elite-centered direction (for example, Sartori, 1987; Zolo, 1991).

ELITE THEORY IN THE NEW CENTURY

The beginning of the twentieth century was marked by the birth of elite theory, and, after the circuitous route we have summarized, the century ended with a marked return to the discussion of elites. References to elites are today ubiquitous in political discourse. Journalists and commentators speak regularly about elites when dissecting events in Washington and Moscow, Belgrade and Beijing. Social scientists and historians regularly assign elites pivotal roles when analyzing political regimes, revolutions, social movements, democratic transitions and consolidations. Elites are at the core of the emphasis on "political" causation that is now so prevalent in macro political analysis, even though many scholars continue to use synonyms such as leaders, rulers, power groups, power networks, and state actors.

The discussion of elites is once again in vogue. As yet, however, elite theory has not been renewed. Scholars have not followed up on the attempts of Mosca, Pareto, Michels, and, in his own way, Weber to make elites the centerpiece in theories of political and social change. Consequently, the many who today focus on elites in their analyses do so in something like a theory void because there is no well-accepted body of definitions, interrelated concepts, and propositions guiding their focus. "The elitist paradigm," George Moyser and Margaret Wagstaffe have observed, "suffers from argument and confusion over key terms, a relative dearth of testable hypotheses, a failure clearly to separate normative from empirical theory and, not least, the lack of a firm data base in which the latter could be solidly grounded" (Moyser and Wagstaffe, 1987: 1).

This book has tried to address some of these problems, but it is obvious that much remains to be done. The kinds of overall elite configurations that exist among contemporary societies, the means by which transformations from one configuration to another occur, the limits that mass publics place on elite actions, and the examination of what is, therefore, possible in the political world of the twenty-first century demand better theory and analysis. These are complex and difficult issues. In concluding, we can only list some of the suppositions that underlie the theories and analyses presented in this book and that, we believe, must inform further thinking and research if elite theory is to be renewed. Stated in their baldest form, these suppositions are:

- The internal workings, commitments, and patterned actions of elites constitute the basic distinctions to be made among the political systems of all independent countries.
- The extent to which elites do or do not trust and cooperate with each other is logically and factually prior to constitutional and other institutional arrangements, to the existence of political stability or instability, and to any serious degree of democratic politics.
- The existence and centrality of elites make all utopias impossible to achieve; major political and social changes stem mainly from basic transformations of elites.
- Elite transformations take place within, and are somewhat limited by, wide parameters that are set by the political dispositions and orientations of mass populations; to this extent, the relation between elites and mass publics is interdependent.
- At the end of the day, basic choices in politics pertain mainly to the desirability of some kinds of elite configurations over others, and to the wisdom, in any concrete situation, of trying to modify or transform an existing elite configuration.

BIBLIOGRAPHY

Adorno, Theodor, et al. 1950. *The Authoritarian Personality*. New York: Harper & Bros.

Arendt, Hannah. 1951. *The Origins of Totalitarianism*. New York: Harcourt, Brace.

Aron, Raymond. 1950. "Social Structure and Ruling Class." *British Journal of Sociology* 1: 1–16, 126–43.

Bachrach, Peter. 1967. *The Theory of Democratic Elitism*. Boston: Little, Brown.

Barton, Alan H., Bogdan Denitch, and Charles Kadushin. 1973. *Opinion-Making Elites in Yugoslavia*. New York: Praeger.

Beck, Carl, ed. 1973. *Comparative Communist Political Leadership*. New York: David McKay.

Beer, Samuel H. 1965. *British Politics in the Collectivist Age*. New York: Knopf.

Beetham, David. 1977. "From Socialism to Fascism: The Relation Between Theory and Practice in the Work of Robert Michels." *Political Studies* 1 and 2: 3–24, 161–81.

Briggs, Asa. 1961. "The Welfare State in Historical Perspective." *European Journal of Sociology* 2: 221–58.

240 J. Higley & J. Pakulski

Brown, Archie, ed. 1989. *Political Leadership in the Soviet Union.* Bloomington: University of Indiana Press.

Bunce, Valerie. 1981. *Do New Leaders Make A Difference?* Princeton, N.J.: Princeton University Press.

Burnham, James. 1943. *The Machiavellians.* New York: Gateway.

Dahl, Robert A. 1960. *Who Governs?* New Haven, Conn.: Yale University Press.

———. 1971. *Polyarchy: Participation and Opposition.* New Haven, Conn.: Yale University Press.

Diamond, Larry, Juan J. Linz, and Seymour Martin Lipset, eds. 2nd ed. 1995. *Politics in Developing Countries: Comparing Experiences with Democracy.* Boulder, Colo.: Lynne Rienner.

Etzioni-Halevy, Eva. 1993. *The Elite Connection: Problems and Potential in Western Democracy.* New York: Basil Blackwell.

Evans, Peter, Dietrich Rueschemeyer, and Theda Skocpol, eds. 1985. *Bringing the State Back In.* New York: Cambridge University Press.

Field, G. Lowell, and John Higley. 1980. *Elitism.* London: Routledge.

———. 1986. "After the Halcyon Years: Elites and Mass Publics at the Level of Full Development." *Journal of Political and Military Sociology* 14: 5–27.

Fromm, Eric. 1941. *Escape From Freedom.* New York: Farrar Rinehart.

Hamilton, Richard F. 1995. "Marxism." Unpublished manuscript. Department of Sociology, Ohio State University.

Higley, John, Tong-yi Huang, and Tse-min Lin. 1998. "Elite Settlements in Taiwan." *Journal of Democracy* 9 (April): 148–63.

Higley, John, and Jan Pakulski. 1993. "Revolution and Elite Transformation in Eastern Europe." *Australian Journal of Political Science* 27: 104–19.

———. 1995. "Elite Transformation in Central and Eastern Europe." *Australian Journal of Political Science* 30: 415–35.

Hough, Jerry F. 1997. *Democratization and Revolution in the U.S.S.R., 1985–1991.* Washington, D.C.: Brookings Institution Press.

Huntington, Samuel P. 1991. *The Third Wave: Democratization in the Late Twentieth Century.* Norman: University of Oklahoma Press.

Johnson, Chalmers. 1982. *MITI and the Japanese Miracle.* Stanford, Calif.: Stanford University Press.

Kataoka, Hiromitsu. 1998. "Japan: The Elite Legacies of Meiji and World War II." In *Elites, Crises, and the Origins of Regimes,* ed. M. Dogan and J. Higley. Lanham, Md.: Rowman & Littlefield Publishers.

Kornhauser, William. 1959. *The Politics of Mass Society.* Glencoe, Ill.: Free Press.

Kotz, David, with Fred Weir. 1997. *Revolution from Above: The Demise of the Soviet System.* London: Routledge.

Lane, David S. 1988. *Elites and Political Power in the U.S.S.R.* Brookfield, Vt.: Edward Elgar Publishers.

———. 1996. "The Gorbachev Revolution: The Role of the Political Elite in Regime Disintegration." *Political Studies* 44: 4–23.

Lasswell, Harold D., and Daniel Lerner. 1965. *World Revolutionary Elites.* Cambridge, Mass.: M.I.T. Press.

Linz, Juan J., and Alfred Stepan. 1996. *Problems of Democratic Transition and Consolidation.* Baltimore: Johns Hopkins University Press.

Lipset, Seymour Martin. 1960. *Political Man*. New York: Free Press.

Mannheim, Karl. 1940. *Man and Society in an Age of Reconstruction*. New York: Harcourt, Brace.

Meynaud, Jean. 1965. *The Politics of Technocracy*. London: Faber & Faber.

Mills, C. Wright. 1956. *The Power Elite*. New York: Oxford University Press.

Moyser, George, and Margaret Wagstaffe, eds. 1987. *Research Methods for Elite Studies*. London: Allen & Unwin.

Myrdal, Gunnar. 1960. *Beyond the Welfare State*. New Haven, Conn.: Yale University Press.

Pakulski, Jan, and Malcolm Waters. 1996. *The Death of Class*. Los Angeles: Sage.

Parry, Geraint. 1969. *Political Elites*. London: Allen & Unwin.

Putnam, Robert D. 1976. *The Comparative Study of Political Elites*. Englewood Cliffs, N.J.: Prentice Hall.

Rose, Arnold M. 1967. *The Power Structure*. New York: Oxford University Press.

Sartori, Giovanni. 1965. *Democratic Theory*. New York: Praeger.

———. 1987. *Democratic Theory Revisited*. Chatham, N.J.: Chatham House Publishers.

Schumpeter, Joseph. 1941. *Capitalism, Socialism, and Democracy*. New York: Harper & Row.

Thoenes, Piet. 1966. *The Elite in the Welfare State*. London: Faber & Faber.

Tingsten, Herbert. 1955. "Stability and Vitality in Swedish Democracy." *The Political Quarterly* 26: 140–51.

Tökés, Rudolf L. 1996. *Hungary's Negotiated Revolution*. New York: Cambridge University Press.

Wallerstein, Immanuel. 1974. *The World-System*. New York: Academic Press.

Welsh, William A. 1979. *Leaders and Elites*. New York: Holt, Rinehart & Winston.

Wesolowski, Wlodzimierz. 1977. *Classes, Strata, and Power*. London: Routledge.

Zolo, Danilo. 1991. *Democracy and Complexity*. University Park, Pa.: Penn State University Press.

Zuckerman, Alan. 1977. "The Concept 'Political Elite': Lessons from Mosca and Pareto." *Journal of Politics* 39: 324–44.

Index

adaptive reconstruction of elites, 130–39; blocked transformation, 130; elite circulation, 132–33; ideological reconstruction, 137–39; personnel reconstruction, 132–35; reconstruction of material positions, 135–37; separation of politics and economy, 130
administrative elite, 79–80
adversaries, political, 100–101
age and elite, 37, 168–69, 187, 201–2, 219–21

bankers. *See* financial elite
BSP. *See* Bulgarian Socialist Party
Bulgaria, 199–207, 214, 215; age and gender of economic elite in, 201–2; career patterns of economic elite, 205–6; economic elite in, 200–207, 218, 221, 222, 223; economy of, 199, 206; education of economic elite in, 203–4; elections in, 199; elite circulation in, 11–12, 204–5, 206–7; family backgrounds of economic elite, 202–3; fragmented elite in, 17; institutional mechanisms in, 8; party affiliations of economic elite, 204; political elite in, 206; reproduction circulation in, 13; transition from state socialism, 199–200, 206

Bulgarian Socialist Party, 11–12, 17, 199, 204
business elite. *See* economic elite

capitalism, 147–51, 165; Croatia, 150; and democracy, 148
career patterns of elite: Bulgaria, 205–6; economic elite, 223; financial elite, 171–74; managerial elite, 171–74
Carnogursky, Jan, 50, 51
Center Alliance (Poland), 90, 91
chaotic economic formation (in Russia), 195, 196
Christian Democratic Movement (Czech Republic), 31, 50, 51, 56
Christian National Union (Poland), 90, 91
civic competence, 105
Civic Democratic Party (Czech Republic), 15, 31, 39, 40, 42
Civic Forum (Czech Republic), 29–30, 49–50
civic participation and democracy, 97
class (social): and elite theories, 123–26; and state socialism, 128; and transformation from state socialism, 126–30. *See also* Marxism
classic circulation, 5, 7, 128, 144; Croatia, 160; Czech Republic, 11, 13, 43; examples of, 9–11; Hungary, 13; Poland, 13; political elite, 43. *See also* elite circulation

About the Editors and Contributors

Attila Bartha is a lecturer in sociology at the Budapest University of Economic Sciences.

József Böröcz is professor of sociology at Rutgers University in New Brunswick, New Jersey.

John A. Gould is a doctoral candidate in political science at Columbia University in New York.

John Higley is professor of government and sociology at the University of Texas at Austin.

Dobrinka Kostova is a fellow in the Institute of Sociology at the Bulgarian Academy of Sciences.

Mladen Lazić is professor of sociology in the Faculty of Philosophy at the University of Belgrade.

David Lane is reader in sociology at Emmanuel College, Cambridge University.

György Lengyel is professor of sociology at the Budapest University of Economic Sciences.

Bogdan Mach is a research fellow in sociology at the Polish Academy of Sciences.

Pavel Machonin is senior research fellow in sociology at the Czech Academy of Sciences.

Jan Pakulski is professor of sociology at the University of Tasmania in Australia.

Ákos Róna-Tas is associate professor of sociology at the University of California, San Diego.

Dusko Sekulic is associate professor of psychology at Flinders University of South Australia.

Zeljka Sporer is a lecturer in sociology at Flinders University of South Australia.

Soňa Szomolányi is professor of political science at Comenius University in Bratislava.

Milan Tucek is senior research fellow in sociology and director of the Project on Social Transformation and Modernization in the Czech Academy of Sciences.

Rudolf L. Tökés is professor of political science at the University of Connecticut and fellow of the Collegium for Advanced Studies in Budapest.

Christian Welzel is a research fellow in politics at the Wissenschaftszentrum in Berlin.

Wlodzimierz Wesolowski is professor of sociology in the Polish Academy of Sciences.